When
Labor
Organizes

By ROBERT R. R. BROOKS

Assistant Professor of Economics, WILLIAMS COLLEGE
Sometime Fellow of Trumbull College, YALE UNIVERSITY

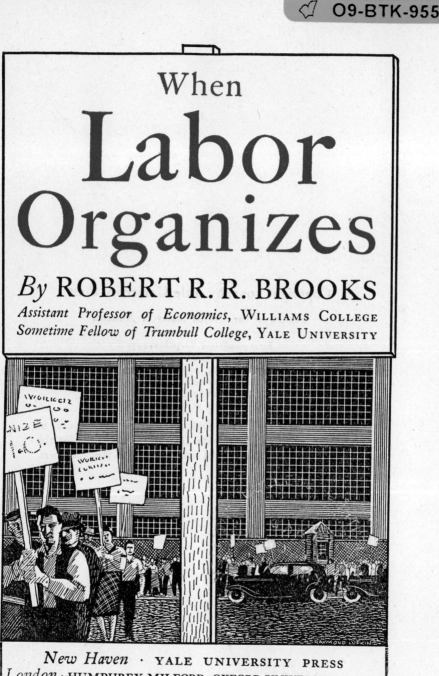

New Haven · YALE UNIVERSITY PRESS
London · HUMPHREY MILFORD · OXFORD UNIVERSITY PRESS

To

Mary, Patricia and Robin

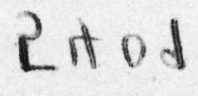

Contents

Illustrations

Harris & Ewing
FRANCES PERKINS
Secretary of Labor

Harris & Ewing
WILLIAM GREEN
President of the American Federation of Labor

Harris & Ewing
JOHN L. LEWIS
President of the United Mine Workers

Soibelman Syndicate
WILLIAM S. KNUDSEN
President of General Motors

WHEN LABOR ORGANIZES

CHAPTER I

Organizing a Union

A UNION organizer has been assigned by his national office to the task of forming a local union in a section of the country to which organized labor has never penetrated. The shop upon which the union has designs pays lower wages and runs for longer hours than those in the organized area of the industry. This threatens the standards which the union is trying to maintain. Some of the employers whose shops have been unionized have been protesting to the national officers that if the union does not push up the wages and shorten the hours in the unorganized shops, the union shops will be driven out of business. This pressure in addition to the national officers' desire to extend their membership leads to the decision to assign an organizer to "that sweatshop down in Tomkinstown."

The organizer, whom we shall call John O'Mara, arrives in Tomkinstown by train and puts up at a modest hotel. The seven dollars a day plus a restricted expense account which the union allows him does not permit lavish expenditures. He has a wife and two children whose demands are increasing as school age comes on and he always hopes that he can save a little out of his expense account to add to his weekly salary. Each week, however, he finds his expenses cutting in a little on his salary and although his wife doesn't say anything, O'Mara feels it necessary to explain to her that he met a couple of old-timers who were dead beat and he just couldn't turn them down. O'Mara has a brogue as broad as his smile, is physically robust, has a high-school education and is intelligent. He is not too good-looking to be considered dangerous by the men among their women, consequently both men and women like him.

Having hung up his extra suit on the only coat hanger in the hotel room closet, O'Mara washes the soot from his hands and face and goes out for a walk. As far as he knows there is no trace of the labor movement in Tomkinstown and he has no acquaintances there. He decides that he needs a shoe shine and while this is in process he engages the bootblack in conversation. He is in luck. The bootblack turns out to be the town's leading liberal. A reference to an article in *The New Republic* hazarded by O'Mara as a feeler brings an easy reply from the bootblack and O'Mara knows that he is on safe ground. Guarded inquiries disclose the fact that there are a "coupla old union men" at the post office, a retired professor who is regarded by some as a "radical," and a few men at the shop who are "pretty griped" by the conditions there. O'Mara pays for his shine and goes to call on the people the bootblack has told him about. They give him a line on conditions in the town and the shop and, after following two or three leads, he secures a list of workers who might be interested.

O'Mara covers his list of prospects in two evenings of door-to-door calls. Most of them are suspicious. Some understand what O'Mara is driving at but are afraid to do anything about it and tell him not to come to their houses again until after dark. Others are apathetic about the whole situation. Others have no idea of what a union is about and "can't see how it's going to do us any good." Some of them say that they don't want anything to do with "outside agitators." A few workers, however, turn out to be good prospects. O'Mara concentrates on them. He tells the whole story of the union and of comparative conditions in the industry. He gives them enough information and special "selling points" so that they can go out on the door-to-door and man-to-man calls and do the talking while O'Mara remains in the background. The squad of half-a-dozen leading spirits begins to produce results. Some workers fall for the personal attack on the "boss." Others see that if wages are not pushed up in Tomkinstown they will soon be cut elsewhere and that the employer will offer that as a reason for a further reduction in Tomkinstown. Some are impressed by the fact that "we oughta stick together in this." Two are interested because they hear that "there's something going on here, and we wanta be in on it." Finally this group is called together in the home of one member. A little ceremony and a good deal of secrecy are observed. The organizer explains the condition of the industry, how this locality compares with others, what the union stands for, what the union is prepared to do, what the union has been able to accomplish in the past, what the limitations and dangers of union activity are and what the plan of action is. The members of the group agree to go to work on others. The organizer stays away from the shop in order not to attract attention to himself or to anyone seen speaking to him. He is able to take the week end off "to run down and see the wife and kids."

When he gets back he finds that good work has been done at a beer party put on by the temporary chairman of the group. On Monday night he goes up on the hill to visit the professor. They have three scotch and sodas and fall to speculating over "the coming revolution." "In the South," says the professor, "there are great disparities between the upper and the lower social classes. The middle classes are not fully developed, and yet industrialism has proceeded far. This produces a condition comparable to that in Russia at the beginning of the War. When the cultural and industrial education of the negroes develops sufficiently to make it impossible for the upper classes to play them off against the poor whites, the revolution will come." "Maybe you're right," replies O'Mara, "but I'll put my bets on the Middle West. Those boys out there have taken a beating during the depression, and it's getting so even the union officers can't hold 'em back. There's going to be plenty of trouble in Akron, Toledo, Flint and Detroit when they get going." The professor lets O'Mara out the side door into the quiet night and O'Mara grins to himself on the way back to the hotel. "I wonder what the boys down at the shop would say if I tried to sign them up for the coming revolution. They'd probably sign me up for a ride on a rail."

Eventually a solid nucleus of 40 per cent of the workers is secured. O'Mara's smile and his care in protecting the active union workers from observation have overcome their fear. The attitude that O'Mara is an "outside agitator" and that unionists are "justa buncha reds" has been changed to the opinion that "they're pretty good guys, after all." Apathy toward things as they are has been altered by descriptions of things as they might be, or things as they are somewhere else. O'Mara now expands his activities. Enough of the secrecy is dropped so that other workers hear that "some of the guys are gettin' together." A charter is received from the national office and an initiation is held with a district officer present. The district officer gives the initiation oath and delivers a stock address on "Labor and the Nation."

The appeal of the union workers now changes from persuasion to shame and perhaps to fear. The distinctions here are subtle. One worker says to another, "All of my crowd have gone in, you better come along." The next time it is, "You wouldn't scab on us, would ya?" O'Mara's smile has developed a peculiar habit of ending in a sudden underthrust of the jaw and a narrowing of the eyes. Twenty per cent more of the workers come in. Another meeting is held and a bunch of the weak sisters are invited. The organizer makes a speech which flatters, shames and frightens them. Ten per cent more sign up. "Some of the boys are beginning to wonder a little about you. 'Course I know you're all right, but if I was in your shoes and wasn't looking for trouble I'd come along with the rest of the gang." Another 5 per cent signs up. Three workers' Fords develop a mysterious series of flat tires. O'Mara hears about it and says, "Take it easy on that stuff, boys," with a faintly perceptible wink, "but if you can't be good, be careful." The piston rings in another Ford suddenly wear thin and it is reported that emery dust was found in the crank case. "Who's the dirty bum that done that?" says one worker to another with a broad grin. The union now has 80 per cent of the men in the shop.

The employer is suspicious and worried, but he receives a large order from a firm whose custom he cannot afford to lose. O'Mara calls a meeting of the union. The situation is discussed and O'Mara says he thinks "things are about ripe for a tumble." The meeting puts it up to O'Mara to call on the employer and present the demand. O'Mara phones the employer and asks for an appointment. The employer is glad to get the thing out in the open. O'Mara is recognized as bargaining agent for the men in the shop. A trade agreement is concluded embodying higher minimum wages, differentials above the minimum according to skill, a forty-eight-hour week and seniority in layoffs. The union accepts it. Both sides sign. To celebrate the event there is a dinner at Joe's Tavern with some beer on the side. O'Mara makes a speech telling them that now is the time to get their organization going in good shape so that when the employer's big order has been filled they'll be able to prevent any funny business. "You boys have gotta stick together now and make this organization into a big thing. Regular meetings, two or three socials a year, learn some parliamentary law and get a permanent headquarters. You'll need some letterheads too. The national office will furnish them cheap. You're in good hands here. Your new president, Joe Bagliotti, is a good man. I've been watching him and he's coming along fine. And as for your Executive Secretary, Tom O'Flaherty, well, he's a mick like myself and you couldn't do better. If you get in trouble or need any help, let the district office know and they'll do the best they can to take care of you." While the boys are singing "For He's a Jolly Good Fellow," O'Mara is handed a telegram from the home office telling him to hurry on to a "hot situation" in Jonesboro.

O'Mara often points out to interested outsiders that the basic principle of union organizing is that of selling the idea of group action. The methods used by union organizers vary as much as those used by other sellers of goods and services. Ideas as well as goods may be sold on a wholesale, retail or door-to-door basis. The type of sales talk, the methods of advertising and the nature of the goods itself depend upon the kind of market in which the salesman is operating.

In the labor movement the salesman is the union organizer. He is usually employed and controlled by the national union. Occasionally local unions and central labor councils put organizers in the local field. The State Federations and the Executive Council of the A. F. of L. also have their organizers who are assigned to sections which especially need assistance. The Committee for Industrial Organization has put into the field an unprecedently large force of organizers who are not closely attached to any particular union. In normal periods, however, it is the organizers employed by the national union who form the most important single group. They are usually assigned by the national officers to sections of the country, social groups or branches of the industry to which they are best fitted. French-Canadian organizers are likely to be assigned to New Hampshire, native Southerners to Alabama, women organizers to the girl silk workers of Pennsylvania or the clothing workers of New York. All sorts of motives bring an organizer to his work. Getting a job, excitement, variety and altruism all play a part. There is probably a larger proportion of "the old missionary spirit" among the

motives of the sellers of unionism than among the sellers
of electric refrigerators and vacuum cleaners. At least it
forms a larger proportion of the organizer's sales talk. But
even the Realsilk salesmen must be convinced that the
world needs them and their products if their sales talk is
to carry the ring of conviction.

Until relatively recently, organizers have ordinarily
come from the ranks of the workers. Local union officers
who have done well in their territory, or workers who
have been discharged for union activity, are often taken
on as organizers. They have learned the ropes by experience, have carried on the policies of their predecessors, and
have developed rule-of-thumb methods of their own. The
problems of the organizers, however, have become increasingly technical. In spite of the skepticism of old-time union
leaders, the unions have more and more drawn upon colleges, graduate schools and law schools for the prestige and
the skills involved in the more ambitious organizing programs. In this respect, American unions have followed,
some distance in the rear, the footsteps of American business. Similarly, the labor movement has developed its special training schools for organizers comparable to the sales-
manship training courses of big businesses and the more
elaborate programs of business colleges and graduate business schools. In both cases there has been merriment among
the skeptics, but in both cases the idea of specialized training is winning out. The institutes and training courses of
the International Ladies' Garment Workers' Union, The
Steel Workers and Textile Workers organizing committees, the Affiliated Schools for Workers, the year-round
work of Brookwood Labor College in Katonah, New
York, the similar activity of Commonwealth College in
Mena, Arkansas, and the classes at the Rand and Workers
Schools in New York have already made an indelible impression upon the organizing techniques of the American
labor movement. Although the bulk of the organizers is

still self-trained and up-from-the-ranks, formal training or specialized knowledge will soon be an indispensable prerequisite to organizing work.

A number of other parallels may be drawn between the organizing policies of unions and the sales policies of corporations. The general officers of unions occasionally act in the capacity of organizers. Usually, however, their services are reserved for special occasions when particular skills or the advantages of a nationwide appeal are necessary. The officers act somewhat in the capacity of general managers or vice-presidents of corporations when a sales campaign of unusual importance is afoot. Apart from these occasions the permanent officers are usually reserved for quiet duty at the national or district offices and for the direction of particularly important legislative activities. During the nineteenth century union organizers were often called "missionaries." This was also true of the advance agents of big business in the backward nations. Nowadays, in the interest of greater accuracy, the term has been dropped in both connections.

The remuneration for union organizers has increasingly been placed upon the basis of a monthly salary computed as a fixed daily wage plus an expense allowance. Payment of organizers upon a commission basis has been found to be unsatisfactory because so many of the locals formed or members gained in this way proved to be impermanent. Preinitiation preparation and postinitiation follow-up are almost certain to be inadequate when the organizer is paid according to the number of members or locals gained. Many important businesses are experiencing the same results in the form of lapsed policies, returned goods and discontinued time-payments. Big business, where it has not already done so, may well follow the lead of the labor movement in this respect.

Organizing work takes place upon a great variety of different levels. To illustrate this we may continue to follow the career of John O'Mara.

When O'Mara arrives at Jonesboro he finds that it is another door-to-door job, but much harder. The local minister is interested because industrial homework and child labor are involved. The opening of the average door, however, is hardly wide enough to get his foot into. The minister tells his congregation that collective bargaining and Christianity have elements in common, but Mr. Graves and Mr. Squire who put the fresh five-dollar bills in the collection plate every week don't seem convinced. The Ladies Guild puts on a tea for O'Mara who gives a talk on "Labor Literature." He also produces a sheaf of pay envelopes showing wages of $4.16 for a seventy-two-hour week. One of the Guild members is the wife of the editor of the local paper. She makes a little joke to the effect that there isn't much difference between their Ladies Guild and Mr. Heywood Broun's Newspaper Guild, "which is a real union!" She tries to get her husband to run a "piece" in the paper about labor's constitutional rights. Her husband tells her that woman's place is in the home. Things are not going very well. Only about a dozen workers are interested. They are all suspicious of O'Mara, and he is suspicious of one of them. Soon his suspicions are verified. The local patriots are organizing to protect Jonesboro from outside agitators. O'Mara hurriedly casts up the balance of risks against gains and starts for the railroad station. There is a group of suspicious-looking loiterers on the platform. A few feathers are available and the local contractor has supplied some nice warm tar. After a long and anxious five minutes the train finally moves off. Jonesboro is saved from the Communist menace and O'Mara has an uneasy feeling that he has run out on the job. Irritated, he snaps to his wife when he pulls in late Saturday night, "This is a hell of a job. Why didn't I pick out a nice soft racket like selling Fuller brushes?"

On Monday morning O'Mara goes down to the district office and finds that things are really stirring. The Executive Council has decided to put ten thousand dollars into organizing the Jonesboro territory. They are sending the sound truck, several bales of literature, three extra organizers and a vice-president. The vice-president and auxiliary equipment arrive. The territory is mapped out. A thorough study of the "economics" of the area has been made. The map is dotted with red, blue, yellow and black flags showing shops with various wages, hours and conditions. Publicity stories are written describing the working conditions from a "human interest" point of view. There is the case of Anna Quinn who worked twenty-one hours for seventy-three cents. Her little brother has tuberculosis. Then there is Sophie, a skilled worker, who paid her boss a dollar a week to "learn" the trade and was fired at the end of the month. The newspapers are not interested in these stories although the reporters from the Newspaper Guild do the best they can. The "strategy board" decides to sink a thousand dollars in dignified advertising. The union's stories begin to appear on page two. On Sunday Anna's picture is in the brown section. The sound truck goes into action at several shop gates during the noon hours. The gospel is set forth with restraint and dignity. The workers can't help hearing it and there is no risk involved in listening. Three society matrons are photographed talking to the union's vice-president. There are protests from the ranks, but the publicity man says, "What's the difference whether they are endorsing Lucky Strikes or the right to collective bargaining as long as it makes the newspapers?" Leaflets printed in large round type on smooth paper are distributed at shop gates as the workers come out. This is slower than the sound truck, but the organizers have a chance for a word or two with the men and can get an idea of what they are thinking.

The Central Labor Union of one of the towns in the area has at last swung into action. The officers of the C. L. U. are politicians in a small way and are pals of the

United States Congressman from the district. It happens that he is at home repairing his political fences. Contact is established. A big meeting is arranged with the Congressman, two union officers and an associate professor from a near-by denominational college as speakers. The Congressman opens the meeting and makes a full-bodied speech in which he says that the Republican party has always stood for free speech, freedom of assembly ("just as we are doing now"), and the right of the workers to bargain collectively. A union officer tactfully closes him off at the end of his third peroration and just before he begins on the tariff question. The other speakers are more specific and the vice-president finally gets down to the actual situation. Literature is distributed along with application cards. It is announced that a headquarters will be opened for recruiting, but that any workers who want to apply by mail may do so. A handsome woman organizer, borrowed for the occasion from another union, sings a few songs and smiles at the boys. The meeting is adjourned with the singing of "America the Beautiful."

Membership applications and initiation fees pour in. Charters are issued. The organizers preside at the opening meetings of the locals. Officers are elected and the position of sergeant-at-arms is carefully bestowed upon the town comic. Cracks are made about "the small-town lad who made good." The rudiments of parliamentary procedure are instilled. Local bylaws and a constitution are drawn up. A program of meetings is decided upon. There is the usual trouble in getting the people with ideas to do the talking and to keep the people without any ideas from talking all the time. Eventually a common program for the whole area is ratified by all the locals. Demands are served upon all employers at once and the organizing stage of unionism passes either into the business or strike period of its life. This might be described as the retail or chain-store type of organizing.

The wholesale method may cover a wider field and involve even more elaborate techniques. O'Mara did such a good job on this last case that he has been appointed general organizer for the union and is assigned the task of taking on a whole industrial area. He packs up his belongings in two suitcases and piles them into the second-hand Buick which the union has assigned to him along with an enlarged expense account. His wife, who is always worried and who recently has been reading the LaFollette Committee reports, says, "Be careful, won't you, John?" as she kisses him good-by. On reaching the central city in the industrial area, O'Mara sets up headquarters in a good hotel and has a direct telephone connection put through to his room. The telephone establishes contact with all the important local and central labor union officers in the vicinity. A conference is called and general plans are laid. The conference is subdivided into committees on publicity, finances, legal affairs, physical equipment, personnel, fraternal contacts, interunion coöperation, political contacts and others of this order. These committees are drawn together at the top by the Board of Strategy. Stenographers and business equipment are installed at the headquarters. Regional and local offices are set up. Trained public relations counsels and newspapermen establish contact with local and metropolitan newspapers. Funds are raised by nation-wide appeals. A staff of trained organizers is built up. These in turn assemble groups of voluntary organizers who are able to establish direct relations with workers in the industry who carry on the man-to-man and door-to-door work that O'Mara usually had to do himself in his earlier days. The coöperation of fraternal groups and other unions is solicited and plans are made for the special fields of their activity. Statisticians and economists are retained partly for their names and partly to give the Board complete information about every phase of the industry: its financial structure and history, its profits record, the nature of foreign competition, disparities in wage rates and hours, differentials between minimum rates and those above, seasonality of operation, the chief markets and interlocking financial connections. Efforts are made to secure a senatorial investigation of the financial or employment conditions in the industry. The Secretary of Labor and other important Government officials are invited to address mass meetings. These occasions are used as sounding boards for union publicity. If there are company unions in the industry they may be induced to come over bag and baggage to the union cause. "Progressive" employers are asked to explain publicly why they have always dealt with the union in their industries and what they think the union has to offer to business. When locals have finally been set up and the workers have had some experience in operating as a group, demands are made and the situation, as before, moves forward into the strike or business stage of unionism.

There is a very large amount of organizing which takes place as a result of spontaneous strikes. When a strike breaks out before any organizing work has been done by a union, the leading spirits among the strikers are very likely to appeal to near-by union offices for help, or union organizers may hear of the strike situation themselves and hurry to the scene. Most union leaders and organizers much prefer not to have a ready-made market for organizing provided in this way. The risks of failure and consequent discredit to the union are greater than when a careful period of preparation has preceded the presentation of demands. The organizer is placed in something of a dilemma. If he refuses to respond to appeals, his union is likely to be discredited. If he does respond, and fails to bring the strike to a satisfactory conclusion, there is usually talk of "sell-out" and "bungling" which will rankle in the minds of workers in the vicinity for a decade after the event. In the cases in which the organizer accepts the invitation, his task is that of organizing the strike, rather than securing members. If he is able to secure any sort of concession from the employer, his inclination is to settle the strike as soon as possible and then get down to the job of developing a cohesive group of workers with funds, experience and machinery of their own before pressing on for further gains.

Although most unions try to avoid this type of organizing activity, some unions have specialized in it. The I.W.W. had a flying squad of organizers like Big Bill Haywood and Elizabeth Gurley Flynn, who spent a large part of their lives rushing from one section of the country to another as fast as strike situations developed. That the organizations set up during these strikes proved to be ephemeral was not of great importance to the I.W.W. leaders. Somewhat the same thing was true of the Communist unions set up in the 1929-35 period of the Trade Union Unity League. Although the T.U.U.L. leaders were more anxious for permanent organizations than the I.W.W., the locals which they did succeed in establishing were almost invariably the result of strike situations and rarely survived the settlement of the strike by more than a few months.

In industries where the wages are very low, hours long, cultural heterogeneity of the workers great and the hostility of employers to unionism determined, the strike may be the only form of organizing technique which has any hope of success. In the New Jersey and Pennsylvania silk industry, the Massachusetts and New Jersey woolen industry and the Southern cotton industry, it has always been very difficult to establish permanent organizations. The characteristics of these industries which make organization difficult nevertheless provide a basis for spectacular strikes. Such organizing work as has been done in these industries and others similar to them has of necessity taken the form of providing leadership for frequent and large-scale strikes with a subsequent struggle to preserve the organization after the settlement. In industries such as these the influence of the union cannot accurately be judged by membership alone, since the immense number of workers who pass through such unions without paying more than the initiation fee, if that, is not reflected in the tax-paying membership figures of the national union. The influence of such unions as the United Textile Workers, the I.W.W., and unions among metal miners, agricultural laborers, longshoremen, lumbermen and sailors has been very much greater than can be judged by their figures for per capita tax. Since the primary function of the organizer, however, is to build strong and stable organizations with the ultimate goal of rendering strikes unnecessary, most unions regard organizational strikes as unavoidable means to this end.

Organizing Through the Employer

THE organizing methods which have thus far been described are pursued without the connivance and usually in spite of the resistance of the employer. In addition to these methods there is another set in which the employer, willingly or otherwise, occupies a key position. The first of these is the demand by the union for recognition as sole bargaining agent. Although this demand is basically considered a prerequisite to collective bargaining, rather than an organizing technique, its significance in the latter capacity is becoming increasingly important. In the mass production industries when an employer agrees to bargain collectively with an industrial union for its members only, as in the case of the 1937 General Motors and Chrysler strikes, it means in effect that the trade agreement concluded with the union will apply to union and nonunion members alike. It is in fact next to impossible to have one set of wages, hours and conditions applying to union men and another set applying to company union or nonunion men working alongside. This means that the demand for sole bargaining power has a purpose which is ulterior to securing uniformity in wages, hours and conditions. It may be assumed that this ulterior purpose is to use the fact of sole recognition as a means for extending the membership of the union in the shop or plant. Having secured sole recognition, the union is enabled to use the double argument that there is no use in the workers' joining any other organization and that, since the union has improved the position of the nonunion workers, it would be decent of them to join and help pay the expense of maintaining the conditions which the union has established.

The second step in using the employer to assist in extending the membership of the union is to try to secure what is called the "preferential union shop." An employer who grants this demand agrees to give preference to union men in employing new recruits, in promotions and in layoffs. This gives the union a further talking point in selling itself to the remaining nonunion workers. "You better join the union, brother. Slack times are coming, and if you haven't got a card, you'll be the first to go."

The third step in selling the union through the employer is the "closed shop." When good union organizers smile in their sleep, they are dreaming that they have secured the closed shop and that all their troubles are over. Many American employers resist this demand to the very end, even if they have long since recognized the union, granted sole recognition and found that relationships with the union have been profitable. When the closed shop is agreed upon, the employer is obliged to discharge any workers who refuse to join the union. The vigor with which the union presses its demands and the strenuousness with which the employer opposes them often depend on the percentage of the workers who are already union members. Sometimes the employer says, "If you can get 95 per cent of the workers, I'll grant the closed shop." But more often in American industry the employer takes the position that he will go out of business before meeting the union's demands, regardless of the percentage of members the union may have. The employer says, "It's against all the principles of freedom and democracy to force workers to become members of any organization." The union says, "They're getting the benefits of the union. Why should they sponge on us? It won't hurt them to come into the union and pay our modest fees. Furthermore, isn't it the basic principle of democracy that the minority should abide by the decisions of the majority and pay the taxes which the legislature imposes, even if it is controlled by the opposition?" The employer replies, "But in the political field there is an explicit agreement before the election takes place that the minority will abide by the decision of the majority. When a worker takes a job in a factory, he makes no such agreement either explicitly or implicitly." The union counters, "How much freedom of choice does a native-born citizen of this country have in determining whether he will or will not abide by the laws and pay the taxes imposed by the majority? The courts say to the citizens of this country that if they don't like it here they may go elsewhere. Well, that's what we say to the workers in this plant."

Back of this argument of the union there is more than the desire to collect dues. In the history of American unionism, union leaders have amassed a volume of evidence to show that in the majority of cases in which the employer opposes the closed shop, the real reason behind the argument is that the employer hopes, by limiting the expansion of the union, to take the next favorable opportunity for getting rid of the union altogether. The phrase "open shop" has become almost identical in workers' minds with "antiunion" shop. The industries which have been most successful in eradicating unionism have organized under the name of "Open Shop Associations." In England, where collective bargaining has been very generally accepted by industrial management for more than a generation, the "closed shop" has not been an issue. If acceptance of unionism in this country becomes equally general, it may be anticipated that both the demand for and the resistance to the "closed shop" will decrease in intensity. In the meantime it remains an important instrument in the union's organizing kit, and a source of bitter conflict between union and management.

Both the 1934 and the 1936 maritime strikes on the Pacific Coast really centered around this issue of the closed shop. The method of enforcing it among the seamen and longshoremen is through union control of the "hiring hall." Although both parties to the strike talked in terms of safety at sea, efficiency and the public interest, it was apparent enough that if the employers retained control of the hiring halls in 1934 or secured control in 1936, nonunion men, as far as possible, would be given preference. Whereas, since the union actually secured control of the hiring halls in 1934 and retained it in 1936, the opposite has been true. The industries in which unions have been most successful in securing the closed shop are coal mining, the building and printing trades in many areas, and men's and women's clothing.

Close on the heels of the closed shop as an organizing device operated through the employer comes the "checkoff." This is a system under which the employer agrees to collect union membership dues from the pay envelope of the workers. It is understood that the dues shall be collected from every worker regardless of his willingness to have such a deduction made. The checkoff, therefore, is in effect an extremely efficient method of enforcing the closed shop. The average employer's opposition to the checkoff is even more intense than to the closed shop. Union organizers and leaders, by the same token, are likely to consider it the *summum bonum*. In addition to enforcing the closed shop, it eliminates a vast amount of trouble in collecting individual dues, and reduces the bookkeeping problem to a minimum. The most important single instance of the use of the checkoff is in the coal-mining industry where the United Mine Workers have successfully applied it to something over 90 per cent of the tonnage of coal produced in this country. In this particular instance the Mine Workers have used the additional argument that in the coal industry employers have for generations had their own "checkoff" in the form of deductions from pay envelopes for bills at company stores, rent in company houses and fines.

Somewhat different in method, but identical with the foregoing tactics in that they operate for organizing purposes through the employer, are the union label and boycott. The union officer says to the employer, "If you will recognize our union and grant the conditions which we ask, we will sell to you, for a nominal price, labels which you may use on your product. This will help you to sell your product among union men and union sympathizers." The conditions which the union lays down may refer simply to wages, hours and shop affairs, or they may include a demand for the closed shop or the checkoff. In almost every case, however, union recognition is a *sine qua non*. The resistance of the employer may thus be broken down and the work of organizing facilitated. In the case of the boycott, the converse procedure is employed. "If you do not recognize the union and adhere to the conditions which we ask, we will see to it that your products are not bought by union men and union sympathizers."

The use of both the boycott and the label is very limited. They are unlikely to be effective unless the products are sold at retail. If the products on which the workers are employed are not consumable, the only way of making the label or boycott policy applicable is to secure interunion agreements not to handle goods which have not been made under union conditions. In the past these agreements have been difficult to arrange. Recent examples may be found in the refusal of East Coast longshoremen to handle "hot" cargoes from the West.

In the retail field the products which lend themselves to the boycott or label policy are those which are purchased primarily by working-class families. Boots and shoes, over-alls, work shirts, cigars, stoves, barbering services, beer, hats and bread are the products among which the greatest successes of the past have been achieved. Even in these fields, however, the success of the policy depends upon a high degree of union consciousness among consumers. Un-less the tradition of the labor movement is very strong, working-class families are likely to think in terms of price and quality rather than in terms of the conditions under which the goods are made. Throughout the history of the A.F. of L. strenuous efforts have been made to render the labor movement label conscious. The matter is emphasized at least once in almost every local union and central labor union meeting. Specific examples in the neighborhood are pointed out. A delegate rises and says, "Speaking for the Barbers' Local No. 204, I'd like to say that the shop on the corner of Willow and Prospect is nonunion and we advise the brothers to stay away until they see our card in the window." This reminds the chairman of several other cases which he recites. Delegates may be seen making a note of these matters on an old envelope for report to their local unions. Unless it is a period of considerable excite-ment in the labor movement, however, the frequent repeti-tion which is given to this question is very likely to dull any interest which there may be in it.

National unions often press the label and boycott ques-tion in the pages of the union periodical and by attention to it at the annual conventions. Some unions try to make their members label conscious by requiring that every dele-gate to the national convention shall have on his person a certain number of union labels. As might be expected, the practice often leads to a good deal of hilarity when, for example, it is discovered that the presiding officers have not passed examination and must retire to purchase some labeled cigars, a labeled tie, a pair of labeled shoes, some labeled socks and a labeled suit of underwear. Someone yells, "Say, he's got a *union* suit on. Wyncha leave him alone?"

The Label Trades Department of the A.F. of L. is made up of all the unions in the A.F. of L. which pursue a label policy. The function of the Department is to provide common advertising of the labels used by A.F. of L. unions. In 1936 there were fifty-two national union labels, ten shop cards and seven groups of directly affiliated federal unions using the A.F. of L. label. These last included the Horse Nail Workers, Suspender Makers, Sausage Seasoning and Spice Workers!

The legal status of the label has never been questioned. It has been placed on the same basis as the trade-mark and is protected by patent law from infringement. The legal status of the boycott, on the contrary, is very questionable. The primary boycott, under which a union seeks to influence only its own members, has generally been allowed by the courts. The secondary boycott, however, in which the union attempts to influence the buying public, has been repeatedly outlawed by the Federal courts under the conspiracy doctrine of common law and under the statutory prohibitions involved in the Sherman and Clayton Acts. The state courts have in many instances been more lenient, but have usually limited the manner in which the boycott may be applied. As a result of the Buck's Stove and Range Case in 1908, the A.F. of L. was forced to discontinue its "We Don't Patronize" list. To some extent the A.F. of L. has evaded the force of this and subsequent similar decisions by bringing in resolutions to the annual convention which refer to "unfair" products. These resolutions are discussed at some length and then tabled without action. Delegates, however, are as likely to be as much affected by this procedure as by the formal list which the A.F. of L., and the Knights of Labor before it, were wont to publish. On the whole, the increasing complexity of the market and the hostility of the courts has rendered the boycott ineffective except in its local applications. The label, on the other hand, will probably increase in usefulness as an organizing device as the membership of labor organizations expands and as workers become more union conscious.

The most elaborate method used by unions in organizing through the medium of the employer is the policy which during the 'twenties came to be called "union-management coöperation." This policy involves the application on a wider basis of the principle which lies behind the use of the label. This principle is the theory that the interests of union and management are to some extent identical. In the case of the label, the union says, "If you will recognize the union and grant certain conditions, we will help you in selling your goods. If we both play ball together, each of us will gain." In the case of union-management coöperation, the union agrees that in exchange for recognition and the granting of certain conditions it will make every possible effort to regularize employment, increase efficiency, stop industrial conflict by arbitrating disputes, and reduce labor costs in every way which does not involve a reduction in wage rates or an extension in working hours. In some cases the union also agrees to extend the sale of the product by the use of the label and through the advertising channels of the labor movement.

Union-management coöperation is nothing new in the history of the labor movement. It is at the bottom of every business relationship between the two groups in industry. It becomes explicit whenever a trade agreement is signed. During the 1920's even the conservative unions in the A.F. of L. lost ground. The relationship between wages in many industries and the general price level was such that real wages showed some increase simply as a result of what is called "fundamental economic law." The appeal of unionism as a protection for labor standards was consequently minimized. The idea of the "New Capitalism" was in the air: "The interests of workers and management are identical; all that is necessary is that the two groups in industry get together and talk things over." Specific applications of this theory were made in the form of employee stock-ownership and profit sharing, company "welfare work" and company unionism. It was a period of effective opposition by management to the "interference of outside agitators"—meaning the labor movement. Both consciously and unconsciously the labor movement adjusted itself to this changed situation. The A.F. of L. developed a new "sales talk" to meet the new resistance of management. This sales talk in its bluntest form was "let us come in and help you run your business. It will be worth while for both of us."

At least two attempts were made by the A.F. of L. to adopt this policy as a general organizing technique. During the year 1926 there was a good deal of talk about organizing the automobile industry. Accordingly, the A.F. of L. convention of that year was held in Detroit to direct attention toward the automobile industry. The convention resolved that the Executive Council should put on a campaign beginning as soon as the convention adjourned. The Executive Council obtained conferences with management and put the case before it. Management was not impressed so the organizing campaign came to an end. In 1929 and 1930 the A.F. of L. undertook to assist one of its constituent unions, the United Textile Workers, in organizing the South. The union-management coöperation tactic was again decided upon. President Green of the A.F. of L. and President McMahon of the Textile Workers launched upon what the radicals called a "hat-in-hand" tour of the

South. University groups were interested and chambers of commerce were polite. As soon, however, as particular employers were approached, strikes, lockouts and evictions became the order of the day. In the end the campaign was an entire failure.

In a large number of particular instances some success attended the formal adoption of a union-management coöperation program. Among the railroad shop workers, in the clothing industry, among the printing pressmen, hosiery workers, upholsterers and sheeting workers union-management coöperation enjoyed a much publicized success for limited periods before the depression. In these instances, however, the policy was not so much an organizing tactic as it was a business relationship established after some degree of recognition had already been achieved. There is little evidence that employers who had an antiunion attitude were much interested in the conciliatory mood of the labor movement during this period. In the postdepression period, consequently, unions have fallen back almost exclusively upon the direct organization of workers in an atmosphere of conflict.

The policy of union-management coöperation has been attacked as "class-collaboration" by the radicals and as "racketeering" by the friends and enemies of organized labor. The first charge rests upon a social philosophy which need not at the moment be elaborated. The second charge is one which must be seriously considered in this connection. It is unquestionable that all of the organizing tactics, from the closed shop to union-management coöperation, which involve an approach through the emloyer, lend themselves to labor racketeering.

The word "racketeering" in the labor movement needs careful definition according to one's economic interests and social point of view. To an antiunion employer all unionism is racketeering if it results in the extraction from him of more money or power than he would otherwise surrender. To the consumer who is not primarily a wage receiver unionism may appear as a racket if it takes from him in the form of higher prices more than would be taken in the absence of a labor movement. To the organized worker, however, his union is a racket only if it delivers gains to him which are small in relation to the income received by the organizers and leaders of the union. This is admittedly a loose definition, but it is more real from the worker's point of view than those offered by the employer and the nonunionized consumer.

When the union leader operates through the employer in securing his hold upon an industry rather than by direct appeal to the interests of the workers, the leader is to that extent less dependent upon the support of the workers for the maintenance of his position of power. The closed shop makes unnecessary the same intensity of effort on the workers' behalf that is necessary if the leader's position is dependent upon his ability to satisfy his membership. If there is discontent among the membership, the leader may avoid difficulties by expelling the troublous members from the union and compelling the employer to discharge the workers in accord with the terms of the closed-shop agreement. It is therefore possible for the union leader and the employer to come to an agreement under which the leader receives a consideration for carrying out the wishes of management. The union leader thus becomes the official dispatcher of troublemakers, the management escapes the difficulty of being known as an anti-union firm, and as long as the local exists at all it constitutes effective protection against other organizational efforts. When the closed shop is combined with the checkoff and the label, an almost foolproof racketeering arrangement is possible. The management receives the benefit of the label and protection against "labor troubles." The union leaders receive the membership dues direct from the employer. Difficulties may be avoided by dispensing with union meetings altogether. Elections may be held with great infrequency and with the union leaders as the tellers! In the case of the more elaborate union-management coöperation program much the same thing is true. Coöperation may be carried to a point at which the union leader engineers wage reductions, progressive speeding-up and layoffs for the benefit of the employer and with dubious blessings to the workers.

It by no means follows that the adoption of the closed shop, the checkoff, the label and the policy of union-management coöperation inevitably results in the development of labor racketeering. It must be emphasized, however, that to the extent that a union owes its position in a plant or industry to the acceptance by management of any of these devices, the temptation to allow this situation to develop into racketeering and the possibility of accomplishing it are perceptibly increased. It becomes imperative under these conditions for an honest union leader constantly to subject his motives to the most thoroughgoing scrutiny. It becomes even more important for the membership of a union to be more persistent in their attention to leadership policies than is otherwise necessary.

The technique of organizing lies in selling the idea of group action and in making such action effective once it has been stimulated. It is the basis of all social power whether it is achieved by money, credit, ownership, legal devices, reason, eloquence, habit, inertia, love, shame, hate or fear. The motives behind the drive toward power based on organization run the whole gamut of combinations between sheer altruism and pure self-interest. In organizing workers, the basic appeal is to their self-interest as non-propertied wage earners. Upon this basis may be overlaid an appeal to dignity, group ethics, excitement, romance or beauty. The success of the organizer depends upon his ability to adapt the form of his appeal to the circumstances in which he operates. His instruments may vary from stethoscopes [1] to brass knuckles; from statistics to the harmonica; from animal strength to parliamentary procedure; from cold brutality to the rhapsodic overtones of inspired eloquence; and from Hegelian dialectics to fraternal affection. His task is inspiring or degrading, elevating or depressing, depending upon the motives which bring him to it, the objects toward which it is directed and the success with which it is attended.

[1] John Steinbeck, in his novel *In Dubious Battle*, describes an instance in which an organizer secured his entrée to a group of fruit-pickers by assisting at a child-birth.

CHAPTER II

The Evolution of the Labor Movement

FOR nearly one hundred and fifty years American workers have been acting in groups. The ink on the American Constitution was scarcely dry when the first craft unions came into existence. Workers turned to group action because they discovered through trying experience that social rights and economic status rest upon the power of the group rather than upon individual desires or the fiction of natural law.

In pursuing their economic and social ends the participants in the American labor movement have developed a variety of forms of organization. The key to the understanding of unionism lies in recognizing that its evolution has been determined chiefly by workers' efforts to adjust their unions to the changes in the industrial and social world in which they operate. In this adjustment there has inevitably arisen a lag based upon human inertia, habit and vested interests. The development of unionism has consequently been irregular and uneven. There have been periods during which the form and methods of labor organization fell far behind the contemporary changes in the environment. These have been succeeded by periods of extraordinarily rapid alteration in union policies which have profoundly influenced the following periods of relative quiet. The phenomenal rise of the Knights of Labor in the 'eighties, and the spectacular activities of the Industrial Workers of the World during the World War period provide examples of this aspect of union evolution. The present conflict between the Committee for Industrial Organization and the Executive Council of the American Federation of Labor is an even more striking illustration of tardy adjustment of old forms to new conditions.

The earliest unions confined their activities to the immediate locality in which they came into existence. Thus the unions of printers and shoemakers which appeared between 1794 and 1805 in Philadelphia, New York and Baltimore established no connections among these cities except those of occasional correspondence. They were local unions of one craft and one place and gave their attention exclusively to matters of their own trade.

District organizations, however, soon appeared. Between 1827 and 1834 there were developed in Philadelphia, New York and elsewhere Trades' Councils or Mechanics' Unions composed of the representatives of the different craft unions. Since the different crafts in these Trades' Unions had various economic interests at stake, it was unlikely that they should consider matters of trade policy. Consequently they sought their goals through political channels. They were successful in securing concessions from the major political parties in the form of mechanics' lien laws, freedom from imprisonment for debt and widening of the suffrage. In addition to this, local unions flourished in greater numbers than before and a few short-lived national unions made their appearance.

During the 1850's the first permanent national unions were formed. They were permanent in the sense that many of them remained intact for several decades and a few, such as the Typographical Union and the Mulespinners' Union, have maintained a more or less continuous existence down to the present time. Since the 'fifties, the national unions have gradually developed in power until they have become the core of the labor movement. Many national unions have assumed the more imposing title of "International Union" as a result of securing locals in Canada.

The process by which the national union has increased its power and importance is exactly parallel to the similar development in the relationship between the states and the Federal Government. In the early days of the national union, the locals were very jealous of their autonomy. Upon joining the national union, the local surrendered only a limited number of powers specifically delegated to the national. The national unions, therefore, consisted of very little more than an annual convention attended by delegates from the local unions, presided over by officers receiving little if any salary and devoting themselves primarily to exchange of information upon matters pertaining to their craft. Between conventions the officers occasionally engaged in part-time organizing, but were chiefly occupied by actual work at their trade. The locals made scant financial contributions to the national treasury and surrendered little of their power over the calling and settling of strikes, signing of agreements and dispensing of benefits.

Changing economic and social conditions, however, made necessary a change in union methods. Transportation improved, markets broadened and the scale of production increased. The products made in one locality began to compete with those made in another. Local unions were forced to consider the advisability of maintaining uniform scales of wages, hours and conditions throughout a whole trade or industry in order to protect the worker from becoming the shock absorber for the entire competitive process. Local union leaders, furthermore, were forced to recognize the necessity for organizing the unorganized workers in order to prevent a wage reduction from originating in the unorganized shops and being communicated to the unionized centers. In those industries such as the railroads, steel, distilling, in which monopoly rather than competition was the result of the development of large-scale production and the modern corporation, local unions found themselves impotent in the face of the massed power of capital. Finally the employers themselves began to organize for action in their relations with labor even though they were competing against each other in selling their products. Gentlemen's agreements among employers not to compete in hiring labor, or agreements to blacklist union leaders or to help each other during strikes developed into full-fledged employers' associations against which a local union was powerless.

As a result of these changes, local union leaders began to see that it had become necessary to grant the national union increased powers in order to cope with the forces arrayed against them. The basic transfer of power from local to national unions has taken the form of an increase in the taxes which the locals pay into the national treasury. This has increased the services which the national organization can perform and has enabled it to control the local unions by making the granting of services or financial benefits to the members of the locals conditional upon good behavior by the local.

A typical modern national union has the following elements: An annual or biennial convention usually presided over by the permanent officers of the national union and attended by delegates from local unions elected upon the basis of some form of proportional representation; a board of permanent officers intrusted with carrying out the decisions of the convention and having large power granted by the constitution; an executive council having advisory and administrative powers to whom the president is responsible between conventions; a set of offices constituting the headquarters where records, business machinery, a library and legal, technical and stenographic services are available; regional offices directed by subordinate national officers; a treasury to which contributions are made by the locals and from which payments are made by the officers; traveling organizers attached to certain districts and responsible to the national officers.

Parallel with the increase in the power of the national unions, a change in their structure has developed. The earliest unions were craft in form. Although modified craft unionism still remains the backbone of the American Federation of Labor, industrial unions and labor unions have repeatedly challenged the dominance of the craft unions in the past, and may well engulf them in the immediate future.

The shift from the craft toward the industrial form of organization has been brought about by the same economic and social developments which have transferred power from the local to the national union. The craft union came into existence before the rise of the factory system, mass production, minute specialization of tasks and semiautomatic machinery had become the major characteristics of the industrial system. The craft form of organization was based upon the special skills of clearly distinct occupations whose common interests with other occupations were not apparent. This form of organization remains valid and effective only where special skills and clearcut separations of occupations and interests still prevail. This field has been steadily reduced in extent and importance by the inexorable forward march of modern industry. A labor movement based exclusively upon the craft form of organization would have found its scope increasingly limited and its powers exhausted by continual conflict between old forms and new needs. Crafts have been federated and amalgamated. Industrial unions have appeared and grown powerful. National unions have been brought together for common action through the American Federation of Labor and its subordinate agencies. All of these developments have been in the direction of greater solidarity of the labor group.

The evolution of the modern industrial union has been a process which has included a good many transitional stages. A national craft union is composed of locals, all of which accept only the workers in one specialized craft as members. Thus in the brewing industry there might be

national craft unions of coopers, engineers, teamsters, firemen and oilers. The next step in the direction of greater
solidarity is the federation of national craft unions. In this
stage the national craft unions retain their separate identity
but come together in annual conventions to consider matters of mutual interest. Local craft unions may also federate to deal with affairs of common concern. For example,
in 1898 the American Federation of Textile Operatives
brought together into a loose group the national craft
unions among mulespinners, loomfixers, weavers and
carders. In Fall River and New Bedford the local unions
of these crafts were grouped in the Fall River and New
Bedford Textile Councils. The third step is amalgamation.
Under this form of organization the national craft unions
usually go out of existence and each of the craft locals
becomes directly attached to the new national union
formed as a result of the merger proceedings. In the early
stages of amalgamation each craft has its separate local
union in each organized center. When the United Textile
Workers, for example, was formed in 1901 it was made
up of separate local unions of loomfixers, weavers, spinners and so forth. In a well-organized center like Fall
River there might be four or five locals in one mill all
affiliated with the United Textile Workers, but each having separate meetings, policies, officers and treasuries. In
other industries, or in later stages of amalgamation, several
crafts might combine in one local as in the case of the
Amalgamated Association of Iron, Steel and Tin Workers
which until recently was composed of locals admitting
workers in three metal crafts to membership.

The fourth stage in this evolution is industrial unionism.
In this final form the national union is composed of locals
each of which admits to membership all the workers in
and around a given production unit. In a typical iron
foundry, for example, there are between fifteen and
twenty separate occupations in addition to a group of

casual and relatively unskilled laborers. Under the industrial form of organization now adopted by the Amalgamated Association of Iron, Steel and Tin Workers all of these occupations, including the casual laborers, are placed in one local union.[1]

The "labor" union, in which all workers in a given territory regardless of industry are organized in one local union attached directly to a national organization, has had only a limited development under the Knights of Labor, the I.W.W. and the One Big Union. Extension of this form is unlikely except among migratory and agricultural workers. Further evolution is likely to take the form of close affiliations between related industries such as clothing and textiles; coal, steel, automobiles, rubber and glass; seamen and longshoremen; and agriculture, canning and lumbering. In addition to the development of national industrial unions, a second process has helped to provide unity in the labor movement. This has been the rise of the American Federation of Labor to a position of dominance which has only recently been seriously threatened. The A.F. of L. was founded in 1886 by Samuel Gompers as the result of a long series of preliminary efforts to bring together the national craft unions. For the first fifteen

[1] The use of the words "horizontal" and "vertical" has purposely been avoided as being more misleading than helpful. The most common use of these words makes "horizontal" identical with "craft" and "vertical" identical with "industrial." Confusion arises from the fact, however, that the industrial union is horizontal in the sense that it connects all workers with each other who are engaged in a certain stage of production. Thus the iron miners, the steel workers and the automobile workers are horizontally organized at each level of production although each of these groups is organized in industrial unions. The word "horizontal" may also be used accurately to describe craft unions which connect all workers of a given occupation, such as carpentering, regardless of the industry in which the carpentering takes place. The word "vertical," on the other hand, may be applied to "company" unions each of which has no connection with any other union, or it may be applied to the Carpenters' Union which until recently pushed its jurisdiction backward into the earlier stages of the manufacture of wood and included sawmill hands and wood finishers.

years of its life the Federation consisted chiefly of Samuel Gompers and a series of annual conventions. National union officers were suspicious of the new organization and were reluctant to surrender to it either powers or funds. In the generation after 1900, however, the present characteristics of the A.F. of L. were gradually developed. The central core of the Federation is the hundred or more national unions which are affiliated with it. These unions send delegates to the annual conventions and from among the leaders of these unions are chosen the members of the Executive Council of the A.F. of L. The Executive Council has at least four meetings a year and conducts the important business of the Federation between conventions. It is the center of the machine which has for a long time ruled the affairs of the Federation with an iron hand. Its personnel has been composed almost exclusively of craft union leaders, some of whom have held their positions for many years. Through the powers of committee appointments, presiding officers, personal contact and political relationships the Executive Committee and its officers have been able to enforce a common policy upon the constituent unions in spite of the loosely federated structure which is established by the constitution of the Federation.

Although industrial unions have been admitted to the A.F. of L., their importance in its affairs has been relatively slight. Even during the heyday of the N.R.A., industrial unionists did not constitute much over one third of the total membership of the A.F. of L. and they were sparsely represented on convention committees and the Executive Council. The policies of the A.F. of L. have consequently been the policies of craft unionism somewhat modified by the diversity of interests which it represents and by the necessities of its titular leadership of the American labor movement.

Centralization of power within the Federation has resulted not only from machine control but also from the extension of its financial powers. In the period before 1900 Gompers gradually persuaded the national unions to increase the contributions which they paid to the treasury of the A.F. of L. The constitution of the A.F. of L. came to require that each national union pay into the A.F. of L. treasury one cent a month for each member the national union claimed to have. The compulsion applied to the national unions to secure the observance of this requirement has been partly moral suasion, but it has been chiefly the provision that the voting strength of a national union at the annual convention depends upon the amount of monthly per capita tax which the national has paid during a preceding period. This has resulted in both underpayment and overpayment of per capita tax, depending upon the voting strength which the union delegates have wished to have at A.F. of L. conventions. The important consequence, however, has been that the officers and Executive Council of the A.F. of L. have had money placed in their hands. This money has made possible the provision of organizing, technical information, lobbying, propaganda and other services which are available to the national unions on condition of good behavior.

One other important development within the structure of the A.F. of L. has very much increased its power and importance. This has been the provision of local, state and departmental federations of unions. These federations have been the machinery back of what the A.F. of L. officials call the "family of labor." In each city or town where unionism has progressed, there have been set up organizations variously called trades' councils, city centrals, central labor unions or city federations. The primary purpose of these federated groups has been to provide local clearing houses for the common problems of all organized workers in the vicinity. Local unions send delegates and funds to these councils and receive in return services and support.

In spite of the diversity of interests among local unions, the trades' councils represent important advances toward solidarity of labor, especially on the political front. Very much the same thing is true of the forty-nine state federations composed of delegates from both the city centrals and local unions in each state and in the District of Columbia. The primary purpose of the state federations is to protect workers' interests in the state legislatures, although they also act as publicity devices and organizing centers for the state as a whole. In addition to the local and state federations, the A.F. of L. has grouped in departments those crafts and industries whose interests link them closest together. Thus the building workers', metal workers', railway workers' and label trades workers' unions have been placed in departments of the A.F. of L. whose councils or conventions meet and act on both a local and national basis. Finally, the A.F. of L. has created another adjunct called the Federal Trade or Labor Union whose function is to absorb workers for whom there is no national organization in existence, or who exist in insufficient number in a given locality to make it worth while to set up separate locals of the crafts with which they would otherwise affiliate.

Apart from the fact that each of these devices constitutes a step in the direction of common action among all workers, their primary significance lies in the fact that they are all directly affiliated with the A.F. of L. without the intermediation of a national union. The city centrals, state federations, trades departments and federal unions pay their taxes directly to the A.F. of L. Executive Council. They send their delegates directly to the A.F. of L. convention and they take their orders from it. The officers and Council of the A.F. of L., therefore, are furnished with a powerful implement of compulsion which may be brought to bear upon the national unions. If national unions or their locals refuse to carry out the mandates of

A.F. of L. conventions, or the decisions of the Executive Council, they may be expelled from all the federated groups to which they are attached. This means ostracism from the "family of labor." The moral effect of this upon the ostracized national or local union is great. Beyond this, however, assistance in organizing, striking, lobbying and publicity may be shut off; the fund-raising channels of the labor movement may be closed; competing organizations may be founded; and even the strikes of the "renegade" union may be broken by the activities of "good" union men.

As a result of machine control, increased financial resources and the elaboration of the principle of federation, the American Federation of Labor, in spite of its technically loose structure, has therefore successfully achieved a high degree of centralization of power within the American labor movement. The diagram on the opposite page may serve somewhat to clarify the very complicated structure of the organization which has become the backbone of American organized labor.

In spite of the gradual progress of industrial unionism, however, and the emergence of centralized control within the A.F. of L., the "orthodox" trade-union movement has by no means kept pace with the changes in its industrial and social surroundings. Trades' councils, state federations, trades' departments and federal unions have failed to meet the problem of jurisdictional disputes. The slow progress of industrial unionism within the A.F. of L. has failed to meet the problem of organizing the unskilled mass production workers in most of the basic industries. Centralization of power within the A.F. of L. has failed to promote unity in the labor movement as a whole. The consequences of this failure have been the wasting away of the strength of existing unions and inability to realize possible powers.

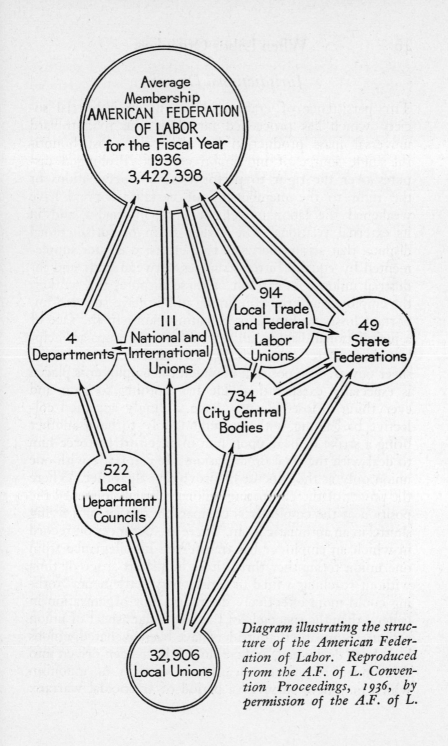

Diagram illustrating the structure of the American Federation of Labor. Reproduced from the A.F. of L. Convention Proceedings, 1936, by permission of the A.F. of L.

Jurisdictional Disputes

THE persistence of craft unionism in an industrial society which has proceeded far along the road toward universal mass production has been the most bountiful single source of interunion conflict. Prolonged disputes over the right to perform certain occupations or the right to the membership of certain workers have weakened the labor movement both internally and in its external relations. The earlier form of jurisdictional dispute, that arising between two crafts, was later supplemented by equally bitter struggles between craft and industrial unions. As a result of these disputes the worker, the employer and the consuming public have suffered important losses without any palliating gains. In the face of a jurisdictional dispute, all three of these groups are helpless since there is no solution ultimately except that of sheer power. The position in which the employer is placed is especially exasperating. He has nothing to gain and everything to lose. He may have willingly accepted collective bargaining with one union only to have another bring a strike to bear upon him in an effort to force him to deal with the rival organization. He can settle with one union only at the expense of provoking the other. Where the power of the competing unions is evenly matched the position of the employer is comparable to that of a flying shuttel in an automatic loom. There are instances on record in which an employer has transferred his allegiance from one union to another three times in a short space of time without reaching a final or satisfactory settlement. Nothing could more effectively discredit labor organization in general than the spectacle of this particular aspect of union activity. Sympathetic outsiders have been alienated, unions have been decimated, and employers have been driven into determined resistance toward any vestiges of unionism which may have survived a period of fratricidal warfare.

Jurisdictional disputes between crafts are the most virulent and futile form of interunion conflict because they are completely insoluble as long as national craft unions retain their absolute autonomy. Changes in materials, tools and methods, increasing specialization, and the consequent substitution of unskilled for skilled labor have blurred the lines of demarcation between crafts. This has been especially true in the building industry. Materials have changed from wood, stone and brick to metals, cement and composition products unknown in the nineteenth century. Increasingly the building industry has become a process of assembling more or less completely prepared products. Tools have therefore changed; the open-end wrench is replacing the hammer and saw, processes have been specialized, and unskilled labor encroaches upon the domain of the craftsman. The vertical assembly line may one day become as familiar as the skyscraper. Consequently the carpenters have fought with the joiners, woodworkers and sheet metal workers. The plumbers have fought with the steamfitters. The elevator constructors have struggled with the sheet metal workers, the machinists, the structural iron workers and the carpenters. And so on. A lengthy catalogue may easily be made.

It is easier to emphasize the cost and the futility of jurisdictional disputes than to offer solutions. In the first place, there are so many possible tests which may be applied to the laying down of jurisdictional lines that to propose any given test is simply to shift the dispute to the question of the type of test which should be applied. Custom, the type of materials, the nature of the tools, the form of skill and precedence in relations with the employer are all possible tests which might be used. Each party to the controversy, however, chooses the test which favors its cause, and the struggle continues.

Amalgamation of the crafts concerned has satisfactorily settled some of the conflicts of the past. The process is slow, temporary in its effect and limited in its applicability. Amalgamation involves the surrender of autonomy, the sacrifice of perfectly understandable personal ambitions on the part of the leaders of the competing unions, and the merging of previously accumulated funds. The fusion is not likely to take place until the conflict has reached a considerable degree of intensity. The constant changes in methods and materials make these amalgamations a temporary solution at best.

Federating the competing unions into local councils and national departments of the A.F. of L. has been the chief hope of the past. The Structural Building Trades Alliance, founded in 1904, became the Building Trades Department of the A.F. of L. in 1908. Similar departments in the A.F. of L. have been set up for the metal trades and the railway trades. Superimposed upon the Building Trades Department in 1919 was the Board for Jurisdictional Awards in the building industry, a board composed of representatives from technicians, the Building Trades Department and employers. On the whole, the effect of the setting up of these agencies of arbitration has been merely to provide a new arena in which the struggle has continued, with the outcome determined by the relative power of the litigants. In the conflicts, for example, between the carpenters and the sheet metal workers over the right to install metal trim, the Carpenters' Union has repeatedly withdrawn from the Building Trades Department when the decision has gone against it. Neither the Department nor the A.F. of L. could afford to lose the support and the per capita tax of the Carpenters. Consequently, power has won, the decision has been reversed and the Carpenters have been reinstated as often as they have withdrawn. This conflict has been going on within the Department for twenty-eight years. It had had an informal status for years before the establishment of the Department. Discussion of the issue occupied a major portion of the time of the

San Francisco convention of the A.F. of L. in 1934 while
the convention was faced with general problems of prime
importance. There is little likelihood that the matter will
reach a final settlement in the near future.

Progressive labor leaders, labor sympathizers and "intel-
lectuals" have for years been insisting that industrial
unionism is the only possible basis upon which final eradi-
cation of this type of jurisdictional dispute may be made.
Although this is true, the development of industrial unions
claiming jurisdiction over fields already partially occupied
by craft unions has in the last forty years been the basis
for even more determined conflicts than those between
craft unions. The first of the strong industrial unions, the
Miners, almost immediately came in conflict with the
Engineers, Firemen, Blacksmiths and Machinists. The
Brewers, a powerful industrial union from 1896 to 1918
and now well on the way to recovery after the repeal of
Prohibition, have had more or less continuous trouble with
the Coopers, Teamsters, Engineers, Firemen and Oilers.
The United Textile Workers have, until recently, faced
the strong opposition of the Loomfixers, Mulespinners,
Lace Operatives, Woolsorters and others. In most cases
the industrial unions have eventually won. It is safe to
predict that in the future the craft unions must inevitably give way to the industrial unions when the two types
come into conflict. The march of industry is inexorably on
the side of the latter.

The contemporary unpleasantness between the Committee for Industrial Organization and the Executive
Council of the A.F. of L. is not, therefore, an isolated
phenomenon in American labor history. It signalizes a
rapid increase in the intensity and scope of the process of
transition which has been going on for nearly fifty years.
Regardless of the personalities and the machinery through
which they operate, the principle of industrial unionism
can be expected to win if for no other reason than that

the problem of the jurisdictional dispute must be met if the labor movement is to survive. To the extent that industrial life continues to change, industrial unionism will not prove to be a final panacea. Unquestionably, however, it will represent an important adjustment which, from the pragmatic viewpoint of the success of organized labor, is long since overdue.[2]

Divided We Fall

A SECOND aspect of the failure of craft unionism to adjust itself adequately to changing industrial society has been the fact that it has often been impossible for workers actually to bargain collectively even when they have been well organized in a given shop or mill. Employers have been able to play off one craft union against another to the disadvantage of the workers by signing agreements which do not end simultaneously. A union which is in the process of renewing an agreement is faced by the knowledge that all other crafts are bound by agreements not to strike for any cause until the agreements are terminated. The union which is bargaining for a new contract is thus forced to rely upon its own power to secure favorable terms. Its power may be insufficient to avoid a worsening of the conditions of its members. Having succumbed to the less

[2] Industrial unionism is by no means a solution for all of labor's jurisdictional troubles. There remain several important difficulties: 1. There are distinct separations of interest among different classes of workers in a given unit. 2. The immense size of some industrial locals makes democratic procedure nearly impossible. 3. Craft workers moving from one industry to another face the problem of joining several unions. 4. The determination of wage rates by industrial unions may lead to the establishment of several different wage rates for the same class of workers in separate industries, but in the same community. Answers to some of these problems are suggested in the chapter on Union Administration. In the meantime it must be pointed out that the C.I.O. does not urge industrial unionism to the *exclusion* of other forms. It is primarily interested in organizing the unorganized. When this requires the industrial form, the C.I.O. urges its adoption. In other cases as, for example, the Office Workers' Union, a combined craft and industrial form has been adopted.

favorable agreement, the union in question is effectively disposed of while the employer is free to deal in the same manner with the union whose agreement is next in order. One by one the faggots in the bundle are readily broken. Although it is possible that unions may secure contracts with simultaneous terminations, the unified power of the employer and the shortsightedness of the separate unions make such agreements difficult to achieve. An industrial union, on the other hand, with a single trade agreement covering a multiplicity of rates and conditions, is distinctly a more effective bargaining instrument. It is possible, furthermore, that in many instances when an employer is not actively hostile to unionism he may be more willing to deal with a single bargaining agent than with a confusing variety of separate unions.

Organizing the Unorganized

For more than fifty years the slogan "Organize the Unorganized" has been spread across the literature of the American labor movement. Solidarity! One for all, and all for one! An injury to one is the concern of all! These have from time to time been the watchwords of powerful movements which have arisen in opposition to the chartered institutions of the orthodox. Apart from the development of industrial unions within the A.F. of L., there have been three great waves of activity in the labor movement which have been based upon the concept of the solidarity of all workers, skilled and unskilled alike. The rise and fall of the Knights of Labor, the brief ascendency of the Industrial Workers of the World, and the upsurge of organization which began at the time of the N.R.A. have been the three major efforts of the labor movement to keep pace with the changing world around it.

The Knights of Labor, beginning modestly enough in profound secrecy in 1869, slowly expanded during the 'seventies as an organized protest against the frailty and exclusiveness of the craft unions which survived the Civil War and the crisis of 1873. The structure of the Knights was flexible enough to encompass all workers, the skilled as well as the unskilled. The basic unit of the organization was the local assembly. Some of these local assemblies were composed exclusively of the members of one craft. Others were industrial in character and included all the workers in and around a given production unit. Still others, called "mixed assemblies," were labor unions composed of all the workers in a given locality regardless of industry, skill and social status. Many of the mixed assemblies admitted small farmers, professionals and even employers. Race, sex or creed were no bar to entrance to the Noble Order. The doors were closed only to bankers, lawyers, stockbrokers, gamblers and the makers and sellers of intoxicants. These were excluded on moral rather than on economic grounds!

The unit next superior to the local assembly was the district assembly, organized upon a territorial basis and clearly cutting across craft and industrial lines. The district assemblies were held together at the top by the General Assembly with its annual conventions, its executive council, its constitution, treasury and permanent officers. The structure and the constitution of the Order indicated a strongly centralized organization with power closely held by permanent officers at the top who controlled the calling and settling of strikes and the distribution of funds to an extent unimagined even now by the executive officials of the A.F. of L. In actual fact, however, its heterogeneity of membership, the far-flung boundaries of its empire, and the uncontrollable rapidity of its growth gave the Knights less centralization of control than is now exercised by the officers of the Federation.

In 1881, no longer having its weakness to conceal, the Order threw off the cloak of secrecy which had aroused the hostility of the Catholic Church, and announced itself as the champion of the unorganized workers in the developing mass production industries. After 1883 its growth was meteoric. By 1886 it had 700,000 members. Its prestige was immense. The country at large surveyed the prospect of its further growth with dread or with extravagant enthusiasm. A victory of great symbolic and actual importance was won over one of the railroads controlled by the powerful Jay Gould. The Order decided, somewhat reluctantly, to stake its future on one throw of the dice. A call was sounded for a nation-wide strike for the eight-hour day to take place on May 1, 1886. The strike was an almost complete failure. The dice were loaded against the Knights. The explosion of the Haymarket bomb in Chicago created a wave of hysteria which turned the tide of jittery public opinion against the Order. The huge organization was too amorphous to be disciplined and held together. Conflict between the mixed assemblies and the craft assemblies affiliated, or about to become affiliated, with the American Federation of Labor, became increasingly determined. Personal jealousies, local rebellions and strategic mistakes completed the process of disintegration. By 1890 the membership had dwindled to 100,000 and, although the Order retained a technical existence until 1917, it was practically dead by the turn of the century.

After the Knights of Labor had been smashed, Samuel Gompers, who had a hand in the smashing, went busily about the country collecting the pieces. He and others put them together in the form of national unions, predominantly craft, and drew these unions into the A.F. of L. Gompers staked his future and that of the labor movement upon craft exclusiveness, "pure and simple" methods and the philosophy of the "here and now." The victory, for the moment, was his. Solidarity, democracy and the power of a great vision had failed. It became stock in trade for the A.F. of L. leaders to point to the debacle of the Knights as a warning against the distressing fate of organizations based upon the "riffraff," the "fence-jumpers" and the "scum" of the labor movement.

Although the Noble Order was a failure, it was a presage of things to come. The time was not ripe for labor organizations resting upon a territorial basis. Craft consciousness was still the predominant attitude of the American worker and the mass production industries were in their infancy. The development had begun, however, and economic change made imperative the organization of the unskilled. The Knights were scarcely decently laid away in their graves before the thin shoots of industrial unionism sprang from the soil which the Knights had enriched. In 1890 the United Mine Workers undertook the herculean task of organizing all the workers in the mining industry into one powerful union. In 1892, as a result of the Homestead strike, Carnegie and Frick broke the back of craft unionism in the steel industry. In 1894 Eugene V. Debs created the American Railway Union, an industrial organization open to all the workers connected with the Western railroads. This union was sufficiently powerful to cope with the management of the twenty-four railroads entering Chicago, but was no match for the Federal Army, the Sherman Act, the blanket injunction, the United States Supreme Court and the Woodstock County jail. Although the great railroad strike was a failure, the mass of the railroad workers had again been caught up in the net of industrial unionism. In 1896 the Brewery Workers began their long struggle to establish industrial democracy among the skilled and unskilled alike. In 1897 the Western Federation of Miners withdrew from the A.F. of L., created the American Labor Union, and expanded the metal mining strikes of the West into a series of class wars that caused tremors throughout the whole of American society. In 1900 the International Ladies' Garment Workers' Union brought together the existing crafts and began to dip into the reservoirs of the semiskilled. The

Knights of Labor was dead, but the concept upon which it was founded endured in spite of the vested interests of craft union leaders and the united front of a consolidating capitalism.

Industrial unionism, however, was both too much and not enough. In the building trades, on the railroads and in a score or more of the highly skilled operations in the printing and metal working trades the craft form of organization showed a high degree of vitality. From these sources the dominant unions in the A.F. of L. drew enough strength to assert their jurisdictional claims against the encroachment of the rising industrial unions. When these claims were vigorously and successfully asserted by the craft organizations, the leadership of the A.F. of L. sanctioned the conquests with the stamp of official approval. On these occasions doubts were seriously raised as to whether it would ever be possible to organize the mass of unskilled workers within the structure of the A.F. of L. Thus the question again emerged as to the necessity for setting up an all-embracing One Big Union, competing with the A.F. of L., which would aid and sanction the industrial unions in their struggle for power. Beyond this, the industrial unions in anthracite, in metal mining, in brewing and among railroad maintenance and right-of-way men found that though they might be equal in strength to the employers and their associations, they could not beat the law, the courts and the armed forces of society. Real meaning was thus given to the idea of class conflict and the query was raised as to whether unionism in the basic industries was possible without embodying a determined challenge to capitalist society. Finally, there developed industrial areas such as shipping, longshore work, mass production agriculture and lumbering, in which it appeared that the labor union, based upon territorial and cutting across industrial lines, was a more effective organizing instrument even than the industrial union.

Consequently, in 1905, the Industrial Workers of the World came into existence, asserting its sovereignty independent of the American Federation of Labor, throwing down the gauntlet of its syndicalist philosophy in bold challenge to the capitalist system, and providing room within its structure for organization both upon an industrial and a territorial basis. Like the Knights of Labor before it, the I.W.W. was hailed with enthusiasm or received with forebodings or dread according to the predisposition of the observer. The I.W.W. had its first real roots in the Western Federation of Miners. Scarcely had the first convention been adjourned when the I.W.W., as a result of the "confessions" of a labor spy, Harry Orchard, became involved in the murder of ex-Governor Steunenberg of Idaho. Then came the disastrous strike at Goldfield, Nevada, in 1907, resulting in the destruction of the Western Federation of Miners. The field of I.W.W. activity shifted to the casual and migratory workers of the West and Northwest. Fruit, vegetable and cereal harvesters, oil field and longshore workers, sailors and lumberjacks—these were the dispossessed toward whom the I.W.W. held out hope and the red union card. Men without homes, men with casual family connections, denizens of the hobo jungles and "working stiffs" set forth their "revolutionary" philosophy in a new and vivid language which expressed their contempt for traditional concepts of loyalty, patriotism and organized religion. They fought for free speech, fresh drinking water and the liquidation of the bedbug.

From this base among the migratory workers, the I.W.W. stretched out a long arm toward the textile workers of Lawrence, Massachusetts, and led them in one of the bitterest class wars in the history of the eastern United States. In this strike the I.W.W. leaders took on not only the woolen industry but the A.F. of L. as well. From Lawrence the I.W.W. moved into the bituminous and silk fields of Pennsylvania and New Jersey where it engaged in both "dual unionism," and, "boring from within," the textile and mining unions of the A.F. of L. To the consternation of many and the amusement of some, the I.W.W. had the effrontery to wave the red flag in the streets of Greenville, South Carolina.

The class war, however, had to be postponed. National ambitions superseded class aspirations. Making Europe safe for democracy became more important than exterminating the vermin in bunkhouse beds. In many respects the two objectives were mutually exclusive. The orthodox trade-union movement became indispensable to the winning of the War in Europe. The I.W.W., however, was an obstacle. They were antipatriotic in a superpatriotic world. They were antireligious at a time when organized religion had become an important instrument in the military scene. They had no womenfolk to watch them march bravely off into the influenza pandemic and the Flanders mud. They resisted the draft and they persisted in striking. The best people thought there ought to be a law against this and many state legislatures obligingly passed criminal syndicalism acts. The state and Federal forces, ably assisted by unions in the A.F. of L., proceeded to break the I.W.W. strikes, raid its headquarters, confiscate its belongings, disrupt its meetings and imprison its leaders as slackers or criminal syndicalists. The I.W.W. was useful only as a bogey and whipping boy. Fond mothers warned obstreperous children that the I.W.W. would get them if they didn't watch out. Government and business referred to the I.W.W. as the American arm of the Kaiser's secret service and credited it with being responsible for an amazing versatility in sabotage and graft. A.F. of L. officials referred to I.W.W. leaders with more vigor than precision of metaphor as "leeches" and "bloodsuckers" who "thunder out their vomit." The I.W.W. fought back in the economic and vituperative fields but the tide was too strong against them. When A. Mitchell Palmer went on his hunting and fishing expedition, the witches and red herrings which he brought in turned out to be "criminal syndicalists" in so many cases that the ranks of the I.W.W. were decimated. By 1922 the I.W.W. had little left except the sour satisfaction of watching the government and big business, armed with the full dinner pail and the "new capitalism," turn upon the A.F. of L. with such effect that its membership and power were quickly reduced almost to their pre-War status.

The I.W.W. was beaten, but from the wreckage there emerged a renewed tradition of solidarity; a new workers' language, literature and song; a new bundle of techniques; and a handful of leaders. Some of these went into the Communist party and developed the policy of "boring from within" the A. F. of L. unions in an effort to divert their attention to the problem of the mass of unorganized workers. The reaction of the 'twenties, however, was at least equal to the action of the 'teens. The A.F. of L. became engrossed in coöperating with management. The Communist infiltration was purged from the ranks of the garment, textile and mining unions. In 1929 the Communist party, therefore, created a new organization, the Trade Union Unity League, to compete with the A.F. of L. among the industrial workers. Thereafter, Communist unions in textiles, mining, fur, metals, agriculture and half-a-dozen other basic industries fought a losing struggle to organize the unorganized. The shrinking tide of depression and the ineptitude of Communist tactics carried radical and conservative unions alike down to the nadir of the fortunes of the American labor movement.

March 4, 1933, dawned over a dreary and despairing world. American labor, organized and unorganized, partook of this despair as bitterly as any other element in American society. Within six months, however, an electric transformation had been effected. Employment of workers in manufacturing and trade sharply improved as managers, anticipating the higher labor costs of the N.R.A. codes, began to build up their inventories. Prices, stimulated by the restrictive policies of the N.R.A. and the A.A.A. and by the activities of the administration in the monetary and banking fields, began to move upward more rapidly than the general wage level. The real wages of the employed workers began consequently to fall. The expansion of the Federal relief program toward a more nearly adequate basis than that provided by private, local and state charity reduced somewhat the threat to wage standards and union activity involved in the immense volume of unemployment hanging over the labor market. The known liberal inclinations of President Roosevelt toward the labor movement and the explicit recognition of the right to collective bargaining contained in Section 7a of the N.I.R.A. provided a profound psychological stimulus to organizing activity. The doctrine that organized labor was indispensable to the enforcement of the wage, hour and child labor sections of the codes gave union leaders a semiofficial relation toward government. The actual appointment of many labor leaders to governmental positions gave prestige and influence to organized labor. The immense volume of publicity accorded the labor movement both by its friends and its enemies carried the gospel of unionism to the nooks and crannies of the land. These combined forces resulted in a period of expansion of labor activity and union membership comparable only to the mushroom growth of the Knights of Labor. By October, 1933, the American Federation of Labor reported that an increase of 1,300,000 had brought its total membership to 4,000,000. Another million was reported in unions independent of the A.F. of L. Strikes swept over the country. In October, 1934, various estimates placed the membership of the A. F. of L. at more than five and a half million, although for a number of reasons this growth was not accurately reflected in the official figures for dues-paying membership. Independent union membership probably brought the total to well over six millions. The third great wave in labor's rising tide hung over the industrial scene.

A break in the crest of this wave, however, soon became apparent. Management, emboldened by the crescendo music of the cash register and alarmed by the strength of organized labor, rapidly resumed the antiunion weapons which had been rendered relatively unnecessary by the depression. Company unions, industrial espionage, the courts and the militia again demonstrated their effectiveness as protection against the labor movement. The government, although it had provided the original stimulus to labor organization, became worried over the frequency of the strikes which were called to make the declared policies of both government and unions effective. The tendency among union leaders to leave the settlement of difficulties up to government boards was consequently encouraged by the government's increasing hostility toward labor's use of its own strength. The intense disappointment of union members, flowing from the acceptance by union leaders of a series of settlements laid down by governmental agencies, resulted in large-scale defections from union ranks.

The decline of unionism in late 1934 and throughout 1935 was not by any means due entirely to the attack of industrial management and the lessening sympathy of government. The labor movement of this period had important weaknesses within itself. The spectacularly rapid growth in membership involved somewhat the same risks that were inherent in the similar growth of the Knights of Labor. The organizing facilities of the Federation and many of its unions were insufficient to meet the demands placed upon them. Unions hastily put together by hard-pressed organizers were left to their own devices while the organizers hurried on into new territory. Many such unions immediately collapsed upon meeting their first major test. Discipline in the calling and settling of strikes was extremely difficult to enforce. Workers who had flocked into unions in the belief that the millennium was at hand flocked out again when they found that the millennium often took the form of a meager settlement or a whiff of tear gas. Hundreds of thousands of the new members had no tradition of organization behind them, were easily discouraged by failure, suspicious of their leaders and disgusted by factional conflict.

Quite as important as these disintegrating influences, however, was the old and familiar conflict between the craft and the industrial form of organization. A large percentage of the new members came from the mass production industries. Automobiles, rubber, oil fields, cement, chemicals, aluminum, electrical appliances, public utilities, coke and gas were the industries which were profoundly stirred by the clarion call of Section 7a. These industries, previous to the N.R.A., were almost completely devoid of unionization. It was, furthermore, almost impossible to organize them along craft lines. Either there were no craft distinctions, or workers in these industries performed tasks which came under several craft jurisdictions, or the weakness and complications of craft organization were painfully apparent to workers and management alike. The A.F. of L. was consequently forced to organize these workers in industrial locals. In the absence of national industrial unions, the only course open to A.F. of L. organizers was to put these workers in directly affiliated federal labor locals. As has been previously indicated, the function of these federal labor locals was originally intended to be that of acting as a temporary receptacle for workers whose trades had no national union or were insufficiently represented in a given locality to make it reasonable to set up separate craft locals. The federal unions, therefore, had one primary purpose. This was to go out of existence as

Courtesy of Union News Service

During the intense organizing activity of 1933-34 it proved
to be impossible to organize the mass production workers
in craft unions.

soon as possible. During 1933 and 1934, however, the number of federal unions increased spectacularly. In 1932 there were 307. In 1934 there were 1788. There was danger that the tail might wag the dog. The members of the federal unions were anxious to join themselves together by industry into new national industrial unions. Craft union leaders, however, cast envious glances toward the new membership and asserted that the federal locals should be sliced up into appropriate segments and apportioned among the existing craft internationals.

This was a major issue before the San Francisco convention of the Federation in October, 1934. Such time as could be spared from the perennial jurisdictional dispute between the Carpenters and all comers was allotted to the question of disposing of the federal unions. A compromise was reached which conceded the right of federal unions in several mass production industries to form national industrial unions. The terms of the resolution, however, and the discussion which attended its adoption made it clear that the craft unions did not intend to surrender their claims over any workers who might be identified as coming within their jurisdictional grasp. The Executive Council, furthermore, was granted large powers of interpretation of the resolution and supervision over the formation of the new national unions. Trouble inevitably ensued. Craft union leaders continued to press their claims for members among the federal unions. The officers and Executive Council of the Federation arrogated to themselves a dominant influence in the newly-formed nationals. Nearly six hundred federal unions disbanded in disgust or were suspended for failure to comply with Federation rulings. Thousands of workers quit the federal unions which survived.

By the summer of 1935 it had become clear to the leaders of several major unions in the Federation that the rapid gains made by the labor movement during 1933 and

1934 were speedily being erased. The strongly antiunion position taken by management in the basic industries had proved as effective as it had been in the 'twenties. The inadequacy of organizing facilities and methods had borne fruit in cumulative defections from the workers' ranks. The blunder of allowing the labor movement to become dependent upon the good will of the government had become painfully apparent as a result of a series of unfavorable decisions and settlements laid down by governmental agencies. The nullification of the N.R.A. climaxed the process of labor's education in this respect. Most important of all, it seemed clear to these leaders that the Executive Council of the Federation could not itself and would not allow others to retain and extend the gains which had been made in organizing the industrial workers. These were the issues which faced the Atlantic City convention of the A.F. of L. in October, 1935.

Throughout the convention these issues were debated with vigor and persistence. The matter reached a dramatic climax in the physical conflict between John L. Lewis, leader of the industrial union block, and William L. Hutcheson of the Carpenters. Although Mr. Hutcheson was worsted in the fisticuffs, the convention sustained the craft union position by a vote of approximately 18 to 11. The decision reached was in effect a restatement of the compromise of 1934, i.e., that charters should be granted to industrial unions in the basic industries, but that the craft unions need not surrender their claims to any workers in these industries whom they might identify as suitable members.

Shortly after the convention a group of industrial union leaders and one amalgamated craft union leader met at the inspiration of John Lewis, president of the United Mine Workers. The result of the meeting was the setting up on November 10, 1935, of the Committee for Industrial Organization. This was not a "dual" organization in the

Courtesy of Union News Service

On September 5, 1936, the Executive Council of the A.F. of
L. suspended ten unions affiliated with the C.I.O. The
C.I.O. published the above cartoon over the caption,
"Suspended."

sense usually accepted by A.F. of L. tradition. It was designed to expedite organizing work on an industrial basis within the A.F. of L. During the following year fifteen national unions, through their national officers, affiliated with the committee. All but two of these were affiliates of the Federation. The Executive Council of the A.F. of L., however, determined to oppose this move upon the legalistic ground that it represented defiance of the decision of the convention and therefore was a "dualistic" movement. After several warnings, the Executive Council on August 5, 1936, directed the members of the committee to withdraw from it by September 5, 1936. The committee refused to disband and the ten unions among its members specifically referred to by the Executive Council were automatically suspended from membership in the A. F. of L. on September 5. The suspended unions lost the right to vote and voice and the suspension was upheld in the November, 1936, convention. Attempts to effect a compromise in succeeding months failed. The enlarged activities of the C.I.O., its setting up of district councils, its phenomenal success in organizing and strikes, and the intensified bitterness between its leaders and the members of the Executive Council made it more and more clearly a distinct entity in the labor movement. President William Green, on March 4, 1937, took steps to lessen the remaining connection by directing all central labor unions and state federations to reaffirm their loyalty to the A.F. of L.

During the late spring of 1937 the conflict between the A.F. of L. and the C.I.O. became more intense. Several more national unions left the A.F. of L. and affiliated with the C.I.O. On May 24, 1937, the leaders of unions remaining in the A.F. of L. held a conference in Cincinnati. In the course of the three-day proceedings, the A.F. of L. declared "war" on the C.I.O., announced that it would engage in an intensive organizing campaign in fields already occupied by C.I.O. unions, began chartering or-

Courtesy of Union News Service

A C.I.O. version of the A. F. of L.'s declaration of "war."

ganizations in opposition to those affiliated with the C.I.O., and called upon state federations and city centrals to expel C.I.O. delegates. In the meantime the C.I.O. had already been chartering unions in opposition to existing A.F. of L. unions. On this basis, the Transport Workers' and Maritime Unions had come into existence. The C.I.O. had also begun chartering locals in direct affiliation with itself and setting up its own district, state and local coördinating councils. The action of the May 24 conference formalized the opposition between the two organizations and created a condition of apparently irreconcilable "dualism."

Apart from the legal technicalities of the question as to whether the Executive Council and the C.I.O. have kept faith with the tradition and the constitution of the A.F. of L., the basic significance of the activities of the C.I.O. is that it represents another effort in the long history of the labor movement to make the forms and the methods of organization conform to the necessities of industrial life. It is a determined effort to organize the unorganized in the only way in which it can effectively be accomplished, that is, by allowing industrial workers to join industrial locals free from the interference of other vested interests; banding these locals together in strong national unions, and placing at the disposal of these national unions the unified financial, technical and moral support of all workers whose predominant interests are in the industrial field.

At the present time, common action is being secured through close personal relations among the leaders of the C.I.O. and by the immediate necessities of the situation. When the current organizing drive has been carried through, the most important problem facing the C.I.O. will be the determination of the constitutional relationships between itself and its constituent unions. Jurisdictional conflicts are not a peculiar attribute of craft unionism. They are just as likely to occur between an industrial union in steel and an industrial union in automobiles, where the lines between these two industries are blurred, as they are between carpenters and sheet metal workers.[3] Whether the conflicts between the new industrial unions can be solved will depend upon the extent to which the national unions are willing to surrender their autonomy to the co-ordinating committee in the matter of jurisdiction. Completely centralized control in this matter is not inconsistent with a large degree of democracy within the national unions. If the C.I.O. successfully solves the problem of organizing the industrial workers, it will quickly be faced, therefore, with the necessity for reconciling autocratic control over jurisdiction with democratic control over methods, goals and personnel. This question and the even more important matter of determining the relationship between unionism, government and business may be the great issues with which the labor movement of the next decade will be concerned.

In conclusion it may be repeated that the labor movement has been and, if it is to survive, must continue to be, more than a tradition and a body of precedent. It is an evolving institution whose forms and methods are ultimately determined by the environment which surrounds it. For nearly one hundred and fifty years it has haltingly and painfully adjusted itself to changing economic society. The present period of intense activity within the labor movement represents a belated effort to overtake the immense alterations which, during the last generation, have transformed American industrial society.

[3] There is already some question, for example, as to whether the workers in the automobile parts plants should be organized in the Auto Workers or the Steel Workers when the plants in question make parts for machines other than automobiles.

CHAPTER III

Antiunionism

THE average American employer is not enthusiastic about dealing with his labor force througth the intermediation of independently organized unions. Some of the reasons for this attitude are fear of financial loss, unwillingness to surrender power, stereotyped beliefs and the pressure brought to bear upon him by other members of the employer group. That financial loss is not the only reason for opposition to unionization has recently been demonstrated in a striking manner by the introduction of testimony before a Senate committee to the effect that the American Bridge Co., a strongly antiunion firm, spent $289,462 in "protection" of various sorts to avoid employing union iron workers on the Pulaski Skyway in Jersey City. The amount which the company saved by employing nonunion men was $51,849. The net loss of this particular transaction would appear to be about $237,-613. It does not necessarily follow, of course, that this would be a net loss in the long run. The company might, after very careful consideration, decide that successful resistance to unionization in this instance was worth more than $237,613 if spread over a sufficiently long nonunion period. On the reasonable assumption, however, that the union was determined to persist in its efforts to organize the iron-working industry, the company might be expected to conclude that the protection was not worth the cost if the size of the wage bill were the only consideration facing the company.

This, usually, is not the case. Many employers resist unionization because they do not want their business interrupted through strikes called in their plants by a union seeking gains in other plants. For example, in the general

textile strike in the autumn of 1934, the plants of employers who were dealing with the United Textile Workers as well as those of employers who were strongly antiunion were affected. This is one of the most frequent
objections raised by employers who compare "company"
unions with "outside" unions to the discredit of the latter.
Many employers fight off unionism because of the natural,
and more or less universal, disinclination to be told by
others what to do. The union may ask for no more than
the employer is already giving, but the fact that the union
asks for it may be enough to provoke the employer into
taking away part of what he has given. "This is my business. You mind yours and I'll mind mine." Moreover, although labor costs may not be increased by the rates and
hours imposed by unions, the shop rules embodied in the
trade agreement may result in an inflexibility of production practices which is vastly irritating to the employer
accustomed to have his way in his plant. "Before I can
transfer two men from inside to outside work, what do I
have to do? I have to get down on my knees to a business
agent who, after due deliberations, says, 'H'mmm, I should
think so,' as though he were General Grant." Thus to his
wife. "How do they expect me to meet my pay roll on
Saturday noon? I'd like to see them run this business for a
week."

The idea that "this is my business and I can do as I please
—within limits, of course," has a multitude of variations.
It is basic in capitalistic philosophy, but it is powerfully
affected by the type of economic institution through
which it operates. In the two hundred large corporations
which dominate the field of manufacture and transportation, the stockholder, who owns the corporation, is unlikely to have anything to say about the running of the
business. The management, which actually runs the business, is unlikely to own more than one per cent of the
stock. The Ford and, to a lesser extent, General Motors

companies are classic exceptions to this general rule. Consequently, the management cannot accurately say, "This is my business to do with as I please." The management may be able to do as it pleases with the business, but management does not own the business. There is very little in law or in self-interest to prevent the management from operating the business to its own considerable advantage and to the loss of owners, as well as workers and consumers. That this does not always happen is largely due to the development of an ethical concept of trusteeship. "It is my primary duty to protect the interests of the owners while doing as well as possible for the workers and consumers." There are those who object to this pouring of the sweet syrup of social service over the hard facts of corporate management. The concept of trusteeship, however, may be more than pure publicity material. It may actually become a part of the managerial code and profoundly affect corporate behavior. Where this is true, the idea of trusteeship is likely to take the form of refusing to allow the "outside" forces of the labor movement to interfere with the carrying out of the trustee's obligations to investors.

A great variety of other nonpecuniary motives also affects the relationship of employers to the labor movement. In the behavior of many employers there is a strong coloring of *noblesse oblige.* "I do the best I can for my men, in good times and in bad, but let them keep their place, I say." Some employers seriously believe that the labor movement represents the Communist menace incarnate, and think of it in terms of the "nationalization of women." Others have some difficulty in distinguishing between Bolshevism and Fascism but generously associate both in their minds with trade unions. In the North union organizers are considered "foreigners who ought to go back where they come from" even though that may mean New Bedford. In the South organizers are "damned

Yankees, and a menace to the flower of Southern woman-
hood." There are those who think of labor leaders in terms
of their private morals and their contamination of the
probity of good honest workers. "He has a penthouse in
New York and a suite at the Mayflower Hotel." It may
seriously be contended that these attitudes are not conscious camouflage for the economic self-interest of the
employer. They are beliefs which may be entertained in
spite of, or without reference to, economic self-interest,
and they have a powerful influence in determining the
antiunion attitude of the great number of small-scale employers who constitute the fringe of the industrial scene.

To these antiunion forces there must be added the compulsions of group action among employers. Many employers might be willing to deal with unions as the bargaining
agents for their workers were it not for the interdict
placed upon this kind of behavior by their fellow employers. The same appeals to reason, ethics, shame and
fear are often made by the employing group to a wavering
member that are made by unions to reluctant workers.
"You may save a little now by dealing with the union, but
in the long run it will pay to keep it out of your plant."
Or, "It's all right for you to talk about running your business on a union basis, but what about the rest of us? If you
let them get in your place, we'll be next. We've got to
present a solid front, whether you like it or not." The compulsions of fear are not likely to be applied in terms of
threats or physical violence among very small employers.
The business fraternity has the more powerful weapons
of control of credit, interlocking directorates, holding
company controls, and the posting of bonds for the fulfil-
ment of employers' association agreements. Thus the
United States Steel Company, formed in 1901 at a time
when there were signs of increasing willingness of employers to deal with unions in some industries, successfully
applied an antiunion policy to all of its constituent com-

panies in the United States Steel group. It is interesting to note in this connection that in the case of the American Bridge Company, cited at the beginning of this chapter, the decisions of the president of United States Steel were referred to in the testimony as being influential in determining the policy of American Bridge during its "labor troubles."

Fundamentally the resistance of employers to unionism is based upon individual and group economic self-interest. This, however, is overlaid with a bewildering variety of nonlogical considerations which sometimes completely obscure the basic economic motive. These paternalistic, religious, traditional, collaborationist, sectional, moral and political beliefs become a part of the antiunion arsenal of the employer. When he believes them himself, he expects (and with some accuracy) that workers will believe them too. As he rises in the industrial scale, these beliefs may be sloughed off to a sufficient extent to lay bare the economic motive beneath. He may continue to use them, however, simply because they are more effective in carrying his fellow employers and his workers along with him in his antiunion position.

In the actual tactics of resistance to unionism, as opposed to the motives behind this resistance, somewhat the same variety of levels of action may be found as in the organizing methods of unions. In addition, however, to these parallel levels of action, there are others open only to the employer because of the superior legal status of property relations. The simplest form of opposition to unionism exists in the form of personal relationships between the employer and his workers. In the small shop the problem is that of retaining the personal loyalty of individual workers. The employer, hearing that an organizer is in the vicinity, has merely to walk through the shop, pat one or two workers on the shoulder, ask about the wife and children and walk out again. Occasionally he may take off his coat and show a worker how things were done "back in the good old days, when men really knew their trade." Sometimes this causes resentment, but a judicious mixture of sympathy and encouragement will often save many dollars in wage bills. In the larger plants this task must be performed by the superintendents, "straw-bosses" and foremen.

If trouble persists, a word or two about "these Communists," "outside agitators," "labor racketeers," "professional radicals"; a few stories about the seduction of a local girl by a labor leader; or the fantastic demands made by unions in other localities may be all that is necessary. These stories need not have foundation in fact, although it may not be impossible to secure a factual basis. It is important, however, that they be believed by the teller in order that his words carry conviction. Constant repetition may develop in time into an adequate substitute for belief. In a large plant, this kind of activity is most effectively carried on by confederates planted among the workers. Such confederates are not difficult to obtain. In every social group there are always those who are willing to achieve a modicum of self-importance by carrying tales. If these are not present in sufficient numbers, financial rewards, or fear induced by petty blackmail or threat of discharge may be used. In some plants relatives of the employer often perform the tale-bearing task. In the Ford and a few other large companies the setting up of a spy system inside the plants is a part of personnel management policy. These channels of communication also accomplish the reverse function of providing the employer with information as to the sources of discontent or the activities of union-conscious workers. The disgust of workers with this system of espionage is adequately summed up in the phrase "stool pigeon." If it is discovered, as it usually is sooner or later, it is likely to arouse intense resentment which may result in strikes or in permanent organization of the workers. There is so little that workers can do to eliminate it, however, short of determined collective action, that it may be successfully employed to defeat organization for an extended period. The widespread use of the "stool pigeon" system in American industry may or may not be testimony to its success as an antiunion device.

A somewhat more formal method of achieving the same result is the employment of professional spy agencies. Such institutions as Pinkerton, W. J. Burns, Railway Audit and Inspection, Bergoff, and Sherman Service, among a host of others, usually maintain one department of activity which is expressly dedicated to this form of service to the employer. The investigations of the Senate subcommittee on labor espionage have given widespread publicity to a type of antiunion activity which goes back in labor history at least as far as the time of the Molly Maguires in the 1870's. The employer who suspects that trouble is developing in his plant and who is himself entirely out of touch with his workers, calls a professional spy agency and asks that operatives be assigned to his plant. The operatives are taken on with other recently hired workers. The employer may or may not be aware of their exact identity. The operatives keep their eyes and ears open and record their findings in reports which are usually sent direct to the spy agency. There they are "edited" and sent on to the employer. Instructions are sent to the operative via the general delivery of the local post office. The operative is more or less carefully trained in methods of avoiding suspicion. If he successfully spots the troublemakers in the plant, a large part of his task is accomplished. If he cannot discover the source of agitation, he may begin fictionalizing his reports, or decide that the time has come for him to start his own agitation. If the operative himself becomes the agitator, he may be able to discover from the responses who the interested workers are. If he secures no responses, then he may have to imagine enough enthusiasm to keep his reports well filled out. After this has gone on some

time, the agency may decide that the time has come to
deliver the goods by eliminating the employer's labor
troubles. This is accomplished with very little abracadabra
simply by recalling the operative and presenting a bill for
services rendered.

The process of organization may, however, have passed
well into its stable period. The operative receives instructions to join the union and work his way up. His dues and
assessments are paid by the agency and, incidentally, by
the employer. He rises fast in the union and enters its inner
councils. He reports the union's plans, financial condition
and membership rolls. Or he may prefer to remain in the
rank and file. There he does his best to stimulate factionalism, suspicion of the leaders and ill-considered action.
Being a good parliamentarian, he may continually obfus-
cate procedure and disgust the membership by insisting
on the observance of minutiæ.

Whispering campaigns within the union may not prove
as effective as whispering campaigns in the workers' community. Many of the large spy agencies are now developing specialists in the latter. Door-to-door salesmen, having
secured entrance to the kitchen of the worker's home by
the traditional methods, finish their sales talk quickly and
go on to general subjects. The weather is dismissed somewhat more rapidly than usual and the talk passes on to the
children. "Nice boy you have there. Children are a great
comfort, aren't they, but in times like these it's pretty hard
to make ends meet. I don't blame the men at the mill for
getting restless. But what I always say is, don't make a bad
matter worse by having anything to do with these outside
agitators. They're just a bunch of racketeers. Why I had
it straight from someone who knows that the president of
this union has a penthouse in New York where he keeps
his mistress. Well, good day, Mrs. Brody, I must be going
along, though I don't know why I bother, I haven't had
an order all morning, times are that bad."

In spite of the hundreds of thousands of dollars spent

every year on these methods, there is some question as to their effectiveness as antiunion policy. Unions are beginning to develop methods of counterattack. The spy question is frequently discussed at union meetings and members are asked to be on their guard for peculiarities in the spending, telephoning and mailing habits of others. When definite suspicions have been aroused, traps are set by giving false information to the suspect and waiting to see whether it reaches the employer. Every time a spy is caught, an effort is made to secure his picture. Such pictures are widely circularized in order to limit the future usefulness of that particular spy in other localities. Unions are themselves beginning to send their own members to apply for jobs at spy agencies. The employer is thus forced to pay the bill for counterespionage. Recently, evidence has been given before the Senate subcommittee to the effect that spies sometimes come over to the union's cause. One spy on the witness stand reported with delight that he "never sent but one truthful report back to the International Auxiliary in the ten weeks I was there, and the workers knew what I was doing." The public reports of the Senate committee and its special reports to heads of unions make available to the labor movement the names and descriptions of industrial spies. As a result of this there was during the first two or three months of 1937 a general housecleaning among local and national unions, city centrals and state federations.

Nevertheless, there apparently remains a rosy future for the industrial spy business in spite of these difficulties and the legal obstacles that have been placed in the way of interstate transportation of spies. Some of the proprietors of spy agencies have indicated that although public investigations may temporarily intimidate the important customers, the result in the end may be good for business. The widespread publicity which attends such investigations informs employers who otherwise would not have thought of this method. One is reminded of the advertising maxim that "any news is good news."

There is, furthermore, the fact that widespread exposure of the spy system, and the extent to which it has permeated the upper circles of unionism, leads to suspicion of all union officers and creates an atmosphere of mutual distrust which inhibits group action of workers. Each worker thinks that the only person he can trust is himself. The indications at present are that industrial espionage will remain an important antiunion device unless unions become sufficiently strong in spite of it to render it useless. Developments in the near future will probably be in the direction of greater subtlety. Emphasis is being placed upon "harmonizing industrial relations." Tie-ups with ex-Secret Service or former G-men are increasingly possible. Operatives may pass as Federal officials collecting information for government boards of various types. The administration of the Social Security Act offers opportunities for securing information with respect to the union affiliation of workers, although the Social Security Board has stepped in very quickly to prevent this by broadcasting general warnings through the labor movement and the press to the effect that their records call for no information which bears in any way upon the question of unionism. The possibilities of variation in method, however, are great, and employers who are willing to pay the very high prices charged by espionage agencies may not have difficulty in keeping a step ahead of the countermaneuvers.

The second possible level of antiunion activity is that of publicity. The simplest form of publicity is the posting of notices in the shop or mill which express the good will of the employer and advise against commerce with agitators and other persons of this sort who may be in the vicinity. This has its limitations because of the impersonality of the appeal and because there are always people in any group who fancy themselves as wags and insist on decorating such notices or distorting their meaning by judicious additions or deletions. Meetings of the workers may be called and the entire situation discussed on the basis of fraternal good will. This method enjoyed popularity in managerial circles during the early 'twenties and was described by some as the "man-to-man" relationship in industry. In more recent years, however, the large shop meeting has declined in popularity because many workers remain obstinately unimpressed by the rich Sunday-school atmosphere of such a gathering. The man-to-man approach has increasingly been delegated to the field of personnel management which will be discussed later. As an antidote for mill-gate meetings held by union organizers, some employers have found it worth while to install loud-speakers at the gates connected by wire to phonographs within the mill. Union organizers have reported to their offices that a good swing number, well amplified, raises havoc with their best speeches, especially if the phonograph is intermittently operated so that the audience is uncertain as to whether the dance is over or not.

Within the last few years a great deal of very effective publicity designed apparently to check the rise of independent unionism has been issued through press releases, pamphlets, advertisements and the radio. The antiunion position in the publicity material is implicit rather than obvious. Although the words "open shop" are still generally used among employers opposed to unionism, it is becoming more clearly recognized that even the general public, apart from the labor movement, identifies these words with a clear-cut stand against organized labor. Frank opposition to the right of workers to organize in unions has not been an especially popular position during the last forty years.[1] For nearly a hundred years the courts have formally recognized the right of workers to bargain col-

[1] Henry Ford is among a small minority of employers who openly and frankly state their hostility to organized labor.

lectively. This recognition has been made more specific by the Clayton Act, the Norris-LaGuardia Anti-Injunction Act, Section 7a of the N.I.R.A. and the Wagner Labor Relations Act. To take a stand for the open shop is likely to be construed by the reading public as placing oneself in opposition to statute law. The more advanced antiunion firms and associations, therefore, present their position in increasingly general terms.

The Horatio Alger philosophy still has a strong grip on the thinking of the American workman. Emphasis upon the identity and worth of the individual, the belief that there is plenty of room for good men at the top, and that the way to get ahead is to rise out of your class rather than to try to improve the position of that class are deeply imbedded in American life. Several generations of union activity and thought have not been able to make much of an impression upon it. Even when pilloried as "ragged individualism," this set of beliefs remains important among workers' attitudes. Consequently, when the automobile industry accepted its code under the N.R.A., although it did not assume an open-shop position, it affirmed the right of the employers in the industry to hire and fire, promote and demote in accordance with the merit of the individual workman. This affirmation is just as effective as a declaration that "anyone joining a union will be discharged" since it leaves "merit" to the determination of the employer. The employer who is hostile to unionism may discover without difficulty that good union men are always dropping tools or arriving late in the morning. But for publicity purposes the "merit clause" was much better than frank antiunionism since it appeared eminently fair and reasonable to the bulk of the public, including a great many workers.

The best recent presentation of the Horatio Alger point of view has been put out by the American Steel and Iron Institute in the form of a handsomely printed and illus-

trated pamphlet. This pamphlet explains how much wages
have risen in the last generation, how the hours of labor
have been decreased, how safety and the conditions of
work have improved, how well the employee-representation plan works, and how many of the presidents and vice-
presidents in the steel industry have risen from the ranks.
There is no crude implication that *anyone* can become a
vice-president, or that the labor problem can be settled
by making *everyone* a vice-president, but still there is no
getting around the fact that a lot of vice-presidents rose
from the ranks.

The judiciously worded advertisements of the General
Motors and Chrysler Corporations in 1936 and 1937 may
be pointed to as excellent examples of the newer approach
of antiunion firms to the publicity question. Dignified in
language, reasonable in demands and long-suffering in tone,
it is difficult to imagine that there was a single tongue-in-
cheek in the whole copy room while they were being
fabricated. General Motors has also specialized in the
"American Way of Life" in the advertising intervals of
its radio concert series. Still more recently, the National
Manufacturers' Association has been covering the countryside with billboards depicting the American way of life
in specific detail. The hero of the series is married to a
beautiful wife and has two children, a dog and a car. The
words "Highest Wages in the World" or "Highest Standard of Living in the World" figure prominently in the
picture. There is a good deal of country scenery (without
billboards), picnics and rides through the scenery, and
the hero coming home in the midafternoon all clean and
fresh from an easy day's work at the office, factory or
mine. There is some question, however, as to whether this
particular campaign may not be a little too subtle. A popular magazine with an immense circulation has recently
published a picture of one of these billboards as a background for a soup line. The possibilities for irony are

considerable. In a small survey of popular opinion as to
the sponsorship of this campaign (there is no indication of
this on the billboard), the guesses ran all the way from the
American Oil Company to the United States Government.
It may be, therefore, that if an amount of money equal to
the cost of this enterprise had been put into a whispering
campaign, the results might have been more tangible.

The atrocity story method of antiunion publicity has
also been extensively used with impressive results. The
open-shop trade papers usually carry one or more such
stories in each issue. Daily papers with a nation-wide circulation may rearrange or headline the stories of even their
Guild reporters in such a way as to give the desired effect.
The more elaborate efforts take the form of pamphlets or
even small books. The early examples, in the 1890's and
the 1910's, were so highly fictionalized and melodramatic
as to be useless nowadays. Pictures of union agents with
long flowing mustaches and black snake whips driving
honest labor to a fate worse than death are ineffective at
a time when people have become accustomed to taking
their crime neat. The *Wall Street Journal's* "History of
Organized Felony and Folly," however, is a useful com-
pilation of labor crime and racketeering which is accurate
enough to pass muster in fairly select historical circles.

In the writings of several well-known contemporary
magazine writers may be found examples of the most
subtle and effective techniques of antiunion publicity.
Innuendo, association of ideas, stereotyped beliefs, rumor
and spectacular exaggerations are skilfully blended with a
few verifiable facts to produce an important contribution
to the science of propaganda. The influence of this propaganda is heightened by repeated statements by the authors
that they admire the honest worker and believe in the
"principles of trade unionism as such." In a recent article
one author refers to the huge "*secret* political slush fund"
which organized labor has available for campaign purposes

Early forms of antiunion publicity were melodramatic.

in this country. The fact that this fund is "secret" apparently makes it unnecessary to document the statement. It is unlikely to occur to the average reader that union contributions to political campaigns are as faithfully reported to the Senate committee concerned with this matter as are the sums donated by any other contributor. After making a rapid calculation of the membership dues collected by C.I.O. unions, the author concludes that this would amount to about $16,000,000 a year. He says that this gives some idea of the "huge amount" collected by labor unions and spent "to a large extent" for political purposes. Few readers realize that the bulk of union funds is used for strike relief, financial benefits to members, administrative and organizing expenses and overhead costs. Effective propaganda, however, is not expected to go into details of this sort. Another author's method has been to emphasize his approval of the principles of trade unionism in two or three sentences and then devote many brilliantly written pages to associating labor leadership with every known variety of gangsterism and racketeering. When combined with stereotyped ideas about silk-hatted and whip-cracking "walking delegates," this method produces a powerful effect even upon the mind of a disciplined and unsympathetic reader. The author concludes with a demand that unions be incorporated in order that labor union racketeers shall be shriveled in the glare of publicity attendant upon state inspection. Able columnists and political commentators have recently joined the swelling chorus of those who demand the incorporation of trade unions in order to convert them into "responsible bodies" or in order to "protect them from racketeers." Many of those who press this demand are presumably sincere in their beliefs that incorporation is valuable as a method of eliminating labor racketeering. This is eloquent testimony of the effectiveness of the type of propaganda described above. It is quite possible that the technique is so good that its users fall victims to their own wiles. In any case manufacturers' associations and chambers of commerce which have long been in favor of incorporation of unions have recently enjoyed a favorable public response to bills directed toward union incorporation which they have caused to be introduced in numerous state legislatures. Liberal and trade-union publications are faced with a difficult task in explaining that incorporation of poultry, artichoke, florist and cleaning and dyeing businesses has not protected them from racketeers and gangsters; that the A.F. of L., most national unions and many local unions do give publicity to their financial affairs; that since the state possesses the right of "visitation and inspection" of corporations any member of an incorporated union, a spy for example, might by appeal to the courts expose the membership rolls of a union to an agent willing to relay information to employers' black lists; that if a court decides that a union is not "living up to the purposes of its charter," the union's funds may be attached and a receiver appointed for its affairs; that since a corporation technically exists forever, a small minority of shareholders planted by a spy agency in the union may prevent it from transferring its allegiance from the A.F. of L. to the C.I.O. by holding on to funds, records and other assets; that there is no law in Great Britain providing for the incorporation of unions (as is often implied by proponents of the plan); [2] that responsible labor leaders whom no one would think of associating with racketeering, have for a full generation opposed incorporation as a device for facilitating the destruction of unions through repeated damage suits; and that employers' associations are not themselves incorporated although they are in the fore of the drive toward union incorporation. These matters are so highly technical, however, that their

[2] English law requires the registration of unions as friendly or benefit societies, publicity for the accounts of union funds and written permission from union members to allow the use of funds for political purposes.

recital can only with difficulty match the convincing power of innuendo, exaggeration, spectacular misstatement, inaccurate association of ideas and emphasis upon stereotyped beliefs.

A third general method of resisting unionism is the use of the black list and white list. Although these methods considerably antedate the development of the spy system and the permanent employers' association, they have been rendered more effective by these agencies. In the early 1830's both black lists and white lists were used among New England textile manufacturers. The white lists took the form of certificates of honorable discharge. These could not be obtained by mill girls who had taken part in collective activities. Without a certificate, employment was difficult to obtain. The black lists of the period contained the names of those who had "conspired" against their employer or caused him trouble in any way. During the last hundred years the principle of the black list has been made more effective by the development of modern means of communication and employers' associations.

Although there is no question of the legality of the employer's right to refuse employment to anyone, there is some question of the legality of drawing up the lists and circularizing the information. Moreover, the general public is likely to consider the use of the black list an unsporting practice, at best. Consequently a large degree of secrecy is usually maintained. This is not difficult since the use of the telephone, the mails, private conversation, central hiring offices and secret card record files makes it very difficut for a worker to prove that the reason for discharge or refusal to hire is that he is on the black list or not on the white list. There is little accurate evidence as to the exact extent of the use of this device. Workers themselves believe that its use is very general. It is understandable, however, that many workers who are not hired simply because no work is available believe that the reason is the existence of a black list. The effect of this reasoning is to increase the effectiveness of the black list as an antiunion method since workers believe its use to be more general than it probably is.

The worker's only defense against the black list is to get out of the industry or to change his name. The first is often very difficult to do, especially when any degree of skill is involved. Workers, like anyone else, usually have an attachment to their names which makes them reluctant to change them. There is also a context of immorality surrounding the process. In desperation, however, workers often resort to this change and find that after the first two or three aliases, the process is as easy as taking off your coat. Leaders and active workers in the I.W.W. during the period of its extermination developed, especially among the casual laborers, what amounted almost to a habit in this respect. In at least two ways, nevertheless, even this escape may be blocked. When the white list takes the form of a "continuous discharge book," as it may under the terms of the Copeland Act affecting the employment of seamen, it becomes impossible for seamen to secure employment unless they bring with them a numbered book containing a record of their previous employment in the shipping industry. Employers are enabled to make notations in each seaman's book at the conclusion of a voyage. If the employer wishes, he may write "troublemaker" and thus debar the seaman from further employment. Or employers may circulate a list of the numbers of the discharge books carried by "bad actors." This was one of the issues at the center of the 1936-37 shipping strike in the East. Supporters of the bill assert that the books will not be used in this way. This is possible. But it is also true that since the books *may* be used in this way, they constitute an effective discouragement to union activity.

The second method by which alteration of names may

be rendered useless is through the operation of the Social Security Act. Although it is true that the forms issued by the Board do not require any information which would be of use to an antiunion employer, each recipient of benefits under the Old-Age Annuity sections of the Act is assigned a social security account number. This number is of necessity available to the employer as well as the worker and the Board, since the employer must pay premiums into the account of each worker in his employ. In order to change his name, therefore, a worker would also have to drop his account number. This can be done only by denying previous employment in the industry. To do this is to deny any skill or training and to reduce chances of employment. The employer, on the other hand, is furnished with a means of identifying "undesirables" which is much simpler and more accurate than anything except the actual fingerprinting of industrial workers. There appears to be little reason, therefore, to think that the effectiveness of the white list or black list as an antiunion device will be reduced, even if the courts should apply the doctrine of conspiracy against them more actively than has been done in the past.

A fourth method of resisting the advances of union organizers has been the use of the "yellow-dog" contract, either with or without the use of the injunction. The yellow-dog contract or "ironclad" has long been used in American industry to discourage unionization. It is an agreement signed by the worker on receiving employment which provides that he will not join a union or encourage the formation of one while he is in the company's employ. The effect upon the worker of signing these contracts is usually greater if he is conscious of what he is doing than if he is informed at a later date of what he has done. Both policies, however, may be pursued. In the past, two results have been achieved by these contracts. One has been to discourage men from joining unions and the other has been to make possible the issuance of injunctions against union organizers approaching the workers and thereby inducing breach of contract. The first purpose has been achieved through moral pressure rather than legal action. Although the courts have held that these contracts are enforceable, there has been little point in employers' bringing suit against workers since it is difficult to prove that damages have been suffered as a result of breach of contract. Employers have therefore successfully relied upon the effect of these contracts upon the worker's mind. In 1930 it was estimated that well over a million workers were affected by agreements of this sort in force at their place of employment. In the Hitchman decision in 1917 the Supreme Court of the United States took the position that since these were enforceable contracts, any effort by a union agent to organize workers might be enjoined in a plant which was covered by a yellow-dog agreement. This position was reaffirmed and strengthened in a number of subsequent Supreme Court decisions and by state court decisions in several important jurisdictions including Pennsylvania and Massachusetts.

This relationship between the courts and antiunion employers has, however, been sharply restricted in recent years. By 1933 seven states had made such contracts nonenforceable as being contrary to public policy. Although workers may still be compelled to sign them as a condition of receiving employment, the contracts may not be made a basis for injunctive action by employers against union organizers in these states. Furthermore, the Norris-LaGuardia Act of 1932 made yellow-dog contracts nonenforceable in all Federal courts. Both Section 7a of the N.I.R.A. and the Wagner Labor Relations Act in 1935 further limited the possibilities of these contracts by specifically inveighing against any interference with the right of workers to bargain collectively. There is still important room, however, for effective use of this device. In many states the yellow-dog contract has not been outlawed. In others it may be used for its moral effect, presumably still considerable in spite of the advertising which the N.R.A. and subsequent events have given to "labor's right to organize." Although the Wagner Labor Relations Act was validated by the Supreme Court on April 12, 1937, its enforceability in the face of more subtle forms of the yellow-dog contract has yet to be determined.

During the 1920's management developed a policy which the prophets of the New Capitalism called "welfare work." This was labeled by organized labor "hell-fare work," and was more specifically described by management as profit-sharing, employee stock-ownership, old-age and other insurance benefits, company recreation and social service plans. The motives back of the development of this policy were as complex as those which determine the antiunion position of the average employer. "Good business sense," paternalism, group example, experimentalism, pure altruism and antiunionism were part of the complex which propelled the program into existence. Setting aside the question of weighing the importance of any one of these motives, it was soon apparent that most of these policies were effective antiunion devices and perhaps worth their cost on this ground alone. As such, they were espoused by many antiunion firms.

Profit-sharing may be introduced as an alternative to wage increases and thereby shift a part of the risk of ownership to the shoulders of labor. Employee stock-ownership may provide a new source of capital or enable the management to buy into large outside holdings which threaten the control of the existing management. Stock, widely distributed in small parcels among employees, is very unlikely to be voted as a block against managerial wishes. The important consequence of either profit-sharing or employee stock-ownership, however, from an anti-union point of view, is their influence upon workers' attitudes toward the labor movement. "Every worker a capitalist" was the slogan of the 'twenties. If every worker has a share in profits, either through ownership or otherwise, he will become interested in the welfare of the company rather than in joining labor organizations. It need not cost the management anything to inaugurate either of these programs. It may be worth a great deal as antiunion insurance.

It is presumably clear to the management that the effect of profit-sharing is upon the worker's mind rather than his pocketbook. Since the profits or losses of a company are profoundly affected by the success or failure of managerial speculations in raw materials, inventories and equipment, the individual worker who thought the matter over carefully would probably decide that the effect upon his share of profits resulting from doubling his efforts would probably not be startling. If he can be sold the idea, however, that he is now in the profit-taking class, he is much more likely to be antipathetic to "agitators" who propose collective action against employers. The same is true of stock-ownership. If the average dividend rate of a company is 5 per cent, a worker with a wage income of $1,000 a year would have to own $20,000 worth of stock before his economic interests as an owner would equal his economic interests as a wage earner. In 1927, at about the height of the employee stock-ownership program, workers' holdings amounted to about a billion dollars. This was distributed among a million workers with the "bulk" of the holdings in the hands of executives, included under the heading "employees." The average holding of the workers covered by stock-ownership plans was therefore well under a thousand dollars. Assuming a 5 per cent dividend, the average return on all "workers'" stockholdings would be $50.00. On the basis of these figures, it would take a 100 per cent increase in dividends to equal a 5 per cent increase on $1,000 of wage income. If workers consistently approached this matter with a pad and pencil, they would probably conclude that agitation for a 5 per cent wage increase was more promising than working hard enough to double the company's dividend payments. It may be concluded, therefore, that the appeal of employee stock-ownership plans is to workers' nonlogical attitudes, rather than to their pocketbooks. This seriously limits the effectiveness of this program as a permanent antiunion institution, although it may be effective for some time. Workers' skepticism toward stock-ownership as an alternative to collective action is somewhat sharpened when they find themselves during a depression, as many nonexecutive workers did, keeping up time-payments on a stock whose current market value is little greater than each time-payment. There are signs, nevertheless, of the revival of both profit-sharing and stock-ownership plans which are chronologically if not logically related to the intense organizing activity of 1936-37.

In several respects, the program of retirement and other benefits which was a part of the New Capitalism was a more important antiunion instrument than employee stock-ownership. Within this program there was an immense variety of detail. Savings and loans plans, mutual benefit associations, group insurance, industrial pensions, unemployment benefits, dismissal wages and employment regularization were among the most important forms. The operation of the plans was formal or informal, voluntary or compulsory, contributory or noncontributory on the part of the workers, employer-controlled, or joint-controlled and contractual or noncontractual. The motives behind the introduction of the plans are as complex as their forms. Prominent among them is the desire to ward off unionism. This may be accomplished in two ways: In general, by increasing the loyalty of the worker to the company; in particular, by tying the worker to the company. The latter can be accomplished by making the plans noncontractual so that the contributions of the employer to a benefit plan are recoverable at will, in case of strikes or at the termination of a worker's employment. When noncontractual plans are adopted in lieu of, or to forestall, wage increases, workers feel that the contributions made by the employer are really coming out of the workers' envelopes. This gives the employer a further hold upon the workers' movements and actions. The threat of discharge becomes a more compelling reason for remaining tractable than otherwise holds, since discharge means not only loss of employment, but loss of equities in the benefits plans. The employer, on the other hand, need not incur heavy obligations since most noncontractual benefit plans may be dissolved by merger, by reorganization or at the will of the employing company.

During the depression more than a quarter of the industrial pension plans went out of existence. The depression rendered them both insolvent and unnecessary from the point of view of retaining the loyalty of the worker. There was very little labor movement left to which workers might transfer their loyalty, and jobs were so scarce that few dared to transfer their allegiance from one company to another. It goes almost without saying that most of the unemployment benefit, dismissal wage and employment regularization plans quickly became inoperable. The Social Security Act also dealt all of these plans a heavy blow. There are signs, however, of a revival of industrial pension plans among companies in a relatively favored position. The motives back of this revival are again highly complex but appear to include a desire to keep a jump ahead of the parallel revival of the labor movement.

The final aspect of company welfare plans has been an expansion of the Christmas turkey to something approaching magnificent proportions. Here again the motives run all the way from good business, through the spirit of Santa Claus, to antiunionism. Swimming pools, basketball courts, playing fields, rest and reading rooms, educational programs, shop and plant papers, picnics, dinners, dances and various competitions are some of the forms which welfare plans have taken. As will be pointed out later, these plans have paralleled, although well in advance, the similar policies of the more important unions. Whatever the motive behind the introduction of welfare work, its most important by-product has been to increase the loyalty of workers to their companies, except when the satisfaction gained by workers through the operation of any or all of these plans is obviously less than would have been provided by possible wage increases or reductions in hours.

Some employers have followed the lead set by many of our institutions of higher learning in realizing the extensive possibilities of substituting vicarious athletics for actual physical exercise. The sports programs of most companies began as spontaneous gatherings of workers who "picked up" a game during noon hour in a near-by lot. This led to intercompany challenges and the development of informal sports leagues. In some instances this has been followed by the construction of grandstands and bleachers by the company, and the employment of semiprofessional players. This has extended the field of interest in company athletics to nonplaying workers and even into the surrounding community. The development of organized cheering for "dear old Ronoco" would complete the analogy with collegiate athletics. This analogy should perhaps not be pressed further, but it is possible that stressing the immediate issue of the Red Rovers of Ronoco vs. The Tenoco Tankers may keep the question of wages and hours as presented by the Oil Field, Gas Well and Refinery Workers' International Union from assuming compelling importance in the mind of the average worker.

The period of the 'twenties saw a rapid expansion of the employee-representation program in American industry. Organized labor applied to this program the term "company unionism" and in spite of dissent by management the phrase has stuck. Although there were about a dozen experiments in company unionism before 1914, the World War gave the movement its great impetus. The bloody mine wars in Colorado induced John D. Rockefeller, Jr., to begin experimentation in the Colorado Fuel and Iron Company in 1915. This plan was followed by a rapid development of company unionism in the industries which were primarily affected by European war orders. After America entered the War, the movement was accelerated by encouragement from government boards and employers' associations. In 1919 about half a million workers were covered by company unions. This increased to about a million and a quarter in 1924 and to more than a million and a half in 1928. But in 1932 it dropped to about a million and a quarter. The N.R.A. revived the growth of company unionism so that by the autumn of 1934 the number of workers covered was estimated at about two and a half million. Recent defections of company union members to the ranks of independent unions have probably reduced the number considerably.

There is a great variety in the forms which company unions assume. This variety is indicated to some extent by the names attached to the various forms. Employee-representation plans, employees' associations, industrial relation plans, shop councils, works councils, industrial assemblies, company brotherhoods, good-will clubs, protective associations and industrial democracies are some of the names which are used. There are two essential features, however, which may be offered as a definition of company unions. They are almost always subject to some degree of employer control, and they are usually limited in membership to the workers in one company or plant. As usual, the employer's motives in introducing company unionism to his business are mixed. At the extremes, there are, however, two clear-cut positions. One is that the employee-representation plan is a personnel management device designed to acquaint the management with the sources of irritation and the possibilities of improvement in personnel policies. The employers at this pole are in a very small minority. At the other pole are those employers who frankly assert that the company union is introduced only to ward off independent unionism. This group is also a small minority. Between these two positions there is an immense confusion of motive and policy which includes the great majority of company union employers. Within this group the bulk of company union plans indicate by their origin and nature that they are antiunion agencies. They are a means of avoiding collective bargaining rather than providing it. They become methods of acquainting the workers with the decisions of management. As such they do not fulfill the personnel management function of acquainting the management with the sources of irritation among workers, nor do they, by any conceivable elasticity of the phrase, constitute "collective bargaining."

Company unions are an effective antiunion device for two reasons. First, to the extent that they do fulfil real personnel management functions, they eliminate this element from the appeal of independent unions. Second, whether or not they accomplish the first purpose, they offer the appearance of collective bargaining without involving the economic, psychological and social costs which constitute the average employer's objection to independent unionism. The appearance of collective bargaining is important to achieve not only because the labor movement is constantly setting its competitive wares before the workers, but also because the law and, to a certain extent, public opinion, demand that it be allowed. Company unionism offers the appearances at little cost.

The appearances may be maintained by setting up an organization, giving it a name, holding occasional meetings, electing officers, giving out membership cards and granting inexpensive requests. The problem of "Washroom Reds" [3] is one which has frequently been raised through the company union and satisfactorily solved through the good offices of paper products companies.

The costs of independent unions may be avoided by keeping the company union well in hand. This may be accomplished in a variety of ways. First, by starting the organization well in advance of agitation from outside sources. If the workers are not enthusiastic or are actually hostile, compliance may be secured by suggesting that preference in hiring, promotions and layoffs will be given to company union members. Some companies have intimated that the plant was about to be moved but that acceptance of the company union would make this unnecessary. Others have stated that the various welfare plans of the company were an integral part of the company union scheme and that they would stand or fall together. In some instances the foremen have distributed copies of the proposed company union plan through the plant and compelled the workers to sign as indicated. When an outside union has been hard by, a few companies have found it necessary to intimate that a 5 per cent wage increase would be forthcoming as soon as the company union was set up. There have been subtler methods of getting a plan started which have gradually shaded off to a point where it is impossible to say who really began it.

After the company union has been erected, the second problem is to keep it under control. Membership in a company union is usually free and often automatic. But even company unions cost something. Both employee and management representatives must be paid while on union duty. Stenographic costs must be met and occasional meetings

[3] An advertiser's phrase used to describe dissatisfaction resulting from inadequate lavatory properties.

on company time are expensive. All this must come out of the company's pocket. The control of the purse strings is as important to the management of a company union as it is to the leaders of a national union. When membership dues are collected from the workers, control may be maintained by subtracting the dues from the pay envelopes. This may also be a fairly simple way of effecting a wage reduction.

When the matter of money has been settled, the important question is the actual form which the discussion of issues assumes. It is important to have at least one member present who represents the management. Under the employee committee plan, an executive meets with the workers' representatives and guides the discussion into the sunny waters of mutual interests. His function is not to say "No," but to make it unnecessary for anyone higher up to say "No." The joint-committee plan usually provides for equal representation from both workers and management. The function of the managerial representatives in this instance is the same as in the employee committee plan. It is more expensive, however, to have so many highly paid executives sitting around a table discussing common interests. The most complicated method of retaining control of the company union is what is called the "industrial democracy" type. This consists of a House of (employee) Representatives, a Senate of foremen and lower executives, a Cabinet of higher company officials and a President who is also president of the company. Laws passed by both houses must be approved by the cabinet and signed by the president. Company control in this instance is so obvious that the "industrial democracy" plan is becoming increasingly rare. The fourth, and much less common, form of company unionism is the employees' association. These associations closely resemble independent unions. They often have membership rolls, pay dues, meet on their own time, sometimes pay their own representatives, and discuss their affairs in the absence of guidance by management. Such company unions may develop extensive bargaining power or become interested in linking themselves with the outside labor movement. If company unions reach the "association" stage, they may therefore actually simplify the problem of the union organizer.

On the whole, however, the advantages of the company union to the antiunion employer are clear. It is incapable of actual bargaining with the employer because it has no independent treasury, and because the workers' representatives are paid by the company and are therefore dependent upon it. Although many company union plans contain specific guarantees that employee representatives will not be discriminated against, it is not to be expected that representatives will make themselves "unreasonable" by pressing demands toward which management's attitude is negative. If this should happen, the representative's understanding of his position may be sharpened by guarded reference to the possibility of "promotion coming along sometime soon." Company unions, furthermore, are insurance against the exercise of real bargaining power because they do not employ outside experts for advice, as independent unions often insist upon doing; they rarely have membership meetings during which the workers might come under the influence of "mob emotions"; they seldom make use of arbitration proceedings; they do not have the support of workers in other plants; and they are not a part of the labor movement. They have no long traditions of historical struggles behind them, they rarely sign trade agreements, they do not meddle with labor legislation and they are almost incapable of precipitating strikes. Apart from their personnel management functions, therefore, company unions are one of the most effective

forms of resistance to unionism at the disposal of the antiunion employer.[4]

A further possibility of resisting organization of workers
is the use of the legal methods of ridding a community
of the physical presence of union organizers. There are
a variety of charges upon which organizers may be arrested and put quietly away. Trespass, suspicion, loitering,
breach of the peace, vagrancy, littering the streets, and
violation of noise, zoning, fire, building, traffic and public
safety ordinances are convenient charges which may be
preferred if temporary incarceration of the organizer is all
that is necessary. If the employer's political connections
are adequate there is usually little difficulty in arranging
the details. In a company town, owned and operated by
the employer, the matter is simple since the organizer is
trespassing the instant he steps off the public carrier which
brings him to the town.

If the organizer persists in coming back, more serious
charges may be necessary in order to make possible sufficiently high bail to keep the organizer in jail pending trial
or appeal. "Inciting to riot," "criminal syndicalism," "resisting an officer," and "undesirable alien" are suitable

---

[4] The Wagner Labor Relations Act forbids most of the practices which,
taken together, constitute a definition of a company union. Since this act
has been upheld by the Supreme Court, antiunion employers have been
compelled to become more subtle in their methods of controlling company
unions. Many employers have given up the task altogether. Others have
fostered the development of so-called "independent" unions which bear
most of the earmarks of the company unions they replaced. Early in
August, 1937, many of these "independent" unions came together to form
the Independent Labor Federation of America, in opposition to the A.F.
of L. and the C.I.O. Some of the leaders of this organization are identifiable as persons who played an important part in breaking the 1936-37
Remington Rand strike and the 1937 Hershey strike (see chapter V).
Two days after its formation, I.L.F. of A. leaders made an unsuccessful
effort to break the strike of Hazelton, Penn., silkworkers. From an antiunion point of view the danger of allowing these "independent" unions
to federate with each other is that they may really become independent
of the employer.

charges if longer terms of incarceration are desired. It should be realized, however, that considerably greater difficulties are involved in actually securing convictions on these charges than in the case of minor offenses. Prosecuting attorneys must be paid (and the taxes for this purpose often come largely from employers), witnesses must be secured and, in the first three cases, a jury must be selected. Even when the bail has been put at a high figure, the American Civil Liberties Union, the International Labor Defense, or other organizations sympathetic to unionism sometimes provide the bond and release the suspect. When this happens, the organizer may travel around the country making speeches, as in the Angelo Herndon case,[5] or writing books and generally making himself more effective than before his arrest.

The simplest method of removing an organizer from a community is to "take him for a ride." When legal resources are inadequate, this may be resorted to. Care must be exercised to dissociate the employer and the local agencies of the law from complicity in the affair. Often this is not difficult. The right thinking young men and lesser business celebrities in the neighborhood may recognize the organizer as a menace to the prosperity of the community and act accordingly. If this sort of spontaneity is lacking, it may be stimulated by a suggestion from a foreman. "Somebody oughta take that red for a ride." If no one takes the hint, a superintendent may use a favorable opportunity to remark to a foreman, "Why don't you get some of the boys together and find out if that agitator isn't interested in the scenery on the other side of the state

[5] Angelo Herndon, an organizer among the unemployed in Atlanta, was arrested for his part in leading a demonstration of unemployed workers to the city hall. He was convicted of "inciting to insurrection" under an act of 1861, and sentenced to eighteen to twenty years on the chain gang. Pending appeal, bail of $15,000 was set. After two appeals had been unsuccessfully carried to the Supreme Court Herndon's sentence was set aside on the third appeal, in 1937.

line?" The foreman thinks of the time-payments still due on his Ford and says "Maybe I'll do that little thing."

From this point on the procedure is likely to be stereotyped. As the organizer is walking along a street, a car draws up to the curb. A blow at the base of the skull stuns him and he is yanked into the car. There he is beaten; stripped and beaten; or stripped, beaten and killed. There are other possible combinations, but these are the essential elements. Sometimes tar and feathers are added. In other cases sexual mutilation is practiced. Sometimes, after the beating has gone on until the organizer is insensible, there is a parley during which the relative merits of "Let's rub him out" are weighed against "Aw, give him a break, I'm tired."

The risks of this form of antiunionism do not lie as much in the danger of subsequent apprehension as in the publicity which usually follows. Sometimes the organizer survives and can be repaired successfully enough to enable him to renew his activities with increased effectiveness. In other cases the public is likely to jump to the conclusion that the employer is connected with the affair and a decrease in the sale of the company's products may follow. When the local police have also been informally involved, the publicity is likely to be particularly bad. It may therefore become increasingly advisable to use the formal resources of the law, whenever this is possible, in removing organizers from antiunion communities.[6]

[6] Sherman Dalrymple, president of the United Rubber Workers of America, was invited to speak to a group of rubber workers late in June, 1936, in Gadsden, Alabama. When Dalrymple arrived at the hall he found the meeting largely attended by Goodyear supervisors and foremen. His speech was interrupted by the entrance of a sheriff and deputies who removed him and other union men from the hall. In front of the court house, Dalrymple was beaten so seriously that there was some doubt for about a week as to whether he would survive. Other union men were similarly beaten and run out of town. The publicity which this event received increased Dalrymple's effectiveness as an organizer, and weakened the company's antiunion position because of the subsequent investigation of this and other similar events by the LaFollette Committee.

This conclusion is in line with previous conclusions as to the necessity for increased subtlety in antiunion methods, whether these take the form of stool pigeons, spies, black lists, yellow-dog contracts, publicity and legal action, or profit-sharing, employee stock-ownership, welfare work and the company union. There is a distinct possibility, however, that the more subtle the antiunion methods become, the more nearly their economic and psychological costs to the employer equal those involved in the acceptance of independent unions as collective bargaining agencies.

The LaFollette Committee has also made available information about the techniques of antiunionism in Harlan County, Kentucky. Testimony before the committee indicated that: 1. Deputy Sheriff White was in one of three cars from which shots were fired into the house of United Mine Workers' organizer Marshall Musick on February 9, 1937. The shots killed Musick's son and wounded his mother and sister. 2. Deputy Sheriff Middleton was drinking with a group of deputies just before the murder. Middleton was employed by the Harlan Wallis Coal Co. and has been indicted for major crimes six times since March, 1934. 3. Deputy Sheriff Hugh Taylor was shot on February 20, 1937, because he refused to help other deputies attack Musick's house. He was later offered $2,000 to ignore the Senate subpœna. 4. Lloyd Clouse, a union member, was killed by four mine guards on April 24, 1937. 5. Ben Unthank was hired by the Harlan County Coal Operators Association as "head road killer." He was paid $150 a month salary, but in February, 1937, his salary and expenses were $23,000. 6. Chris Patterson was hired by Unthank for $100 in November, 1933, to dynamite U.M.W. organizer Dwyer. Patterson served a year in prison for this crime. 7. United States Coal and Coke Co., a subsidiary of United States Steel, employed J. R. Menefee as head of its espionage. Menefee reported to the head of the H. C. Frick Coke Co. in Pittsburgh. The Frick Company maintained a labor spy and private police training school near Pittsburgh. 8. William C. Johnson was employed by the Harlan-Wallis Coal Co. in June, 1933, to lead a gang in "thuggin'," that is, hunting and beating union organizers. They carried machine guns, shot guns, rifles and pistols. 9. Sheriff Theodore R. Middleton acquired property worth $102,728 in three years on a salary of $5,000 a year. His money was largely invested in mining stocks. 10. Daniel Boone Smith, Commonwealth attorney in the district, was paid a monthly salary by three coal companies in addition to his $4,000 a year from the state. 11. While the committee hearings were in progress, witnesses were threatened in the Senate office building by representatives of Harlan County operators.

The effectiveness of these antiunion methods must be questioned, however, in view of the fact that on May 2, 1937, about 5,000 of Harlan County's 16,000 miners belonged to the United Mine Workers.

CHAPTER IV

The Strike

IN a small town outside a large Eastern industrial city there is an iron foundry which employs about seven hundred workers. There are between fifteen and twenty separate occupations, in this foundry, varying in skill from trades as precise as that of a watchmaker to tasks which anyone with hands and feet can perform. The wages run from twenty-five to forty cents an hour, and the hours worked per week vary from sixty-five to eighty. Eighty hours a week means twelve hours a day on week days and eight hours on Sunday. Sanitary conditions are bad enough to constitute a violation of the minimum requirements set by state law. The workers are a polyglot group, but restricted immigration and common schooling have made communication in one language possible among them. They learn through the newspapers that the forty-hour week has been granted by "Big Steel" with minimum rates well above the maximum in their foundry. They learn that the coal miners are working thirty-five hours a week and are asking for thirty with compensatory wage increases. They hear that the clothing workers have won further wage increases and are working half as many hours as the foundry workers. During noon hour the men begin to talk things over. On the way back from Sunday mass, the women talk in groups and their age-old complaints take on a more specific form. The prices of fish, onions, spaghetti, butter, eggs and even bread are held up for comparison with the twenty or twenty-five dollars their men bring home after an eighty-hour week. One Saturday noon a man in a knot of fifteen or more says, "Let's get together on this." The others eye him suspiciously and say nothing. That night two or three of them mention it to their wives. One wife says, "Now don't do anything foolish, Hugo." Another, "Well, it's about time that bunch of dumb clucks showed they had some manhood left." A third, "Couldn't you get someone in from outside to help you who wouldn't have to risk his job?"

All the next week there are groups of men talking together in low tones. They keep an eye on the office door and when a foreman approaches, the group breaks up looking a little like a gang of children who have been caught smoking cigars. Someone suggests that they choose a committee to talk things over. Each natural grouping, by trade, nationality, shop or residence, selects a representative or two and the men begin meeting after hours at each other's houses. They decide to ask for a fifteen per cent increase; a fifty-hour week with time and a half for overtime; toilets, washbowls and towels in every shop; separate washrooms for the women workers. A natural leader has emerged and been made chairman. He is a little proud and a great deal worried.

In the meantime the employer sees that something is obviously going on and decides to offer a 5 per cent increase with other conditions remaining the same. He posts a notice to this effect on every time clock. When the workers see these notices, there are immediate sounds of protest. They hang around the gates in the half-light of dawn. Someone in the swelling crowd yells, "Let's walk out." The cry is quickly taken up and men begin to shove each other aimlessly in disorganized effort to get out of the entrance corridor. The chairman of the strike committee hurries up and says, "Come on boys, let's get outa this. Ten of you go to each shop gate and tell the rest we're not goin' in." With considerable confusion this is done. Most of the latecomers are turned away without trouble. A few who protest are numbed by the instantaneous fulmination of passion which greets their insistence on going in. There is a little shoving around with elbows, knees and hips but no damage is done. The chairman calls everyone together. He says, "Now fellas, we gotta stick together. We'll hire the Lithuanian Hall for a meeting place. The boss has closed down the plant so we don't need pickets, yet. Let's break this up before there's any trouble. Go home and talk it over with your wives. We'll meet at the hall at ten o'clock." There is a half-hearted cheer and the men begin to wander away. They are beginning to cool off. They feel a little foolish walking along the streets at eight o'clock and arriving at their homes just as their children are leaving for school. The children are curious. Their mothers are anxious and dismiss them curtly toward the front door.

At ten o'clock four hundred men and women are packed in a hall intended for half that number. The committee is meeting in a back room upstairs. There is a half-hour wait. Then the committee wedges its way into the hall and the chairman mounts the rostrum. The people sit or stand in rows, immobile, unseeing, wondering how they came to do it, what will happen tomorrow, how they are going to meet the payment on the gas stove. The chairman says, "Everything is all right folks. I went to see the boss. He says that our demands are unreasonable and that he won't deal with our committee. But he has an order that he wants filled. We got that from one of the stenogs in the front office. All we have to do is to sit tight and stick together. He'll come around." A business agent from a near-by coke and gas union is introduced. He says their demands are reasonable and that they need more committes, a soup kitchen and a shoe repair shop. He promises his help and the moral support of his union. A woman from the clothing workers' union promises the shoe repair shop. Three policemen shoulder their way importantly into the hall. They stand for a while in a cleared space with their day sticks under their arms. Nothing is happening so they stroll out again with a joke or two to cover their rear. "Guess we got the wrong place. This looks like a Quaker meeting."

A sympathetic reporter covers the story and the open-shop paper in the near-by city gives it the front page with generous headlines. Attention is called to the violation of state law with respect to sanitation in foundries. A college teacher who is also a member of the Teachers' Union offers his services in collecting statistics on wages and hours in the foundry industry. Five students do the job in twenty-four hours for two points extra credit on the term grade. The statistics show that conditions in the foundry are far worse than the average for the industry. An organizer from the Radio Workers' Union who happens to be in town appears the following morning and makes a speech. He secures by telegram a charter from the Amalgamated Association of Iron, Steel and Tin Workers and a union is hastily organized.

The employer hears of this and quickly reverses his position. He sends for the chairman and apologizes for his hasty action the other morning; says he hasn't been feeling well lately and doesn't know what makes him blow off the handle that way; agrees that the men's demands are reasonable enough and tells the chairman he's glad to be able to grant them. The chairman hurries back to the hall and gives the news. The settlement is accepted by acclamation. After work is renewed it takes the men a week to clean out and repair smelting furnaces "frozen" solid when the fires were allowed to die. The charter from the Amalgamated Association is allowed to lapse. The business agent from the coke and gas workers says, "Jeeze, that's a shame. If the old man had held out two days longer, we coulda had a swell local of iron workers out here, and we certainly need their support."

Every year in the United States hundreds of strikes as spontaneous, unspectacular and informal as this take place.

They represent nothing more startling than a concerted withdrawal of labor. They are as legal as court decisions and the Constitutional prohibition of involuntary servitude can make them. They are precipitated by a variety of events including discharges of popular workers, arbitrary changes in time-honored shop practices, exchanges of personal insults between workers and foreman, as well as changes in or refusals to change wage rates and hours. Many of them take place without ruffling the surface of the social life which envelops them.

Although concerted withdrawal of labor is the essential element in all strikes, it is far from being the only element. If solidarity of group action could be achieved as easily in all strikes as in the one described above, it is quite possible that organized industrial workers would sometime since have rendered worthless the private ownership of the means of production. In the majority of instances, strikes are not effective unless attended by compulsion of both reluctant workers and resistant employers as well as by effective organization of procedure. It is the methods of compulsion which bring the strike into the courts. And it is the need for trained leaders and organized tactics which makes the backing of the labor movement necessary to the success of most strikes.

There is a variety of reasons for the reluctance of many workers to support a strike movement. Some feel a loyalty to their employer so great that any gesture of hostility toward him is extremely distasteful, even if it is clear that economic gain will follow. Others feel that they stand to gain more as individuals by refraining from strike action than by throwing in their lot with the group. Some are so impressed by the traditional social stigma attached to strike action that they do not view the matter in economic terms. Others are already in such desperate economic want that they feel that a temporary cessation of income would mean disaster even if followed by appreciable gains as a result of the strike. Still others are workers who have been unemployed prior to the strike and look upon it as a heaven-sent opportunity to return to work. Some are young or old workers whose incomes are auxiliary to that of the head of the family and who, therefore, are not much interested in wage rates as long as they can secure some pin money by temporary employment. Others again are outsiders like college students working for short periods for tuition or "experience," who bring with them a reserve of strength which leaves them unimpressed by long hours or intensive application of the speed-up. Still others are workers who have been attracted by advertisements to the scene without knowing that a strike is in progress and who feel themselves forced to work in order at least to earn their return trip train fare. Finally, there are those who are not workers at all but professional strikebreakers employed through agencies to break up picket lines and give the appearance, at least, of operating the plant.

It is the task of the picket to dissuade or prevent by intimidation or force any of these classes of workers from entering the shop or mill. Persuasion may be all that is necessary. The picket attempts to substitute the idea of loyalty to the group for loyalty to the employer. To those who feel they will gain by not striking, the picket explains that if the strike fails, everyone sooner or later will suffer. "You may be better off than the rest of us now, but your turn will come if we don't all stick together. You help us now and we'll help you later." If the worker is worried about the stigma of strike action, the picket says that "Nobody strikes for the fun of it, but you can't take everything lying down." To those who are in desperate want the picket promises relief. Those who work for auxiliary income are told that if the strike succeeds they will not have to work as much, or at all, because the higher wage rates will increase their family incomes. Outsiders like college boys are asked to "have a heart" and allow the real workers to determine their own affairs. Imported workers are fended off by union publicity to the effect that a strike is in progress. If they actually appear at the shop, the union may volunteer to pay their return expenses. Against professional strikebreakers it is usually felt that persuasion is simply wasted breath. Even in this instance, however, strikebreakers may be asked to "take it easy, brother, you can earn your pay without gettin' rough." When individual pickets are used, the picket may simply carry a sign explaining that a strike is in progress or that the shop is "unfair to organized labor."

The transition from persuasion to physical force is accomplished through the medium of appeal first to shame and then to fear. During a recent strike of workers in a New York retail outlet, the pickets took pictures or pretended to take pictures of patrons who entered the place. In another recent strike in the hosiery industry, the pickets, including both men and women, lay down on the sidewalk side by side forming a continuous carpet of human bodies. Whether successful or not, these methods obviously involve an appeal to shame. The traditional appeal to shame is verbal. "Blackleg," "scab," "yellow belly" and "rat" are words expressing an ethical attitude toward strikebreakers which is sharply in contrast to the employers' concept of the "loyal worker." Whether murmured under the breath as a strikebreaker passes the picket or shouted from a distance, their impact, under varying conditions, arouses shame, fear or fury. If fury is the product violence is likely to follow.

Violence, however, is most likely to take place either when use has been made of physical resistance through the mass picket line, or when pickets, because of the nature of the industry, are ineffective. The basic principle of the mass picket line is to form an impenetrable column of strikers which completely blocks entrance to the mill.

When there is a sufficiently large number of pickets, several files in lock step and linked arms may be formed. When a determined effort is made to pass through this column by individuals or by flying wedges of professional strike-breakers, truck loads of "loyal" workers or mounted police, violence is almost certain to result. Individuals are beaten, trucks are stoned or their spark plug wires are yanked out, and open warfare between police and strikers takes place. In the shipping, taxicab, truck driving, building service, longshore, agricultural, lumbering and other industries in which picket lines are impossible and in which unions have been "militant," workers who "scab" are beaten singly or in groups; taxicabs and trucks are stoned, burned or tipped over; and the cars or houses of non-strikers may be damaged. In some instances the families of "loyal" workers have been threatened if not attacked. Violence and mass picketing, therefore, are by no means identical. Much violence takes place in the absence of mass picketing, and in many instances this form of picketing actually reduces the likelihood of violence.

Conservative unions almost always avoid mass picketing if possible. This has resulted partly from the conservative union leaders' acceptance of the letter of court decisions or statute law forbidding it, and partly from the fact that the conservative craft union's reliance has been placed chiefly upon the paralyzing effect of withdrawing the labor of a minority of highly skilled operatives. The radical unions of the past and the progressive unions of the present have depended and now depend almost exclusively upon mass picketing whenever it is possible to arrange it. There are two reasons for this: The first, that temporary inconvenience to the employer, rather than paralysis of the plant, is likely to be the only result of withdrawing the semiskilled labor characteristic of the mass production industries in which the progressive unions operate. Without mass picketing, therefore, the strike is almost certain

Universal Newsreel from Soibelman Syndicate

Striking seamen picketing the office of a ship line.

Universal Newsreel from Soibelman Syndicate

A peaceful picket line shortly before being dispersed by tear gas and State Troopers' clubs.

eventually to be broken. The second reason is the maintenance of discipline and morale. A strike in an automobile, rubber, or large textile plant is likely to create unruly crowds of workers. It is the union leader's job to control these crowds. This can be done far more easily in a massed moving picket line disciplined by squad captains and reduced to the almost mechanical movements of an animate conveyor than in a milling and disorganized mob. There is also the very important influence of the mass picket as a spectacle upon the mind of the participant and the observer. It creates a feeling of group solidarity and purpose difficult to achieve by any other method. For this reason some unions have insisted on employing a mass picket line even when the plant has been closed by the employer and no effort made to reopen it.

The legal status of the picket differs from one locality to another. Most courts allow peaceful picketing which does not pass beyond the stage of persuasion. Some courts have held that picketing is never peaceful, always involves intimidation and consequently is illegal. Court decisions usually limit the number of pickets who may act in a given strike. Often the question of the legal status of picketing does not pass beyond the jurisdiction of the officers on the beat or, at most, the local police court. This leads to a great variety of decisions based upon compromises reflecting the varying political strength of workers and employers. A few states have passed laws legalizing even mass picketing while others have statutes specifically outlawing all forms except individual picketing. It has become common for labor sympathizers to speak of "the Constitutional right to picket." Although this has been effective publicity material, it is unlikely that the Supreme Court, in spite of the changed conditions of recent years, would countenance any form of picketing not clearly covered by the right to freedom of speech. This would outlaw anything but peaceful persuasion.

In spite of the dubious legal status of picketing, it has been accorded an increasingly large measure of social support. The attitude of the courts comes in many localities to be of only academic importance. Either employers are hesitant to risk legal procedures against massed pickets, or legal action is blocked by the subtle or open defiance of the strikers. One method of defying court orders against mass picketing consists of the union leader's announcing that although picketing has been outlawed by the courts, this does not prevent his taking a walk past the mill at six o'clock in the morning and inviting his friends along. The leader then makes it perfectly clear that no one is to picket, but that everyone is invited out for a morning constitutional. When the next morning arrives, it just happens that two or three thousand workers have chosen to work up an appetite by walking around the mill in lock-step formation.

Another method, initiated by the I.W.W. during their free speech campaigns in the far West and perfected during the 1934 Toledo automobile strikes, is to go on with mass picketing as though no court order had been issued. When the police patrol wagons arrive and just before the arrests begin, the picket line breaks up into details of ten. Each detail marches to the rear of the patrol wagon, enters, and quietly seats itself. As fast as new patrol wagons arrive, they are filled and dispatched in perfect order. Before long, the jails are full, no disturbance has been created and the only issue which has been raised is that of feeding the strikers in jail. This helps somewhat with the union's relief problem, and leaves a large force to picket the mill. Inside the jail, classes in parliamentary procedure, trade-union tactics or labor economics may be begun. A variation upon this method is to plant people in the picket line who have prominent social, banking, or legal connections in the community or in the country as a whole. Care is taken to see that these people are arrested and placed in jail. Once inside, they raise a terrific rumpus by demanding legal counsel, better accommodations, or talking to reporters who have been tipped off in advance. Immediately after their release, they continue the rumpus by asking why they have been accorded special consideration while others, guilty of the same offense, are still in jail.

A relatively recent variation of the mass picket line is the "flying squadron." The first large-scale use of the flying squadron in this country was made during the 1922 New England textile strike in the Rhode Island area which was under the control of a "progressive" union, the Amalgamated Textile Workers. A group of active union workers calling themselves the "Iron Battalion" moved from town to town in automobiles, acting as pickets where the union was weak or the employer resistance was strong and also assisting with the organization of relief and the maintenance of discipline. In the 1933-34 silk strikes in northern New Jersey extensive use was made of flying squadrons each of which contained several thousand workers and moved from the highly unionized centers to non-union mills where efforts were made to induce the closing down of plants still operating. The method used in this case was to call upon the workers to come out, to picket entrances when workers tried to enter in the morning, engage in open battles with the police when they attempted to break the picket lines, and stone the windows of those plants which succeeded in continuing operations.

The most elaborate use of the flying squadron ever made took place during the 1934 general strike in the textile industry. The organization of the squadrons was carefully planned in advance by union leaders. When the call to strike was issued, workers in the well-organized plants, especially in the South, left their machines, pulled the power switches, and as soon as it was apparent that the place was effectively closed, quit the mill in a body and entered cars and trucks lined up along the road near by.

The antiquity of most of the vehicles rendered the term "flying squadron" somewhat of a euphemism. When a line had been formed the squadron trundled off to the nearest nonunion mill. There the pickets drew up under the windows of the mill and the union workers began calling to those inside the plant to come out. The effect of the appearance of the squadron was almost immediately to arrest activities in the mill. Everyone crowded to the windows; sometimes they came out in a body; in other cases enough emerged to curtail production seriously; in others, the workers in the mill yelled defiance at those outside; in a few cases, the members of the squadron forced entrance to the mills, shut off the power and at least temporarily stopped production. As soon as martial law was declared by the governors of several states, the flying squadrons were called off in the face of machine guns posted along the highways. During the recent strikes in the Middle West, a further variation of the flying squadron appeared. Union leaders quietly arranged the transportation of thousands of workers from union communities to those in which strikers were faced with especially formidable forces of strikebreakers.

There are several forms of the strike which do not involve the use of pickets because the strikers do not leave their place of work. The first of these, the strike-on-the-job, was originally developed among the casual workers of the West in occupations which do not permit effective use of the picket line. In harvesting, lumbering, casual labor in road construction, longshore work, and so on, many gangs of workers developed to a fine art the technique of appearing to work without accomplishing anything. These strikes-on-the-job were often aimless, long drawn out and inconclusive. They were vague protests without effective organization or precise objectives. On the actual technique of "going slow" a great deal of individual ingenuity has been lavished with results which,

from an artistic point of view, have been highly gratifying
to the participants. But the objectives of this form of strike
tend to run over into the field of "making the job last" or
"getting even with the boss" rather than the accomplishment of immediate positive results.[1]

Out of the strike-on-the-job there developed the sit-
down strike, or "quickie." Again the I.W.W. were first to
make extensive use of this technique, but it has been rather
generally used among unorganized workers and as a regular policy of some local unions in the clothing and mining industries. It is a short, sudden strike for limited
objectives in which the workers simply sit with folded
hands at their benches or by their machines while their
representatives deal with the employer. The precipitating
cause is likely to be relatively trivial although if there is
some degree of organization before the strike, it may be
planned days in advance to coincide with a rush order or a
peak season. The advantage of these strikes is that they are
unexpected; they do not allow the substitution of other
workers; there is little problem of control since shop discipline remains more or less in force; and, since the demands are usually limited, there is a strong probability of
success.

From the sit-down strike, the stay-in strike develops
more or less as a matter of course. If the demands of a
sit-down strike are not met within the working hours of
one day and the workers remain determined, the employer almost automatically has a stay-in strike on his
hands. Stay-in strikes are currently referred to as a foreign
importation. Nothing, however, could be more indigenous
than the strikes-on-the-job and the sit-down strikes out
of which the stay-in strikes logically developed. As a matter of historical fact, the stay-in strikes of the Akron

---

[1] The "slow-down" has recently reappeared in the automobile industry
on the assembly lines. In this case the objectives are precise and the
technique is carefully organized.

rubber workers anticipated by months the wave of stay-in strikes which attended the accession of Leon Blum to the premiership of France in 1936. The epidemic of American stay-in strikes in 1937, nevertheless, was undoubtedly stimulated by the success which met the French workers' use of this technique. The stay-in strike has also been condemned or praised as a revolutionary method. If revolution is defined as a transfer of power from one social group to another, all forms of union activity which involve a challenge to the power of owners and managers are revolutionary. From a symbolic point of view, however, the stay-in strike is more "revolutionary" than the orthodox strike. The ordinary strike involves a forceful stoppage of the income from property and the owner's power to operate it upon his own terms. The stay-in strike accomplishes the same result, but through the actual seizure of property. Even when the results of a stay-in strike are identical with those achieved by the ordinary methods, the dramatization of power which accompanies the workers' physical possession of the property is immensely greater than can be achieved by any other method under comparable conditions.

Stay-in strikes are also more "revolutionary" because they are more effective. Many modern plants in the heavy goods industries are built almost like fortresses. Possession of them, therefore, can be kept by a much smaller group than is necessary to make a picket line effective. Discipline of the strikers is easier to maintain since they are free from the demoralizing forces of the street. Warmth, shelter and amusement are provided within the plant to an extent impossible to afford to a mass picket line outside. Violent physical conflict is rendered unnecessary unless an effort is made forcefully to recapture the plant. If this occurs, the initiative must be assumed by the management operating through the machinery of the law. This may often be both politically and financially embarrassing.

The legal status of the stay-in strike is even more

Stay-in strikers eating in the cafeteria of the Fisher Body plant during the 1937
  General Motors strike.

Stay-in strikers in the Fisher Body plant while away the time reading magazines
  and newspapers.

dubious than that of the mass picket line. Managers and owners have almost unlimited ground in common law, statute law, court decisions and general Constitutional guarantees to which they may appeal in securing injunctions and in setting in motion the machinery of forceful eviction. It is improbable that the stay-in strike could be legalized without a significant modification of the concept of property rights. Such a change is unlikely in the near future. The stay-in strike, however, is equally unlikely to be surrendered as a method of achieving demands by organized or unorganized workers. The evolution of its status is likely to be comparable to that of the mass picket line. Its illegality has already been widely disregarded by both its friends and its foes. Court orders have been subtly or openly defied, in some cases by both sides of the dispute as, for example, when General Motors effected a compromise settlement with the Automobile Workers' Union in complete disregard of a court order issued many days before calling for the eviction of strikers from G.M.C. plants. In this case the governor of Michigan, the management and the union apparently felt that the existence of the court order was a relatively academic factor in the situation. The court subsequently issued a request that at least the nominal aspects of obedience to the court be complied with. This *de facto* recognition of the stay-in strike is little less formal than the similar recognition accorded the mass picket, the sympathetic strike and the simple strike itself in earlier labor history. It may be expected that the attention of society will gradually be shifted from the legality of the stay-in strike to the conditions which bring it into existence and the objects toward which it is directed. It might be predicted that many labor sympathizers will soon come to speak of "the Constitutional right to stay-in" as convincingly and with as little technical accuracy as they now speak of the "Constitutional right to picket."

While calling the roll of strike species, mention

should be made of both the "sympathetic" and "general" strike. Although the sympathetic strike is called by one group of workers to help another, it often becomes a strike for new demands which emerge after the original sympathetic strike action. The strike of the East Coast sailors in 1936-37, for example, was originally called to help the West Coast sailors in their struggle for control of the hiring halls. The East Coast strike, however, soon developed demands of its own. Sympathetic strikes are likely to be successful only when they constitute an effective form of boycott. As such, they suffer from the legal and other limitations of the boycott pointed out in an earlier chapter. As the solidarity of the labor movement increases, they may be more frequently used. Sympathetic strikes may also be effective in plants to which orders have been transferred from plants in which strikes are in progress. In this case, the area of group action by workers is widened exactly in proportion to the area of coöperation among employers.

The word "general" may be applied to strikes covering a whole industry, a whole economic area, or a whole political unit or country. The general textile strike of 1934, the general strike in San Francisco in the same year and the general strike in England in 1926 provide examples of each type. When the general strike covers a whole industry its purpose is to establish the power of a union over the entire industry at once in order that wage and hour conditions may be simultaneously imposed. In a highly competitive industry, such as textiles, unions may consider this necessary in order to establish themselves at all. Piecemeal action is likely progressively to destroy itself if the imposition of union rates and hours on a particular plant hurts the competitive position of that plant. If standard wages and hour conditions are simultaneously imposed on the whole industry by general strike action, the effect is to eliminate wages and hours as competitive factors in that industry, rather than to injure the position of any one producer.

A general strike in a given economic area such as San Francisco is a sympathetic strike with social and political implications. It subjects the entire community to the compulsions usually applied to the employer and his "loyal" workers. It therefore sharpens the issue and hastens decisive settlement. If carried on for long, it is likely to be self-defeating because the strikers are themselves subjected even sooner than the well-to-do classes to the privations which follow from the strike. This is not to say that this form of general strike is not effective. There are indications that the San Francisco strike, although terminated in a desultory and disorganized manner, was an important factor in the ultimate success of the maritime unions in securing control of the hiring halls.

The general strike covering a whole country may be a sympathetic strike called to help a union in one industry, as in the 1926 British general strike. The tacticians of the labor movement are gradually coming to agree, however, that the nation-wide general strike should be almost exclusively political in its objectives, provided that the word "political" is broadly defined. This leaves the general strike with two important functions in the labor movement. The first is that it may be used as a demonstration of the mass power of labor in opposition to other political forces such as Fascist parties, or as a means of demonstrating approval or disapproval of political programs being considered by legislatures. The general strike for these purposes, called for a stated number of hours, has recently been used on several occasions in France. The second function of the general strike is the actual assumption of power by organized labor at the instant of revolutionary crisis. Such a use of the general strike was, for example, long planned by the German labor movement to forestall the advent to power of the Nazis. That this did not take place was primarily due to the failure of the Socialist and Communist parties to agree to coöperate in carrying it out.

In returning to the description of strike policies it must be emphasized that the problem of conducting an effective strike is not merely that of compelling reluctant workers to leave their jobs and preventing others from taking them. There is the task of providing relief, sustaining morale and maintaining discipline among the strikers. There are pressures which may be applied against the employer to hasten the end of the strike. And there is the delicate duty of negotiating a settlement with the employer which will be acceptable to the workers.

The task of providing relief in a strike in the mass production industries is stupendous. It assumes the proportions of a large-scale business operation; it must be set in operation at relatively short notice; and it must be discontinued on equally short notice without heavy losses in inventories and equipment. The earlier and more conservative craft unions have avoided this problem. Most of the small craft unions whose members receive relatively high wages and pay substantial dues contract to pay individual strike benefits to their members who are in good standing at the time of the calling of the strike. The problem is thus shifted to the individual worker to get along as well as possible on a reduced income. The assumption by the union of this fixed obligation to striking workers often makes it impossible for a union to call a strike which members feel is urgently necessary. The payment of fixed strike benefits inhibits the granting of relief to workers who may be ineligible for membership but available as substitutes for the striking union members. This policy is, however, a logical outgrowth of a form of unionism based upon skill and the paralyzing effect of its withdrawal from production.

Fixed individual strike benefits are entirely out of the question in industries in which the calling of a strike means the displacement of thousands, rather than scores, of workers. In the unions which have gradually developed during the last thirty years in the mass production industries, it is difficult to distinguish between union members and nonmembers and between active strikers and those who have been persuaded or compelled to come along. Under these conditions, the union's only possible recourse is to set up its own commissary department, soup and food kitchens and methods of distributing food. Sometimes a compromise between the individual strike benefit and the union commissary is effected by the adoption of a food card system in which the union issues cards which are valid as credit up to stated amounts at designated stores with which special arrangements for reduced prices have been made. Increasingly, however, unions find themselves compelled to enter the restaurant business themselves. This is especially true in the case of stay-in strikes in which the food must be brought in a semiprepared state into the factory. When a picket line is being maintained during a strike, a connection is often established between picket duty and strike relief. At the end of a round of picket service the worker is given a card which permits him to receive a free breakfast, lunch or supper, depending upon the time of day.

The question of rent is usually left up to the resources of the individual. Rents are allowed to go by default because there is little else that the individual landlord can do about a situation in which thousands of tenants are cut off from normal sources of income. When the employer is also the landlord, however, as in the case of company towns or in localities in which the employer has made considerable investments in real estate, wholesale evictions may be resorted to by the employer. Textile, coal and metal mining, steel production and stone quarrying unions are especially likely to find themselves in this predicament because of the large number of company towns in these industries. Unions are forced to resort to the setting up of tent colonies. This involves carrying in stock several thousand tents and supplies of the rudimentary necessities for sanitation, cooking and the provision of water. It also involves medical services, and expert technical and engineering assistance.

The provision of clothes and shoes during a strike is also left as far as possible up to the individual worker. If the strike is prolonged, however, destitution may force the union to attempt to assist its members in this respect. Old clothes and shoes may be collected by the truckload from sympathizers, taken to repair shops established by the workers' womenfolk, and then dispensed according to need. Sometimes committees are set up which investigate the financial and physical condition of the applicants for relief. Shoe repair shops are often considered especially necessary if effective picketing is to be maintained. In these cases, picket duty may be made a condition of receiving assistance.

The funds for relief purposes come from the union's own treasury, from loans and grants by other unions, from credit granted by private business houses supplying union needs, and from gifts by sympathizers among the general public. Some unions maintain strike defense funds which are built up in anticipation of strikes. This makes possible careful planning and leaves only the small details to the final event. Many unions feel that the existence of these funds may make an employer hesitate before forcing a strike issue. Other unions, unable to persuade their membership to build up these funds, are compelled to depend upon special assessments placed upon the membership at the time of the strike. Local unions not involved in the strike are very frequently asked for gifts from their own treasuries. Appeals for this purpose may be sent out through the national office or directly by the striking locals.

The second line of appeal, quickly resorted to by weak

unions, is through the central labor unions in large towns and cities. During a season of high strike frequency, scarcely a central labor union meeting passes without an appeal from a near-by local union for help. A representative usually appears, is given the floor under "good and welfare," outlines the strike situation, asks for moral support and any financial assistance which the C.L.U. can possibly afford. Sometimes the C.L.U. grants a small donation from its meager treasury, sometimes a collection is taken up from the delegates on the floor (although this is often forbidden since it discourages attendance at meetings), sometimes the strike is endorsed after further explanation by the chairman, and the petitioner is given credentials to enable him to carry his appeal to the local unions attached to the C.L.U.

Occasionally, powerful national unions grant large sums as loans or outright gifts. This is done as a gesture of solidarity, or because the winning of the strike will have favorable repercussions upon the donor, or because it is expected that when the doner later gets in trouble it may become the beneficiary of the other union's generosity. The Amalgamated Clothing Workers, the International Ladies' Garment Workers and the United Mine Workers have been especially lavish in this respect.

Many unions have established sufficiently responsible records to enable them to purchase supplies from business houses on open book account or short-term notes. When such credit is granted to the national union, its future receipts from per capita tax stand back of the debt. When it is a local union which is involved in debt, local businessmen who are not under pressure from the employer may feel that credit extended to the union during a strike may be safer than credit to individuals, or they may feel that the risk is worth the favorable advertising they receive in the low income market.

When gifts are solicited from the general public, the

channels of communication may be the national machinery of the A.F. of L., liberal magazines such as *The New Republic* and *The Nation*, or personal appeal to local clubs, churches, fraternal groups, bakeries and so forth. Funds are usually paid in to the local strike committee which issues receipts and writes individual "thank you" notes. Responsible unions make every effort to give publicity to their relief accounts and have them certified by public accountants.

In general, the problem of providing relief in a large strike is so immense and complicated that it places a very great premium upon avoiding strikes and bringing them to a close as soon as possible. Once involved in a strike, however, the union has no alternative but to throw its resources of money, ingenuity, prestige and experience into the provision of as nearly adequate relief as can be afforded.

Second only in importance to the provision of relief is the maintenance of morale. Few workers have had extended experience with strikes. The lightning does not often strike twice in a decade at the same point. Hundreds of strikes take place every year in localities which have had no experience with strikes during a whole generation of workers. The result is that the strikers are often bewildered by the situation in which they find themselves; they do not understand the storm of abuse which is likely to be turned loose upon them by newspapers, fellow townsmen and even fellow workers; they are suspicious of their leaders and responsive to antileadership propaganda; they become discouraged easily, discount the future heavily, and are bored or restless with inaction; and they are oppressed by the strange language, strange behavior and strange attitudes which the situation forces upon them. This may be true even when the workers have long since been organized in unions. The primary business of a union is not to strike but to establish business and bargaining relationships with the employer. The stronger the union, the less frequent the strike may become. Consequently, even the union men and women of long experience are often tenderfeet at the strike game.

It is the task of the union to offset antiunion propaganda, sustain the strikers' confidence in themselves, produce a fighting attitude when necessary, retain the trust of the members, inspire courage, provide recreation and amusement, and use every opportunity to educate the strikers in the tradition, the mechanics and the ethical concepts of the labor movement. Most unions feel that they have succeeded when they have attained half of these objectives. There is immense variety in the methods used. A primary necessity in a modern strike is effective publicity. If local newspapers are not avowedly hostile, they may become a method of communication to the workers themselves as well as to the surrounding public. When a sophisticated union leader speaks of the necessity of maintaining favorable public opinion, he is speaking of the opinion of workers about themselves as much as anything else. He knows how "opinion" is manufactured by modern publicity methods and uses all the techniques at his disposal to create a favorable climate of attitude toward the strike, partly in order to aid in collecting relief funds, but primarily to influence the strikers who are as much a part of the general public as anyone else. He expects that whole classes of newspapers will express themselves against the strike either through editorials or, more importantly, through judicious "editing" of front-page news. He warns workers against this and advises them to read down into the fine print on the seventh page if they really want to find the news about the strike.

If local newspapers are unavailable, a strike newspaper run by the union itself may be set up, or the regular periodical of the union may come out in a series of special issues devoted to the strike. Mimeographed daily bulletins distributed by newsboys to the strikers and through the community, elaborate bulletin boards, daily mass meetings in which the chronological details of the strike are recited —these are frequently used methods of communication. If inaccurate rumors are started, mass meetings are immediately called to scotch the rumors as soon as possible. Workers are repeatedly warned not to believe anything they hear outside, but to come to their own committee heads for news. All possible encouragement is given during mass meetings to the asking of questions in order to air as many doubts as possible at one sitting. Although a smart publicity man colors unfavorable news, it is increasingly becoming recognized that full and accurate details of the exact situation are most valuable in the long run to the maintenance of morale.

Handling a large mass meeting is one of the final tests of leadership. The tricks of the trade are myriad but the essentials can and are being increasingly taught in the training schools for union organizers. The radio and the sound truck are minimizing the necessity for stentorian volume, but tricks of voice, variation in pitch, progression from cozy generalities through solid facts to assertion of opinion are still essentials. Some situations call for simple exposition, humor, anecdote, personalities. Others demand the complicated devices of the professional revivalist through which the speaker translates a kind of rhythmic hysteria into organized action by establishing a pendulum of rhetorical question and mass response between himself and the audience, and then breaking this off into short jerky sentences giving precise details of immediate action. This is called demagoguery or genius according to the predilection of the observer. It is often essential in large strikes, such as those run by the I.W.W. and the radical unions among casual laborers, where the resources at the organizer's disposal consist chiefly of his hands, his head and his voice.

In localities where conservative unions of long standing

have established a tradition so extensive that it amounts almost to a culture, when a strike is called the union members simply go home and sit around or make minor repairs on the Model T until the strike is over. In the mass production industries, however, in most of which unionism is in its infancy, the task of entertaining the idle workers falls primarily upon the union. The purpose of such entertainment is twofold: keeping people occupied and amused reduces worry and the power of other "back-to-work" influences, and second, if the amusement provided is mass amusement, the idea of group solidarity can be inculcated quite as effectively as by mass action on the picket line. Consequently, many progressive unions in both large and small strikes have gone in as heavily as possible for mass diversions. Mass demonstrations, mass theatricals, mass picnics, mass excursions, mass singing, mass contests, field days, dances and moving pictures, all carefully organized by auxiliary agencies of union women or sympathizers, are some of the methods used to accomplish the twofold result.

THE final task of the union leader in sustaining morale is the provision of legal assistance to the strikers. If the union has established relations with a bonding house, or has itself sufficient funds to provide bail for strikers arrested on petty charges, it can often perform a valuable service. When strikers are inexperienced in the labor movement, repeated arrest of the lesser leaders is likly to be very discouraging. If the union can promptly release its people as soon as arrested, morale may actually be heightened. In case of hearings for injunctions, it is up to the union to provide at least nominal opposition as a means of publicizing the union's cause even though the outcome of the hearing is a foregone conclusion. If strikers are brought to trial on criminal charges, it is the union's task to provide as adequate defense as can be afforded. In all of these cases the American Civil Liberties Union and the International Labor Defense, organizations which specialize in fulfilling these functions, may be of invaluable assistance.

Next in importance to sustaining morale is the maintenance of discipline. A union leader or organizer who is running a large strike has men and women on his hands who as individuals are like almost everybody else but who in mass may at any moment become an unruly mob. Mob action is very likely to be pointless as well as destructive, and is almost certain to be uncontrollable. Physical force, if it is to be used at all, is useless unless it is organized and directed. In certain circumstances, organized force may help to win the strike. Since winning the strike is the immediate and primary objective, the union may foresee the inevitability of violence and methodically prepare for it.

For propaganda purposes, the first step is to place the union as clearly as possible upon the defensive. This means that, just as in the case of international war, the first overt act must at least appear to come from the other side. This is usually not difficult to arrange but it requires the application of discipline with military precision. If a massed picket line is being used and there is expectation that police or deputies will attempt to break it up, it may be divided in squads according to customary groupings, each in charge of a natural leader if there is a sufficient number available. A hierarchy of superior officers extends upward to the general organizer in military fashion. When the attack comes an instant of passive resistance by the strikers creates the proper impression and may be followed by a concerted response with brickbats, paving stones, shillalahs and short lengths of pipe. If the forces opposing the picket line are obviously overwhelming, perfect discipline is required to carry out an orderly retreat.

When the situation is such that any form of force is out of the question, even more rigid discipline is required in order to prevent sporadic and irresponsible violence.

This is a major part of the task of the leaders of small strikes in which any occasion for the introduction of police or military forces immediately breaks the strike. Even in the large-scale stay-in strikes in Detroit in 1937 the C.I.O. leaders successfully forestalled the violence which would have attended eviction of the strikers from the Chrysler plants by massing and controlling such immense crowds of sympathizers and spectators in the vicinity of the plants that nothing short of the entire military forces of the State of Michigan could have accomplished their evacuation. Discipline is not only necessary on the picket line, but also in strike meetings, in the distribution of relief, in preventing rioting and looting by either strikers or other elements who enter under cover of the strike, in preventing drunkenness among workers on the picket line or occupying plants, and in protecting the machinery and materials in the plants during a stay-in strike.

In addition to providing relief, sustaining morale and enforcing discipline, other tactics are necessary to bring most strikes to a successful conclusion. There are pressures which may be brought to bear on the employer in order to hasten the end of the strike. These compulsions may be economic, social and political; they are rarely physical. Effective strategy is usually considered to require the calling of a strike at the beginning of a peak season when the labor reserve is reduced and the employer is anxious to make hay while the sun shines. The advantage of securing a contract under favorable conditions which will extend over into the slack season is, from the strikers' viewpoint, obvious. The disadvantage is that it may be difficult for a union to persuade workers to interrupt a period of prospective full-time employment by striking. Against this must be set the fact that employment may be secured elsewhere with relative ease during the rush season. If the strike is called in a competitive industry against an employer whose wage and hour standards are inferior to his competitors, care is taken to see that his competitors have no difficulty with their labor supply so that the struck employer is faced with the prospect of losing his orders to others.

If the employer has borrowed from banks to finish goods in process, the union leader may explain to the banker that the chances of the employer's meeting his obligations are being reduced by the continuance of the strike, and that it would be to the banker's advantage to suggest to the employer that he meet the union leader and negotiate a settlement as soon as possible.

If the employer is making extensive use of professional strikebreakers, the union may decide to go in for professional strikebreaking itself. When several plants are affected by the strike, this is relatively easy. Workers from one plant apply for jobs through the strikebreaking agency supplying another plant and vice versa. The wages of professional strikebreakers are usually well above those being asked by the union for its members. When union men act as strikebreakers, the union's problem of relief is simplified at the expense of the employer. Those who are at work are automatically taken care of. The excess which they receive from the strikebreaking agency above the union wages may be turned over to the union for the relief of those who remain on the picket line. The morale of the pickets is not affected by the presence of the strikebreakers if the union has made the situation clear to its members.

It is almost traditional among professional strikebreakers that they are not expected to do any work once they obtain entrance to the plant. Since the union has allowed peaceful entrance, it may feel that its members are entitled to a good rest, or even a little artistic sabotage. Nothing serious, or course, but there are a number of possibilities. Filing cabinets may be rearranged. The right orders may be sent to the wrong people. Buttons may be sewed down the backs of the shirts, or the sleeves carefully sewed up at the elbows. Packing cases may be filled with sand while their original contents are meticulously stored in the wrong room. This kind of sabotage often involves much less damage to equipment and materials than is caused unintentionally by the activities of bona fide strikebreakers who may wreck valuable machinery with the best of intentions. It causes a mild variety of hysteria among supervisors, injures the trade name of the employer and amuses, rather than shocks, all except those who have received a packing case of sand or have tried unsuccessfully to get into a sewed-up shirt.

The social pressures which may be used against the employer are comparable to those used to maintain the morale of strikers. If the opinion of the employer's own social group can be turned against him, successes may be gained which would be impossible in the purely economic area. To this end, unions increasingly devote time and energy. The type of publicity called for may be somewhat more dignified than would be used at a strike meeting, but the essential publicity techniques are the same. Carefully prepared releases are given out to the newspapers. The radio is being used more and more for presentation of the union cause over nation-wide hook-ups. During the general textile strike of 1934, nearly a dozen broadcasts were arranged free of charge by the United Textile Workers. In the preliminary stages of the C.I.O. organizing drive in 1937, extensive use was made of the radio with emphasis upon the legality of the unions' cause under the Wagner Labor Relations Act. Publicity stunts are coming to rival those of big business in elaborateness. Girl hosiery workers on strike are photographed in brief bathing suits and silk stockings, carrying picket placards. These pictures receive wide circulation in the rotogravure sections under the caption, "Striking Girls, Eh?" or words to that effect. Pickets or demonstrators dress in convict clothes complete with ball and chain and parade through the downtown district bearing signs proclaiming that Simon Legree was a piker compared to their employer.

Perhaps the most elaborate publicity device ever used by a union was put on by the United Textile Workers during the 1934 strike. The union announced that it had a series of carefully prepared "Sealed Orders" which were to be issued during the strike as fast as the development of the strike brought about the eventuality to be covered by each "Sealed Order." This gave an air of both mystery and military precision which considerably enhanced public interest in the union's cause. The mystery was further deepened when it was announced that no one would ever know the contents of those orders which remained unopened.

Unions have also made efforts to bring pressure to bear against employers by presenting the union's point of view at church services, women's clubs and fraternal gatherings. It is to be expected that organized labor will increasingly make use of the growing organization among professional workers as media for presenting their side of the case. The American Newspaper Guild and the American Federation of Teachers are especially important in this respect.

Political pressure may take place on a variety of levels. Its simplest form may be bribing the police officers on the beat to cease arresting strikers on charges of petty misdemeanors. Some philosophers of the labor movement have described this as "bribing the police to do their duty." Many local unions, especially of the conservative craft variety, have built up small political connections which give them "pull" enough to bring pressure to bear upon the employer as a taxpayer or as a friend of politicians. Especially when election time draws near, it may be necessary for politicians to use their influence with employers as a consideration for prospective votes.

The large national unions are using the Federal Government and Federal law with greater frequency as means of placing pressure upon employers. The method here is not so much to influence the government's policy or secure the enforcement of Federal law as it is to use government agencies and laws as sounding boards for favorable publicity in large strikes. The Wagner Labor Relations Act, for example, which created the National Labor Relations Board, requires that when a union has secured a majority of workers in a plant or industry as members, the union shall be granted sole bargaining power for the workers in that plant or industry. The Walsh-Healy Act lays down conditions of labor which must be observed by companies working on government contracts. Until April, 1937, the Wagner Act was successfully tied up in injunction proceedings by most large employers. This did not prevent unions from using the existence of the law as a means of creating unfavorable public sentiment toward the employer.

For several months the application of the Walsh-Healy Act was impeded by the refusal of most large steel companies to bid on government contracts as long as the observance of the act was required. Unions termed this a "sit-down strike" on the part of employers. The fact that labor was allied with government on this issue was a very large factor in the acceptance by major steel companies of collective bargaining through the Amalgamated Association of Iron, Steel, and Tin Workers. Both the National Labor Relations Board and the Department of Labor have been effectively used as sounding boards for favorable union publicity. More and more both unions and employers are becoming concerned with maneuvering their positions to coincide with that of the government during a strike situation.

One of the most important elements in strike policy is the method of terminating the strike. If a strike is clearly going badly, the union is faced with a choice between allowing the strike to drag out to a disastrous conclusion or calling it cleanly off and making an effort to consolidate the union position before trying again. Immense harm to the union cause is often done by the first of these procedures. All feeling of solidarity is destroyed as the workers, a few at a time, break ranks under the pressure of hunger and return to work. The union is likely to be discredited for a generation in that locality. The temptation of the union leader to avoid the issue of defeat by failing to call off the strike is often very great. Union leaders are coming to see, however, that in the long run this policy is disastrous.

Second only in importance to calling off the strike is the actual method used in terminating it. If a slight face-saving concession can be secured, this may solve the problem. If not, there is always the temptation to claim a "moral victory" and call the strike off on this basis. Strikers can often be induced momentarily to accept this estimate of the strike's outcome. In the long run, however, the worker's judgment is almost certain to be "If this is a victory, I'd hate to go through a defeat with this union." Charges of "treachery" and "sell-out" are sure to follow. The 1934 general strike in textiles may be cited as a classic example of a strike which, although cleanly called off, was hailed by the union as a great victory, only to be recognized within a few weeks as a clear defeat. In the interests of their own preservation, unions may well adopt policies of calling a spade a spade, explaining the causes of the defeat, and engaging in intensive follow-up work to hold the union together.

If the strike is moving toward a successful climax, the union is faced with the problem of bargaining tactics. As in good horse trading, an overstatement of demands is required so that space may be left for a compromise in which the employer may save his face and the union reach its original goals. Caution in this age-old procedure, however, is necessary. If the original demands are placed too far ahead of those which the union actually expects to gain, the actual settlement may appear to union members as a defeat. Charges of treachery may follow. An advanced development of horse-trading abilities on the part of the union negotiator is necessary if even a successful strike is to be brought to a conclusion satisfactory to union members.

Finally, it is of great importance that negotiations for settlement be carried on as openly as possible and that union leaders guard themselves against the slightest appearance of collusion with employers. Some union leaders protect themselves against appearances of treachery by taking with them to the negotiations a "rank and file" committee composed of the chronic objectors to the policies of the leaders. Most unions go through the form or the actuality of a democratic membership vote on acceptance of the strike settlement. If the leader's prestige is to be maintained and the settlement to be enforced, this procedure is almost indispensable. In small unions a large degree of democracy in this respect can be achieved. In the immense unions appearing in the mass production industries, members who are interested in preserving the strength of their unions may well attend closely to the necessity for perfecting policies which make possible the application of democratic control of the union by its members.

In summary, it may be said that although many strikes are spontaneous and concerted withdrawals of labor from production, most strikes if they are to be successful involve compulsion, and all strikes involve leadership and some degree of organization. Compulsion is applied to reluctant workers through persuasion, shame, fear and force. Compulsion is applied to employers through economic, social and political pressure. There must be leadership and organization to provide relief, sustain morale, enforce discipline and effect a settlement. In all of these fields there is an immense variety of practice and the widest possible latitude for the exercise of intelligence, ingenuity, subtlety and determination on the part of the leaders of the strike.

CHAPTER V

Breaking Strikes

DURING the summer and autumn of 1936 Remington Rand, Inc., conducted one of the most elaborate strikebreaking programs in the history of the American labor movement. The strike in question took place in seven of the company's plants and resulted from an effort by the company to eliminate the unions which had become strongly organized in these plants. Between 1933 and 1936 approximately 80 per cent of the maintenance and production workers in the Norwood and Marietta, Ohio; Syracuse, Ilion, Tonawanda and North Tonawanda, New York; and Middletown, Connecticut, plants of Remington Rand had become members either of federal labor or international unions. After a short strike in 1934, an agreement was signed by the company which came eventually to apply to all of these unions. During 1934 and most of 1935 harmony between managers and unions prevailed.

In the autumn of 1935, however, the company management apparently became restive under the union agreement. Late in the year a plant in Elmira, N. Y., was acquired and rumors began to circulate to the effect that production was to be transferred there from some of the existing plants. These rumors shortly reached union leaders, who soon requested confirmation or denial by the management. Representatives of the management denied the stories, but they continued to circulate freely in the communities in which the plants were located.[1] All the local unions, feeling that common interests were involved, consequently joined together in forming the Remington

[1] A prospectus of the Elmira plant was filed with the Securities and Exchange Commission by Remington Rand on February 19, 1936.

Rand Joint Protective Board of the District Council of Office Equipment Workers. This Joint Board asked the president of the company for a conference on the subject of the new Elmira plant. The president declined to grant the request but empowered a representative to deal for the company. A conference then took place on April 24, 1936, in which the company representative refused to commit himself on the Elmira question or to consider the Joint Board's request for a wage increase which had been conditionally promised two years before. The Joint Board, therefore, conducted a ballot in all of the seven plants to determine whether union members were willing to go on strike if their representatives were unable to secure a conference with President Rand and come to an agreement on the Elmira and wage issues. The combined vote in the seven plants showed 90 per cent of the organized workers willing to strike under the conditions outlined in the ballot. The Joint Board, on May 10, wrote to President Rand again asking for a conference and stating the result of the union's ballot. To this request Mr. Rand made no direct reply.

Apparently acting upon the theory that the best defense is a good attack, the company took the first step in breaking the threatened strike by presenting, on May 21, its own strike ballot to its employees. The company's ballot stated that the organized workers in these plants were in a minority and indirectly implied that only 3 per cent of the workers had actually voted for a strike under the Joint Board's ballot. The company's ballot stated the issue thus: "Are you in favor of a strike?" instead of in the conditional terms of the union ballot. The company's ballot was conducted by supervisors and foremen who went from man to man in the plant. The union instructed its members not to vote upon the false issue which was being presented. The company counted the blank ballots as being against the strike and announced that from 91 per cent to 98 per

cent were in favor of staying at work. The workers in the
Syracuse factory, however, refused to vote and enforced
their refusal by calling a short sit-down strike. The company discharged sixteen union leaders and closed the factory for a two weeks' "vacation." The Joint Board renewed its request for a conference with the president.
Mr. Rand replied that he would not meet with any union
leader or any representative of the A.F. of L. On May 26,
therefore, the Joint Board declared that the strike was in
effect. All but a handful of the production and maintenance workers in the seven plants remained away from
work. The company had an almost 100 per cent strike on
its hands, backed by unions having approximately 80 per
cent of the workers as members in seven separate plants.

After this preliminary jockeying over the strike ballot,
which provided the company with publicity material to
the effect that the strike was a minority movement led by
outside agitators, the real strikebreaking program was set
in motion. This program in each of the communities
passed through three fairly distinct stages. The first was
an effort to bring public opinion and the forces of public
authority to bear against the strikers by threatening to
move the plant and by organizing Citizens' Committees.
The second was the creation of a Back-to-Work Association controlled and financed by the company but ostensibly
generated spontaneously by loyal employees determined
to return to their jobs. The third was the stimulation of
a screen of violence or news about violence behind which
the company replaced its former workers with strikebreakers. The details and the results of this program varied
among the different communities, but the pattern was
essentially the same.

The Middletown strike is perhaps the most interesting
of all because of the greater complexity of the social forces
involved and the greater difficulty which the company experienced in breaking the strike in this plant. Middletown

is a city with a population of about 22,000 which owes
its economic support to its half-a-dozen medium-sized industrial plants, to its being the trading and banking center
for the surrounding agricultural community, and to its
being the seat of a state hospital, several large landed estates
and Wesleyan University. It is not therefore entirely dependent upon the income from the Remington Rand plant
which employs about 1,200 workers. This made the problem of breaking the Middletown strike more complicated
than at Ilion, for example, where the town and the surrounding community are dependent upon income from
the Remington Rand and Remington Arms plants. In Middletown there was a distinct possibility that public opinion
would insist that Mr. Rand clarify the Elmira situation
and confer with the strongly organized workers. This
made the manipulation of public opinion more important
and more difficult than in any of the other communities
except Syracuse.

Mr. Rand's first step was to print an advertisement in the
Middletown Press, three days before the strike began, calling attention to the $2,000,000 annual pay roll of the
plant, demanding that the community aid the company in
protecting "loyal employees" in their "right to work,"
stating that the company would move away from Middletown "if employees will not coöperate," and expressing
gratification that the mayor and other city officials had
already indicated the "determination of the community
to see to it that all who wish to work are protected." Mr.
Rand also reproduced a letter declining a request from the
central labor union for a conference and giving as a reason
for this refusal a statement that the union represented a
small minority of the workers.

The Middletown unions had a membership of about
1,000 out of 1,200 eligible workers. On May 26 all of the
1,200 production and maintenance workers remained outside the plant. Picketing began without disorder. Mr. Rand

was quoted in the *Middletown Press* as saying that "only 10 per cent of his operatives favored the strike." On the following day about fifteen armed guards, some of whom had been equipped with riot guns, entered the plant. They had been recruited in New York City at twelve dollars a day. For four days there was quiet on the Middletown front with only scattered news from the other strikes.

On May 31 the first big drive began. The company announced that the plant was to be closed. Machinery was made ready for shipment, the windows covered with tar paper, and the plant placed for sale in the hands of the mayor. The mayor immediately requested that the company and the unions confer with a view to a peaceful settlement. The company replied on June 2 with a telegram which appeared in the *Press* as follows:

Parties you refer to have met around the table for two days and the company has learned that organized minority are attempting to terrorize unorganized majority into following dictation of a few radicals Stop We have always had the latchstring open to discuss matters with our own employees who are in good standing but will not discuss matters with discharged employees nor with rank outsiders presuming to represent our employees Stop Because you have failed to give protection to honest workers willing and anxious to go back to work and have allowed radicals to coerce and intimidate them in violation of law the company has decided that Middletown is not a suitable community in which to carry on operations and therefore have issued instructions to close Middletown plant permanently.

EARL HARDING, *Assistant to President*
REMINGTON RAND, INC.

The second move came when on June 3, the mayor was approached by a local attorney, Carlos Ellis, who stated that he had sufficient influence with Mr. Rand to arrange a conference if the mayor wished. Unsuspectingly, the mayor acceded to this suggestion by appointing a committee to accompany him to the conference with Mr. Rand in New York. This committee consisted of three businessmen, a banker, the president of Wesleyan University and Carlos Ellis. At the conference the committee expressed resentment at the tone of the telegram which Mr. Rand had published in the *Press*. Mr. Rand replied that the members of the committee should not let that bother them, that he had sent the telegram "to get you started in the proper direction." He repeated that he would not meet with union leaders and that he would move the plant if proper police protection were not granted. While the conference was in progress a door opened and four or five employees of the Middletown plant walked in. Mr. Rand asked them to "tell the story of conditions in the factory for the past two years." Each worker spoke in turn to the effect that the presence of unions in the plant had made conditions intolerable.

This procedure exactly duplicated a similar conference with a Citizens' Committee from Ilion. The Ilion committee, however, was far more responsive to Mr. Rand's demands. In Ilion it was Barney Allen, a dealer in electrical appliances, who played Carlos Ellis' part in arranging the conference. In both cases they appeared to be acting for the community rather than for Mr. Rand. In both cases the threat to remove the factory and the description of the union as made up of radical agitators were emphasized. And in both cases loyal workers entered the office at an appropriate moment and told their stories. In the case of Syracuse, Mr. Rand varied the procedure by inviting members of the Chamber of Commerce to meet him in Ilion at a time when the community had declared a state of emergency, barricaded the roads entering the village, deputized several hundred sheriffs and created a condition of mass hysteria.

After its conference with Mr. Rand, the Middletown Citizens' Committee was enlarged to seventeen members, including the editor of the *Press*. Meetings took place, but nothing was accomplished in the face of Mr. Rand's refusal to meet union leaders and his demands for protection to loyal workers, although no sign of violence had as yet appeared. Meanwhile Carlos Ellis approached the mayor, the head of the unions in the plant, the business agent of the Central Labor Union and the president of the State Federation of Labor, and suggested that it would be politically worth while for them to urge the union members to return to work. At this point the mayor became suspicious of Mr. Ellis, but the latter denied being in the employ of Mr. Rand. Although machinery was constantly being shipped from the plant during these three weeks, on June 16 an agent of Mr. Rand met with the committee and admitted that the program had not thus far been successful. He felt that resistance to the company had been stiffened rather than lessened by the threat to move the plant. He requested the committee's further tolerance of a trying situation. In Ilion, on the contrary, the program at this point was an almost complete success and rapidly moved into its second and third stages with consequent collapse of the strike.

Having failed in the first part of its plan at Middletown, the company reversed its policy on June 17. An advertisement appeared in the *Press* by the "Remrand Back-to-Work Association" announcing that it had set up offices with telephone numbers through which loyal workers might apply for reinstatement. The *Press* carried a headline: "REMRAND WORKERS WOULD END STRIKE—ORGANIZING TO RESUME WORK HERE." Carlos Ellis immediately identified himself with this organization. The Citizens' Committee asked Mr. Ellis to resign from the committee and then disbanded itself asserting that it had "no part in the inception of this movement." There followed an intensive publicity campaign accompanied by almost daily advertisements from the Back-to-Work Association. Company publicity was then abruptly shut off with the result that the *Press* used the Remrand Association advertisements as sources for news stories and editorials. On June 20 there was a notice that the Back-to-Work office would stay open on Saturday and Sunday to take care of the press of business. On June 23 it was announced that there remained only three days in which to return to work and that by that time the company would have all the workers necessary to resume operations. On June 24 the Remrand Association announced that "The Time Is Growing Short to Return to Your Job." On the following day employees were asked, "Do hired agitators have your personal interest at heart? Or are they more interested in their own salaries than in your wages?" On the same day employees received through the mails literature stating that Ilion, Tonawanda and Marietta had returned to work; that the Syracuse plant was 60 per cent moved, Norwood 10 per cent moved, Middletown 30 per cent moved. Photostatic copies of affidavits by Ilion employees were enclosed stating that they had "voluntarily" returned to work. The *Press* on that day announced that Mr. Rand had agreed to accept an invitation to address the Back-to-Work Association. There was also a significant advertisement for twenty-five millwrights "to start work immediately dismantling and skidding machinery for shipment."

In spite of this advertisement, the back-to-work movement was approaching a climax. As a result of a conference between Mr. Rand and Pearl Bergoff, "King of Strikebreakers," held in New York on June 25, Bergoff agreed to send fifty-nine "millwrights" to Middletown. Mr. Rand provided cards for each of Bergoff's men identifying them as millwrights and assured Bergoff that he would notify the police at Stamford "not to molest any of those men who have a millwright's card." [2] At Stamford Mr. Rand boarded the train on which Bergoff and his men were approaching Middletown. He spoke to the "millwrights" about the Middletown situation, told them that he was going to make a speech, and arranged that the millwrights provide suitable applause.

On the morning of June 26 sixty to seventy policemen, instead of the usual ten or eleven, were assigned to the plant in view of factory officials' "fears of disorders arising from the hiring of the twenty-five millwrights." The millwrights arrived, but no disorders occurred. While entering the plant the strikebreakers wove in and out of the picket line jostling the pickets with their elbows. The union had given strict orders against interfering with the entrance of the strikebreakers and this effort to stimulate violence was consequently unsuccessful. At Tonawanda, on the contrary, the arrival of Bergoff's men was greeted with a shower of stones and other missiles from the pickets. Mr. Rand took moving pictures of the event from the plant and distributed them afterwards as evidence of the violence used by the union. Bergoff later testified "I really believe it was a very good stunt on Rand's part because he took some nice pictures and showed how my men were showered with bricks. . . . Naturally it wasn't bad stuff, because those peaceful pickets were certainly raising the devil."

After the "millwrights" had entered the Middletown plant the morning was spent in preparing for the afternoon meeting. Telegrams were sent to all employees asking their attendance. Announcements were broadcast over the radio. Foremen spent the morning visiting workers. When the big event finally came off, Mr. Rand addressed the gathering through loud-speakers placed around the plant. In con-

[2] The Byrnes Act forbids the interstate transportation in certain cases of persons identifiable as strikebreakers.

clusion, Mr. Rand invited everybody into the plant for "a big surprise." This was the signal for applause and a general rush by the audience, composed chiefly of company salesmen, office force and outsiders, into the plant. Mr. Rand then announced that "the big surprise" was that the company had decided to reopen the plant. The "For Sale" sign was taken down, the tar paper was ripped from the windows, and newsreel cameramen took pictures of the event for later distribution. A telegram was sent to all employees telling them that the plant would open on Monday, that there were places for only 911 men, and that at the end of the first week's work each man who returned would receive $15 "vacation money." One of Bergoff's strikebreakers expressed disappointment over "the big surprise": "I thought we were going to get a drink of beer or something, but I didn't see any."

On the morning of June 29 the plant was opened. Loudspeakers audible "for three or four miles," sound trucks and advertisements in the *Press* and the *Hartford Courant* urged the workers to return. On the first day of operation twenty-three persons entered the plant and on the second, forty-five. It was evident that the back-to-work movement had not been a success. The Remrand Back-to-Work Association disappeared from the scene and the second phase of the company's program came to an end. In other plants, however, the company was more successful. At Ilion the stage of violence and terrorism, accomplished through the "state of emergency" device, was moved forward to coincide with the back-to-work movement. In this way the ranks of the union were broken early in June. Effective publicizing of this success was used to speed the end of the Tonawanda strike. At Tonawanda, also, the defection of one group of skilled mechanics was arranged by taking them to a tavern where "the drinks were on" the manager, and by offering them a 10 per cent wage increase if they would return in a body. On the day of the grand opening, these mechanics marched into the plant and thereby broke the morale of the rest of the group who straggled in until by October there were only one hundred fifty on strike and the union had been destroyed.

After the failure of the opening at Middletown, the company entered the third phase of its program: the stimulation of violence and news about violence as a screen for the introduction of a sufficient number of strikebreakers to operate the plant without the original force. The company announced that it was "Determined to Operate Its Middletown Factory" and stated that it would take on new recruits who would be trained in the plant by "competent instructors." From the beginning of the strike until this time, no disorder had occurred. On June 30, however, the day after the unsuccessful opening of the plant, a house in which three strikebreaking employees lived was stoned. "Four concrete blocks weighing about fifty pounds each were thrown at the house." On the same day the company published in the *Press* an advertisement explaining and illustrating the possibilities of injunction procedure by referring to an injunction which the company had secured against the unions in the Norwood strike. On July 2, Carlos Ellis, acting as attorney for the company, filed suit for injunction against three of the Middletown unions and their leaders. Ellis also acted as attorney for the occupants of the stoned house. Each occupant filed suit for damages of $9,000 against the same three unions and their leaders. After argument, a broad injunction was granted limiting pickets to ten in number and restraining all union members from "following in a mocking, threatening, or intimidating manner" any employees of the company. About nine hundred union members were personally served with copies of this injunction, although they were not individually named in the action. Copies were also served upon some members of the one union to which the injunction did not apply. Between June 30 and July 6, the company took on about five hundred new workers from Middletown and vicinity. The ranks of the union remained almost intact and no further violence was reported.

On July 7, however, a series of stonings of strikebreakers' homes in outlying parts of the Middletown community took place. The *Press* headlined, "MAYOR AND PROSECUTOR DETERMINED TO PRESERVE LAW AND ORDER IN CITY, VIOLENCE HERE STIRS OFFICIALS." In small type the *Press* reported that "There is no evidence to show that the stoning was done by striking employees of the Remington Rand Inc. factory . . ." On the same day, according to the National Labor Relations Board, "an automobile containing Rand, his brother-in-law who was an assistant superintendent, and several foremen moved slowly back and forth along the picket line. . . . One of the occupants was taking pictures of the people on the picket line. [President Rand] . . . was deliberately 'thumbing his nose at the group of pickets.' "[3] On the following day the Riot Act was read to a crowd of strikers. The strikers booed the police captain who read the Act and the *Press* headlined, "STRIKERS DEFY COMMAND TO DISPERSE; MAYOR WILL CALL MILITIA IF NEEDED." In fine type the *Press* reported that the rest of "the morning passed without incident." Sixty-six state police arrived. Soon afterward, a striker was arrested and convicted of intimidation and breach of the peace. Mr. Rand published a telegram in the *Press* announcing that a five-hundred-dollar reward had been given to the individual who had testified against the striker in this case. Mr Rand added, "I want to commend you for your demonstration of good

[3] "The thumb to the nose and the fingers in the air" is "among boys a harmless vent for injured feelings . . . but when boys become men they should put away childish things. In the case at bar the circumstances . . . tend to show a desire to engender strife." Peo. ex. Rel. Shannon v. Garstenfeld, 92 Misc. 388. Reported in the *Reader's Digest*, April, 1937, p. 26.

citizenship in assisting in the enforcement of law and order and hope that your action will encourage all other good citizens in the community to follow your example."

This set the pattern for the activities of the courts and police during the rest of the summer. Strikebreakers, plant managers and Carlos Ellis continuously brought complaints against union members upon minor charges and repeatedly asked for greater police protection. On July 9 Carlos Ellis secured writs charging one of the union leaders and other union members with contempt of the injunction. On July 14 a representative of the management stated that he had received "information that the Noiseless Plant was going to be dynamited tonight." Strikers were arrested on charges of this nature and later released for lack of evidence, or were acquitted after trial. While they were awaiting trial, high bail was set. When convictions were secured, high fines were imposed which rapidly depleted union funds. One judge adopted the practice of giving suspended sentences to union members with the provision that the severity of the sentence would depend upon the amount of subsequent violence. The announcement of such a suspended sentence was frequently followed by a fresh outbreak of disorder. When the state police were withdrawn after a period of calm, new disturbances took place. Strikebreakers arrested for throwing paint at pickets were defended by Carlos Ellis. On September 9 the state police "without any provocation drove pickets away from the plant by means of tear gas and clubs and refused to permit the strikers to congregate on a lot they had leased near the plant. The next day the state police launched a tear gas attack on the strikers who were proceeding in orderly fashion to their lots." [4] This attack heightened the feeling among Middletown residents because the tear gas permeated nearby houses and places of business.

[4] This is the wording of the report of the National Labor Relations Board.

Throughout the summer and early autumn the press played an important part in the strike. News articles, advertisements and editorials kept the public continuously informed as to the violent aspects of the strike to the exclusion of news concerning the employment of strikebreakers. All incidents of disorder, notices of arrests, trials, and fines and statements by city authorities were fully reported. These reports were coupled with news of disorder unrelated to the strike, stories of violence from other Remington Rand strikes, and accounts of violence in strikes not connected with the company. When the union secured permission from city authorities to hold a parade, the company advertised in the *Press* "Will You Parade in Defiance of the Injunction?" The *Hartford Daily Courant*, however, editorialized that "The first acts of violence occurred only after a loud-speaker installed at the factory sent forth comments on the strike and the pickets that might well have incited to riot."

Professional strikebreaking agencies were the third important element in this final phase of the strikebreaking program. Much of the disorder was of a type which has come to be associated, as a result of Senate investigation of the activities of professional strikebreaking agencies, with the technique of *agents provocateurs*. For example: stones were thrown at night, from behind bushes, or by an unknown person in a group of strikers. The guards employed by the company were typified, during later investigations, by Chowderhead Cohen who, in commenting upon his long prison record, said, "You see, in this line of work they never asked for no references." Many other guards admitted in Labor Board hearings that they had extended criminal records. A labor spy by the name of Oscar Fortis made repeated but unsuccessful attempts to secure information about the union from an unsuspecting member. Another spy secured the position of answering phone calls at union headquarters and reported his findings directly to the company. He later became night superintendent. The management approached Captain Nathaniel (Crying Nat) Shaw [5] and asked him to supply "missionaries" for some of the plants. Shaw, being a specialist in "radicals," was unable to provide "missionaries." Captain Shaw, however, was used in Middletown to discover whether there were "radicals" or "Communists" among the union leaders. He spent three days in Middletown upon this mission, but was unsuccessful both in uncovering radicals and in his attempt to bribe the President of the State Federation of Labor. He was thereupon assigned by the company to the task of providing "dry-cleaned" [6] strikebreakers for Middletown and other plants. Although Captain Shaw was offered $5,000 to take some of these men into Middletown, he refused because of the Byrnes Act which forbids the interstate transportation of strikebreakers in certain cases. By December 10, however, the company had successfully employed about a thousand new workers from various sources. The total pay roll of production and maintenance workers was brought back in this manner to about 1,150. Thus, although nearly a thousand union members remained on strike in Middletown, the strike was successfully broken. [7]

Although most of the other strikes in Remington Rand plants were broken with greater ease than in this instance, the essentials, with slight variations in detail, of what came

[5] Described in Levinson, *I Break Strikes*, 1935, p. 257 *et seq.*, as the "Prince of Provocateurs."

[6] "Dry-cleaning" is the process of subjecting the applicant for a strikebreaking job to an examination sufficiently drastic to assure the agency that the applicant has no union affiliations or leanings.

[7] One incident in the strikebreaking campaign was the distribution by the company to its employees in Middletown and Syracuse of about fifteen hundred copies of a book by Edward Dean Sullivan entitled *This Labor Union Racket*. The National Labor Relations Board describes this book as follows: "By emphasis on scattered instances of unscrupulous union leadership and by omission of the principles and benefits of legitimate union organization [this book] presents a distorted view of the labor movement. It is written in a spectacular style and rumors make up a large part of its material."

to be called the "Mohawk Valley Formula" [8] were everywhere applied. These essentials were as follows: Institution by the company of a strike ballot of which the stated issues and published results were completely at variance with those announced by the union and later attested by the National Labor Relations Board; identifying union leaders as "a small minority" of "radicals," "agitators" and "Communists"; an intensive publicity campaign centering around the threat to move the plant to Elmira, N. Y., or to route production to other plants; the use of this threat as a stimulus to the formation of "Citizens' Committees" which in the smaller communities were successful in mobilizing public opinion and legal machinery behind a "back-to-work" movement; the creation of an "employees' Back-to-Work Association" which in its own name set up employment offices and carried on an intensive advertising campaign applying pressure at a constantly increasing tempo; the staging of a dramatic "opening" of the struck plant with flags, speeches, loud-speakers, applause, a rush toward the gate, the singing of the Star Spangled Banner, lowering the "For Sale" sign, and the taking and distribution of a pictorial record of the event; focusing the attention of the community upon the violent aspects of the strike as a screen for the employment of strikebreakers; the introduction of new workers and the setting up of training and instructing agencies; the use of professional strikebreakers in their various capacities as "industrial relations counsellors," *agents provocateurs,*

[8] Mr. Rand gave this name to his program in an article appearing in the Labor Relations Bulletin of the National Association of Manufacturers. The Mohawk Valley Formula was used in even more elaborate and extensive form by the Bethlehem, Republic, Youngstown and Inland Steel companies in the steel strike of 1937. Under the label "The Johnstown Plan" the essentials of Mr. Rand's formula have been given nationwide publicity and organized backing. Back-to-work associations, full-page advertising, emphasis on violence and news about violence, citizens' committees, intense pressure on local authorities to preserve "law and order" (with the result that eighteen steel strikers had been killed by midsummer) all figured prominently in the breaking of the steel strike.

guards, strong-arm men, spies, whisperers, bribers, gun-
men and millwrights-for-the-day; the securing of the state
police wherever possible, of local police and of deputized
sheriffs as protection against "violence"; the provision of
private arms to deputy sheriffs; the creation of mass
hysteria by the use of tear gas, the Riot Act, rumors of
threatened invasion, barricading roads leading into the
village [9] and declaration of a "state of emergency"; and,
finally, the abrupt cessation of all publicity upon the re-
sumption of near-capacity operations. This program was
successful in breaking the strikes at Ilion, the Tonawandas
and Marietta. The Norwood plant was moved to Ilion and
Elmira. In Syracuse as in Middletown an almost entirely
new force had eventually to be hired.[10]

Newspapers frequently refer to the dominating part
played by public opinion in determining the outcome of
strikes. To agree with this, however, does not add very
much to the science of conducting or breaking a strike.
It implies that the essential justice of the cause of one side
or the other is easily determinable and that the laurels will
go to the righteous. The above account of the Remington
Rand strikes suggests that it is necessary to be more precise.
It suggests that there are well-defined methods of manip-
ulating public opinion and that there are very specific
reasons which make such manipulation necessary if a strike
is to be successfully broken. With this in mind, it may

---

[9] Ilion, N. Y.

[10] On March 13, 1937, the N.L.R.B. ordered Mr. Rand to reinstate discharged workers with back pay; offer reëmployment to workers displaced
by strikebreakers; desist from his sponsorship of company unions; and bargain collectively with the Joint Protective Board. Mr. Rand defied the
order at first, but boycott and governmental pressure forced him to confer
with union and government officials. A compromise agreement was eventually reached. On April 10 Mr. Rand and Pearl Bergoff were indicted by
a Federal grand jury for violation of the Byrnes Act. The case was finally
brought to trial in November, and resulted in an acquittal based upon the
grounds that the prosecution had not established: 1. An *intent* by the
defendants to disturb peaceful picketing, 2. That picketing was peaceful
before the arrival of Bergoff's men, 3. That Bergoff's men actually were
the cause of disturbance after their arrival.

be more profitable to consider strikebreaking from the viewpoint of the economic, social, legal and political factors involved.

The central economic element involved in strikebreaking is that the operation of plant and equipment is as important to labor as labor is to the operation of the plant and equipment. The simplest method of breaking a strike, therefore, is to match it with a lockout. An endurance contest then ensues in which the economic resources of the employer are likely to be greater than those of the workers. In a recent threatened strike in the Midwest, it was rumored that slips were enclosed in the workers' pay envelopes stating that the employer's resources would support him and his family for two years and asking how long the workers' resources would support them. This describes the situation at its least complicated level: bankruptcy *vs.* starvation. The fact that lockouts are far less frequent than strikes suggests, however, that they are not generally favored as a strikebreaking method. This is not because of legal inhibitions upon the lockout. The courts have universally held that employers' plants and businesses are their property, from which they may exclude workers for any reason they choose. The infrequency of lockouts as compared with strikes is due to a variety of reasons. The first is that strikes are by no means always the result of purely economic considerations. Employers and union leaders rarely cast up in dollars and cents the balance of gains and losses which results from a strike. Strikes frequently emerge from an emotional situation which demands catharsis. The cathartic required appears to be a fight. Far from being the cool and calculating economic man at the time of the worker's strike call, the employer's attitude is likely to be "I'll break up these boys' little show if it takes every cent I've got." For this purpose a lockout is too peaceful. A second reason why lockouts are relatively infrequent is that complete cessation of production is expensive. Fixed charges in the form of interest, insurance, taxes, depreciation and so on, continue even when the plant is closed. Unless the strike is complete, some income can be secured from partial operation which may help to defray fixed charges. The third reason is that a policy of aggressive action by the employer may speed the end of the strike and perhaps cost less than a policy of passive resistance. The great majority of strikes, therefore, is met by an effort to continue operation of the plant and a positive policy of breaking the strike.

On the purely economic level, a strikebreaking program has two aspects: the first is the weakening of the economic position of the strikers; and the second is the buttressing of the economic position of the employer. The ordinary resources of strikers in the form of savings, family assistance, union benefits, public relief and popular financial support are likely to be extremely limited. But all of these resources, limited though they may be, make possible the prolongation of the strike. One method of lessening the strikers' resources is to precipitate an impending strike before preparation has been made for relief by the strike leaders. This may be and often is accomplished by discharge of popular workers or union leaders, arranging "incidents" which lead quickly to hot temper on both sides, or by breach of existing agreements between unions and management. In company towns or in communities in which employers have extensive ownership of real estate or control over real-estate owners, wholesale evictions of strikers may quickly bring the strike to an end. If the union sets up tent colonies or commissary services, sanitation and public health ordinances are sometimes invoked against such relief activities. If unions have adequate strike benefit funds at their disposal, sweeping injunctions may often be obtained which enjoin the payment of union benefit funds to their own members. The use of political pressure upon relief authorities may inhibit the use of public funds for relief of strikers even though officials may publicly state that the fact of destitution, rather than its cause, is the basis upon which relief is granted.[11] Frequently, employers are able to bring sufficient pressure to bear upon local retail grocers and general stores to persuade or compel them to shut off credit to striking workers. As indicated in the Remington Rand strike, the imposition of high fines or bail reduces the funds of the union available for relief. The possibility of applying any or all of these methods varies from one community to another. The smaller the community the less diversified its economic life, the more readily the economic resources of strikers may be depleted.

Methods of strengthening the employer's economic position center around his membership in a manufacturers' association. Several important manufacturers' associations such as the National Erectors' Association and the League for Industrial Rights came into existence to combat the rise of unionism and to help their members in time of strikes. Others, such as the National Association of Manufacturers and the United Typothetæ assumed antiunion and strikebreaking functions shortly after the formation of the United States Steel Company at the turn of the century. Many manufacturers' associations are interested in other matters, such as opposition to regulatory legislation, general propaganda and industrial research. During their early history, some associations actually engaged in negotiating agreements with unions in their industries. In very recent years, associations in the clothing, garment and coal industries have signed agreements with unions as a result of powerful pressure applied by industrial unions. The traditional attitude of the bulk of employers' associa-

[11] In the general textile strike of 1934, for example, although F.E.R. Administrator Hopkins declared that destitution rather than its cause would be made the basis for dispensing relief, textile and other manufacturers raised a storm of protest against this decision. In a great many sections of the country, especially in the South, relief was in fact denied to strikers. This hastened the collapse of the strike.

tions, however, has been "open shop." In addition to the maintenance of black lists, use of the yellow-dog contract, employment of industrial spies, bribing of union leaders, advocacy of company unions, use of political influence to obtain "protection" by police and military forces, active employers' associations usually assist employers in maintaining their economic resources during strikes. The methods used for this purpose roughly parallel those employed by unions. If the employer is a member in good standing of a strong association, he may count upon outright financial support from reserve funds, refunds of interest on loans from banks whose support has been arranged, the filling of his orders by other members who return the profit to him, a supply of strikebreakers from other members' plants and the provision of vocational instructors or training services for new forces of workers. Any or all of these services may be available to an employer who maintains a strictly antiunion position. If, on the contrary, he fraternizes with unions or actually signs agreements with them he is expelled from the association and forfeits his bonds or claims upon financial reserves. The employer's economic power and his will to resist are thus simultaneously buttressed.[12]

The second general level of strikebreaking is the exercise of persuasion and intimidation upon the mind of the worker. The procedure in small plants may be very in-

[12] Testimony presented before the LaFollette Committee referring to the policies of the National Metal Trades' Association (one of the most important employers' associations) indicated that the Association has: 1. Maintained a black list since 1901 of workers "not suitable for employment." 2. Provided "guards" to break the strikes of member companies. Of the forty-two strikebreakers furnished to Black & Decker Co., Kent, Ohio, in 1935, sixteen had criminal records. The charges ranged from misdemeanors to assault upon a judge who had sentenced one of the strikebreakers. 3. Placed "special service men" in the plants of seventy-five member concerns between March 1, 1933, and July 31, 1936, to break up unions in these concerns. One of these concerns was Yale & Towne Mfg. Co. (see illustration). 4. Maintained a fund of $215,000 "to defray the costs of strikes and guards." LaFollette Committee, *Hearings*, Pt. III, pp. 823, 1011 et seq.; *New York Times*, Jan. 21, 1937.

formal. A simple appeal by the employer to the loyalty of employees, reminders of past associations and mutual favors, reference to strike leaders as "agitators" or "rank outsiders" having only their own interests at heart, mention of patriotism and "the American Way" vs. "foreign importations"—these are the elementary principles. Persuasion passes easily over into intimidation. The employer may threaten strikers with loss of employment, seniority, favored position in other respects and financial benefits unless the worker returns within a limited period. In large plants, the program of persuasion and intimidation may become much more formal and complicated. As has been indicated by the description of the Remington Rand strike, "back-to-work associations," "loyal workers' clubs," "citizens' alliances," and others may be formed to bring pressure to bear upon the minds of the strikers. In the 1937 General Motors strike, for example, the Flint Alliance, organized and sponsored by G.M.C. supervisors and foremen and headed by a former Buick paymaster, took a part in the effort to dislodge the G.M.C. stay-in strikers. Members were recruited in the plants, on the streets and from among local businessmen and politicians. The union directed its members not to refuse to sign the membership cards. Members of the alliance were deputized as sheriffs and provided with arms. Active conflict between the alliance and the union was prevented only by the interposition of the National Guard. In the 1937 Hershey strike a loyal employees' association rapidly organized by the management promptly appeared upon the scene. In some strikes the loyal workers' association may be a completely spontaneous development. In others, the association is a mere front backed only by the employer himself, as in the Remington Rand case. In a number of recent strikes, employers have brought organized pressure to bear upon the women and families of the strikers. For example, in the strike at the Syracuse Remington Rand

Universal Newsreel from Soibelman Syndicate

Violence broke out in the 1937 General Motors strike when police attempted to eject stay-in strikers from one of the Flint, Michigan, plants. Strikers overturned police cars as fast as they arrived.

Wide World Photos

A deputy sheriff assists in the eviction of a sit-down striker from the Detroit plant of the Yale & Towne Co. on April 14, 1937.

plant, Pearl Bergoff supplied forty men and twenty women to visit strikers' families, discredit the strike and its leaders, and urge the men to return to work. In this same strike, another spy agency operating as the Women Investors in America, Inc., sent out questionnaires to the wives of strikers. Subtly worded questions were designed to lead to replies which would discredit the strike: Do strikes encourage drunkenness? Do strikes endanger family life and health? What effect do strikes have on children? Did your husband want to join the union, or was he forced to? Do you favor his payment of monthly dues to it?

Organized intimidation may easily pass over into violence, and frequently does. Citizens' committees become "vigilantes" or "law and order" groups which raid union headquarters, smash furniture, destroy records; pour kerosene over food supplies; shoot up, trample down or set fire to tent colonies; kidnap and beat union leaders and members; break up picket lines, or eject stay-in strikers from plants.[13] On these occasions police frequently are mysteriously absent from the scene, or else appear just in time to arrest union leaders for various crimes and misdemeanors. During the vegetable and fruit pickers' strikes in southern California in 1934, metal mining strikes in Arizona in 1935, Southern textile strikes in 1929-30, seamen's and longshoremen's strikes in 1934, Pennsylvania steel strikes in 1933, recent Arkansas sharecroppers' strikes and scores of other instances strikers and strike leaders have been beaten, tortured, kidnaped and murdered by organized "law-and-order" mobs. Sometimes these vigilante groups appear to be relatively spontaneous undertakings. Occasionally rival unions have a hand in breaking each other's strikes or organizing campaigns in this way.

13 Examples of these procedures will be found in the sources cited in the notes for chaps. III and IV. Examples of most of them occurred in the 1937 steel strike.

Usually, however, there is evidence of careful preparation either open or covert by employing interests. Professional strikebreakers, local American Legion groups,[14] the Ku Klux Klan, the Black Legion [15] and a dozen or more secret or avowed antilabor groups are available in many sections of the country to carry on this form of strikebreaking activity. In industrial or agricultural districts where economic life is not diversified, where social life is monotonous and excitement at a premium, where poverty among workers and the lower middle class is great, and where organized justice has a purely nominal existence, vigilante activities develop as a result of a truly psychopathic social condition. The raw material for group warfare lies constantly at hand. The spark struck by a strike may quickly ignite the dry tinder of hate, superstition, ignorance, boredom, race prejudice, mass poverty, fanaticism and group sadism. A little fanning by the dominant economic interest quickly promotes a conflagration which burns itself out only when bodies have been mutilated, property smashed, the community scarred and a victory won for the open shop.

In an effective strikebreaking campaign it is usually considered necessary not merely to affect the minds of the strikers and their immediate neighbors but also to broadcast antistrike propaganda as widely as possible over the countryside. The purpose of this is to shut off the sources of outside relief, to influence the minds of legislators, executives and judges against the strikers, to invoke the support of stockholders, retail outlets and consumers and to bring the added pressure of outside opinion to bear

[14] Throughout most of the country, American Legion groups have been active in antiunion, strikebreaking, red baiting and vigilante affairs. In the Northeast this activity has not been as pronounced. Recently, progressive unions have been directing their members to join their local posts in order to fend off antiunion action.

[15] The trials and investigations in the Black Legion murder cases showed that the Legion was an avowedly antiunion organization, had had a hand in breaking automobile unions and strikes in 1934, and was related to the espionage systems of large automobile manufacturing concerns.

against the union. The methods have already been illustrated in part by the account of the Remington Rand strike. An advertising campaign emphasizing the reasonableness and tolerance of the management and asking for the patience of stockholders, distributors and consumers; press handouts dwelling upon the unreasonable, radical, irresponsible or violent nature of the movement; reports which underline the losses involved to the community, the stockholders and the workers, implying that the only way in which the losses can be stopped is by the surrender of the strikers—these are the standard methods of influencing public opinion. They may or may not be supplemented by provocation to violence or the actual creation of violence through the use of professional or amateur thugs.

The importance of creating a receptive public attitude toward judicial, executive and legislative acts designed to break a strike cannot easily be overestimated. Injunction procedure allows the judge a great deal of latitude. His attitude toward a case powerfully affects his decision with respect to the granting of an injunction, and the public attitude toward a case determines its enforceability. If the injunction is to be effective, both the mind of the judge and the public should be prepared as carefully as possible.

According to strict equity procedure, injunctions are supposed to be issued only when the defendant has no property which may be attached, or when *irreparable* damage is provably threatened; when the loss which the complainant expects to suffer if the injunction is not granted is greater than the loss to the defendant if the injunction is granted; and when the complainant is himself guiltless of any unlawful conduct. Furthermore, judges in this country have made a practice of including *good will*, *business expectancies* and *the right to do business* as property to which irreparable damage may be done. Finally, judges in state courts exercise great power in determining the number of persons and the variety of actions to be enjoined, and whether the situation warrants granting a temporary injunction upon a hearing of only the complainant's side of the case.[16]

It is apparent, therefore, that considerable amplitude is allowed a judge in deciding whether irreparable damage is in fact threatened to the employer; whether this damage is greater than that which will be suffered by the workers through loss of the strike; whether the employer's loss of good will and right to do business caused by the strike is greater than that which will be suffered by the union if the strike is lost; whether the employer actually enters the court "with clean hands" or whether violation of law by the employer brought on the strike; whether only the strike leaders or all of the strikers shall be served with the injunction; and whether the injunction shall apply only to *unlawful acts* or shall cover calling or advising a strike, paying strike benefits to union members, soliciting relief, peaceful persuasion not to work for the employer, offering to transport strikebreakers back to their homes, mentioning the strike in periodicals or meetings or "in any way interfering with the operation of the complainant's business." When such latitude is allowed to judges, their social background, economic interests and information about the strike itself become the major determinants of the outcome of the injunction process. In most localities it is not difficult to discover judges whose social and economic background cause them to be unimpressed by the doctrines of "clean hands," or "equal loss."

Nevertheless, it is important to "educate" the community to accept a strikebreaking injunction in order that public opinion may identify itself with that of the judge, and in order that the public become willing to undergo the cost in money and perhaps in lives of enforcing the injunc-

[16] As previously indicated, the Norris-LaGuardia Act now places limits upon injunction procedure in Federal courts. Some states have similarly limited injunction procedure in state courts. Great latitude of powers, however, still rests with judges in both Federal and state courts.

tion. This is especially true if it is actually disclosed that the judge is himself a stockowner in the company concerned.[17] The validation of the Wagner Labor Relations Act by the Supreme Court will increase the importance of the "clean hands" doctrine since the Wagner Act prohibits a great many antiunion practices which in the past have led to strikes. It will become important for managers to convince the public that no violation of the Wagner Act is involved in the strike, if public sanction to the issuance and enforcement of strikebreaking injunctions is to be secured. As the dispersal of stock ownership increases, it may also become more difficult to find a judge who is not technically disqualified by his stockholdings in the company concerned. It is to be expected that unions will become increasingly attentive in their scrutiny of the economic and social background of the bench.

In large strikes unions frequently defy injunctions in ways which have previously been indicated. Under these conditions if the injunction is to be carried out sheriffs must be deputized or the militia called in. Both of these procedures involve heavy drains upon local or state funds. The public must therefore be psychologically prepared to accept these expenses. There must be a sufficient number of people willing to act as deputies, and the members of the militia must be willing to undertake strike duty. Occasionally, even after elaborate preparations of the public mind, it is difficult to secure strikebreaking deputies. Usually, however, unemployed workers, small businessmen or small farmers may be secured. In other cases, professional strikebreaking agencies provide strong-arm men who may then be deputized as sheriffs unless local ordinances against deputizing nonresidents are enforced. In many coal, steel, metal-mining and textile strikes of the recent past deputies have been allowed to become semi-

[17] As in the case of Judge Black of Flint, Michigan, in the General Motors strike of 1936-37.

intoxicated as preparation for strikebreaking duty. Hindsight has proved this to be unwise in some instances because of later unpleasant publicity. In the steel strike of 1919, for example, Fanny Sellins, a union relief organizer, was bayoneted and beaten to death by a drunken deputy. Strike leaders arranged widespread distribution of post cards showing Fanny Sellins, her skull crushed, lying in the morgue. Material for "atrocity stories" is especially likely to be provided by drunken forces of the law. This is true also of private company police, whether drunk or not, recruited from the ranks of ex-convicts.

The use of state police or state militia in enforcing an injunction or in maintaining "law and order" is in many ways a very effective antistrike weapon. Often it results in provoking disturbances which would not have otherwise occurred. This may swing opinion away from the strikers and make the public willing to pay the bill for the police and the militia. In some cases when violence does not result, the presence of troops in large numbers is enough to create a condition of public hysteria which breaks the morale of the strikers or influences them not to continue defiance of the injunction. The mounting of machine guns and small cannon at strategic points prevents the movement of "flying squadrons," and the formation of military cordons around disturbed areas can usually be counted upon to permit the peaceful entrance of strikebreakers to the plant or plants affected.

There are difficulties, however, in the use of armed force in the settlement of strikes. Although the militia is usually carefully indoctrinated against unionism through bulletins and training-camp lectures against "Communism" and "radicalism," or through riot instructions in which strikers figure as the hypothetical enemy, the social relations between unionists and militia members become increasingly close as unionism spreads. This leads to the necessity for bringing militia recruited from rural areas into industrial

National Guardsmen covering "No Man's Land" in the Flint, Michigan, strike of automobile workers in 1937.

areas, or exchanging militia units between industrial centers which have traditional antipathies for each other. The result is likely to be resentment on the part of the middle-class elements in the community. Furthermore, the public is becoming somewhat less sympathetic with the actual shooting down of strikers during the enforcement of injunctions or in an effort to preserve "law and order."[18]

There is a growing feeling that force does not eliminate the cause of industrial unrest and may serve simply to intensify it, with the result that its surface manifestations appear more violently on the following occasion. This difficulty may be diminished to some extent by the use of tear and nausea gas rather than bayonets, rifles, shot guns and revolvers. Even gas attacks have their limitations, however. Recent strikes are full of illustrations of this. Gas shells or grenades have been caught by strikers and thrown back among the police or militia. Sudden shifts of wind have enveloped attacking forces in clouds of gas originally directed at the strikers. Gas has drifted into near-by places of business or crowds of spectators and has irritated the mucous membranes and the feelings of respectable members of the community. Middletown, Connecticut, for example, after the Remington Rand strike, was disturbed by stories that children had been hospitalized and places of business closed because of the effects of gas used by state police.

Finally, there are intangibles about the use of force in

[18] The development of newspaper and news reel photography has placed narrower limits on the outright killing of strikers as a means of strikebreaking than formerly existed. The film of the "South Chicago Massacre" in the 1937 steel strike showed police engaged in a wanton and almost unprovoked attack upon a group of terrified men, women and children. The details of the manner in which death was dealt to ten and wounds to scores of strikers were felt to be sufficiently revolting to make the release of the film unwise. The pressure for its public exhibition, however, was great enough to effect its release. This made it difficult for the company to continue the prosecution of strike leaders for "inciting" the "riot" and impossible for it to continue describing the events as a planned and well-disciplined attack by a semimilitary group of Bolsheviks.

breaking a strike which are unpredictable. Violence resulting from the use of force may under some circumstances
crystallize the resistance to the employer more effectively
than anything which the leaders can do. There is evidence
that the strength of the Automobile Workers' Union increased very rapidly in Flint, Michigan, after the first riots
resulting from police efforts to isolate the stay-in strikers
from food supplies. This is especially true when the offen-
sive appears to be taken by the legal forces. It is difficult
to avoid giving this appearance when strikers make use
of either peaceful mass picketing or the stay-in strike.

Mass arrests of strike leaders and strikers have occasionally been used as means of breaking strikes either with or
without resort to martial law, declaration of a state of
insurrection or the reading of the Riot Act. Notable instances of this tactic are supplied by the case of the Colorado mine wars in the early 1900's, the I.W.W. strikes of
the War and immediately post-War period, the California
agricultural strikes of the early 1930's, and the general
textile strike of 1934. Trespass, disturbing the peace,
inciting to riot or insurrection, suspicion, vagrancy, planning trouble, obstructing the sidewalk, criminal syndicalism and illegal entry by aliens are all standard charges
which have been lodged against active strikers and leaders. When relief funds are in the name of arrested leaders,
the morale of the strike may quickly be broken. Otherwise, strikers have developed the device, already described,
of submitting quietly to arrest until the jails have been
filled.

In some instances this strategem has been circumvented
by the construction of auxiliary detention quarters in the
open air. During the Colorado mine wars these were called
"bull pens." This term was modernized during the 1934
textile strike to keep abreast of contemporary developments in Central Europe. "Concentration camps" was the
term applied by newspaper reporters to the barbed-wire

Pictures Inc.

The beginning of the South Chicago "Battle" in which ten strikers were killed and scores wounded.

Pictures Inc.

Strikers fleeing from the clubs of police in the South Chicago "Battle."

stockades and the "clean barn" in Georgia in which about two hundred men and women strikers were detained until the strike was broken. The fact that no charges were lodged against most of these people aroused some resentment, but did not prevent the defeat of the strikers.

It may be repeated, in summary, that it is almost meaningless to speak of "public opinion" as determining the outcome of a strike. Both the winning and the breaking of a strike require the manipulation of public opinion for certain definite purposes.[19] These purposes include breaking the morale of the strikers who are themselves a part of the public; closing channels of outside relief; bringing to bear upon the strikers the pressure of opinion of fellow workers, neighbors and the surrounding community; creating public approval of lockouts, evictions and the introduction of outside strikebreakers; and developing public sympathy for the use of judicial, military or vigilante instruments to protect strikebreakers and employers' property, or destroy union property. The methods of accomplishing these purposes tend to become intermingled with the purposes themselves. The following means, however, may be isolated: personal persuasion and intimidation of, or violence toward, strikers; advertising and control of the press, the use or creation of citizens' committees, back-to-work movements and antiunion organizations; the threat to transfer production to another community; the use of private or professional strikebreaking agencies to conduct whispering campaigns, stimulate

[19] Perhaps the best example of the control of public opinion in recent years occurred in the steel strike of 1937 when, in spite of the fact that notoriously antiunion steel firms refused to sign contracts with the S.W.O.C. in flat defiance of the opinion of President Roosevelt, the Steel Mediation Board and precedents set by the National Labor Relations Board, and in spite of the fact that by August 10 eighteen strikers had been killed and scores wounded while no officers of the law had been seriously hurt and no strikebreakers killed, the steel companies successfully persuaded large sections of the public to think and talk in terms of the "irresponsibility and violence" of the steel union.

violence or plant the blame for it on strike leaders; the use of political influence or bribes; and continual emphasis upon the radical, irresponsible, unreasonable and minority character of the strike movement.

In many strikes a large degree of subtlety is required to handle the complicated economic and social factors involved in modern strikebreaking methods. In others, sheer force is all that is necessary. As the strength of unionism increases and as public understanding of the causes of strikes develops, a greater amount of subtlety and ingenuity in strikebreaking methods will be needed. It may be that the psychological costs to the employer involved in an elaborate strikebreaking campaign will induce some employers and their associations to react toward brute force by extending further support to the terrorist anti-union organizations which during the last fifty years have appeared, disappeared and reappeared. Other employers and their associations, however, will turn their energy and their resourcefulness from the breaking of strikes toward the discovery and elimination of their causes. Which way the tide turns depends not only upon the labor policies of business, but also upon the business, welfare, administrative and political policies of unionism.

CHAPTER VI

The Unions

AMERICAN labor is being reorganized on a scale and with a speed which is unprecedented in American social history. Not merely are unions moving from the A.F. of L. to the C.I.O., but workers who have never before been organized are transferring their loyalties from the symbols of management to the symbols of unionism. The leadership of industrialists and financiers is being discarded by labor for the leadership of union officers and organizers. For half a century the engineering techniques of mass production and the credit instruments of finance have been the major sources of social power. With these instruments the great leaders of industry and finance have carved out empires which have cut across political lines, changed the concepts of ownership and reorganized immense areas of American society. Millions of workers, traders and professionals have found their fundamental loyalties directed toward management and finance. During the last ten years, however, accumulating social maladjustments, depression, new ideas, scandals in high places and new political alignments have sapped the foundations of the old loyalties. The spectacular advent of the C.I.O. provided both an occasion for the further crumbling of these loyalties and a symbol for the reorientation of workers' attitudes and beliefs.

This means not only that power is moving toward a new group of leaders representing a different set of economic interests, but also that this new set of leaders is faced with the problem of determining the outlines of the areas in which they shall operate. Just as the financial and industrial leaders of the last fifty years have been concerned with mapping their respective fields of interest, so the major labor leaders of the present are confronted with the necessity for allocating to the various possible claimants jurisdiction over industrial areas. Should General Motors' electric refrigerator workers belong to the Automobile Workers' Union which covers most of General Motors' territory, or should it go to the Radio and Electrical Appliance Workers' Union? Should brass manufacture go to the Mine, Mill, and Smelter Workers or to the Iron, Steel, and Tin Workers? Should rayon manufacture go with chemicals or textiles? Do utility workers go with a Coke and Gas Union or with Electrical Appliances? In general, should workers group themselves by the skills, the materials, the products or the financial organization of production? Cutting across all this is the fact that workers' loyalties are still divided among A.F. of L., C.I.O. and nonaffiliated unions. A.F. of L. semicraft unions such as the Carpenters and Electrical Workers are pushing their jurisdiction back into the materials upon which they work. C.I.O. unions such as the Mine, Mill, and Smelter Workers are successfully organizing tunnel workers apparently because they both dig holes in the ground!

The problem faced by the student of labor during this period of flux is comparable to that faced by the leaders of labor. Both wish a blueprint of the changing alignments which shall be more than a meaningless tangle of complexities. The one needs his blueprint as a basis for comprehension, the other as a basis for action. Both must conclude that a logical and orderly arrangement is impossible. The leader is driven to the imposition and the student to the assertion of categories which are perhaps illogical, but which serve as a point of departure.

Steel lies at the core of American industrial society. Behind it stand coal and metal mining, aluminum, quarrying, natural gas, cement, oil and giant power. Around it are grouped the producers' and durable consumers' goods:

automobiles, rubber, glass, electrical appliances, machinery and building. Somewhat nearer the observer are the lighter consumers' goods: textiles, clothing, shoes, millinery, furniture, tobacco, printing, food, liquor, paper and the service trades. Off to one side stands agriculture and, on the other wing, the professions. Lacing the whole together are the means of transport and communication: railroad, water, road, telegraph, radio and postal service. Approximately one hundred sixty national and international unions operate in these fields. In the limited space available no more than an outline of the organization of labor in the major industrial groups can be attempted. [1]

The Basic Industries

STEEL is the citadel of American industry geographically, industrially, financially and, more particularly, because it has assumed the historical leadership of the antiunion movement. The Amalgamated Association of Iron, Steel, and Tin Workers was founded in 1876, and by 1892 had achieved some importance as a union composed of skilled puddlers, heaters and nailers. The Carnegie Company, however, determined upon an antiunion policy and successfully broke the power of this union in the Homestead Strike of 1892 by refusing recognition and by using Pinkertons, company police, strikebreakers and the forces of "law and order" in a manner which has since become commonplace in the industry. The union retrenched, its leaders went into reactionary local politics and thereby achieved a modicum of importance and affluence. With the formation of the United States Steel Company in 1901 the employers' associations in the metal industries became belligerently antiunion. United States Steel, unwilling to excite a public which was hostile to the first billion-dollar

[1] The reader will find in the appendix a chart of American labor organizations showing affiliation and membership.

corporation, allowed its antiunionism to drift for a few years. When, in 1906, the Structural Iron and Steel Workers attempted to extend their membership to United States Steel subsidiaries, open warfare was declared by the company against all unions in its domain. Antiunionism drove the Structural Iron Workers into underground terrorism which culminated in the blowing up of the *Los Angeles Times* Building in 1909. The conviction of the union's officers, McManigal and the McNamara brothers, for this crime was a staggering blow to unionism. The labor movement pulled its skirts away from the McNamaras and incidentally from the steel industry. Samuel Gompers and his personal machine became very respectable and helped to win the War. This move saved the labor movement temporarily. A dozen or more metal craft unions such as the Blacksmiths, Drop Forgers, Machinists, Metal Polishers, Molders, Sheet Metal Workers and Stove Mounters eked out a precarious existence in the nooks and crannies of the steel industry. In the great producing and fabricating plants, however, unionism was stamped out, and the twelve-hour day, seven-day week and bimonthly twenty-four hour shift became the rule.

In 1919, under the leadership of one of the labor movement's greatest organizers, William Z. Foster, an immense organizing campaign in the heart of the steel industry was undertaken. Foster and Fitzpatrick of the Chicago Federation of Labor secured the "coöperation" of twenty-four interested craft unions. These unions helped by donating a total sum of about $100 each to the campaign and by sabotaging it when it appeared that its success might threaten the existing leadership of the A.F. of L. The needle trades unions, however, donated generously and about one hundred fifty "liberal" and "progressive" organizers were found to carry out the campaign. In spite of almost insuperable obstacles, Foster gave the American labor movement a magnificent lesson in strategy, discipline, perseverence and courage. Race conflicts, post-War political reaction, the Palmer "red" raids, wholesale discharges of union members, the defection of the craft leaders and the impetuosity of thousands of workers did not prevent Foster and his helpers from organizing about 365,000 members and holding them in line. When the great strike was finally precipitated, the companies turned loose upon the strikers a reign of terror which is classic in American labor history. Thugs, spies, coal and iron police, mounted constabulary, the complete suppression of all the basic civil liberties, the riding down of women and children and an hysterical publicity campaign successfully broke the strike in a little over three months. The metal trades unions retired to the recesses whence their leaders had peeped. The Amalgamated Association returned to its customary practices of failing to call conventions and exacting from its membership a generous salary for its aging president, Mr. Michael Tighe. The seal of success was put upon the open-shop movement and business as usual became the slogan of the day.

In February, 1936, Mr. Lewis, acting on behalf of the C.I.O., offered the A.F. of L. the sum of $500,000 toward a fund of $1,500,000 to organize the steel industry, on condition that organization be upon an industrial basis and under competent leadership. After a month of jockeying, the A.F. of L. turned down the proposal. Accordingly, the C.I.O. offered the same amount to the Amalgamated Association upon the same conditions. Early in May, 1936, progressive sentiment in the A.A.'s convention forced the acceptance of this offer. An agreement was signed between the C.I.O. and the A.A. which resulted in the setting up of the Steel Workers' Organizing Committee. During the remainder of June the plan of campaign was mapped, and early in July operations began. Mass meetings, radio addresses, widespread publicity, the setting up of regional and subregional offices, employment of abundant technical assistance, the training of organizers and the enlistment of voluntary workers consumed most of the summer months. The steel industry replied with wholesale advertising of its employee representation plans, rapid fire discharges of union members and, in West Virginia and Alabama, the kidnaping and beating of organizers. During the late summer, however, steel company unions began coming over to the Steel Workers' Organizing Committee in blocks representing thousands of members. On Labor Day approximately 200,000 people attended a mass meeting arranged by the S.W.O.C. and addressed by Governor Earle and Senator Guffey of Pennsylvania. Protection to organizers and relief in the event of strikes were promised to the steel workers by state executives. In October it was reported that 3 regional and 35 subregional offices had been set up and that 158 staff organizers, field directors and office workers, 80 part-time organizers and 5,000 volunteer organizers were at work. A membership of 82,315 was claimed and it was asserted that 1,534 company union representatives of 2,500 in the industry had joined the union. The S.W.O.C. began a policy of appealing to the Senate Committee on Civil Liberties for an investigation of assaults and kidnapings of organizers. It also brought about investigation of steel company unions by the National Labor Relations Board. Each fresh attack on union organizers, especially in Alabama and in Weirton, West Virginia, brought a burst of anticompany publicity from the sounding board of the Senate Committee or the Labor Relations Board.

During the presidential campaign the S.W.O.C. actively electioneered for Roosevelt with the result that sweeping Democratic victories were piled up in usually Republican territory. In Weirton a union organizer was elected constable. Late in November the steel industries granted wage increases and proposed that for the future wages be pegged to living costs. The S.W.O.C. and numerous company

Courtesy of Union News Service

Cartoon used in the steel organizing campaign.

unions turned down this proposal. President Roosevelt and Secretary of Labor Perkins also rejected it. Company unions continued to melt away. Small steel companies began signing contracts with the union. In December a membership of 125,000 was announced. About 150 lodges of the Association were set up and new members continued to pour in. During February, 1937, attention was distracted from the steel campaign by the General Motors strike. Shortly after the end of the automobile strike, it was suddenly revealed that officers of the United States Steel Company had been conferring with Mr. Lewis and other representatives of the S.W.O.C. with the result that an agreement involving recognition of the union, a five-dollar minimum daily wage and the forty-hour week had been reached. This decision electrified the steel industry and the entire country as well. Subsidiary and independent companies hastened to conclude similar agreements with the S.W.O.C. Members flocked into the union as fast as organizers could issue cards and collect the one dollar first month's dues.

Early in May there were indications that a "united front" of eight independent steel companies employing about 230,000 workers had been formed to resist the advance of the union by refusing to sign contracts with it on the ground that such contracts would "inevitably" lead to the closed shop and the checkoff. At this time the union had signed contracts with about 135 companies covering approximately 330,000 workers. After a short strike in Jones & Laughlin, the company, in spite of heavy pressure from other independents, agreed to hold an election under N.L.R.B. auspices. The S.W.O.C. won by a two to one vote and the company signed a contract granting the union sole bargaining power over 27,000 workers. Shortly after, Pittsburgh Steel and Crucible Steel, companies covering 23,000 more workers, also broke away from the united front. There remained the Bethlehem, Republic, Youngstown, National, and Inland steel companies employing about 175,000 men.

On May 26, 1937, strikes involving about 77,000 workers were declared against the Republic, Youngstown and Inland companies. The S.W.O.C. decided to withhold action against Bethlehem (the largest of the independents, with 72,000 workers) and National, headed by Ernest T. Weir, one of the most determined antiunionists in the country (22,000 workers). Shortly after the beginning of the strike, however, it was extended to cover the Cambria plant (15,000 workers) of the Bethlehem Steel Company. The four combined companies fought the strike with an elaborate version of the Mohawk Valley Formula. Martial law, militia, and state police were repeatedly used in Pennsylvania, Ohio, Illinois and Indiana. In Pennsylvania and to a less extent in Indiana, the forces of the state aided the strikers' cause, while in other states they were used in general to aid the "back-to-work" movement. In a "battle" between strikers and police at Republic's South Chicago plant, ten strikers were killed and more than a hundred were wounded. The union conducted a militant campaign which included the enlistment of every available form of governmental assistance. The companies succeeded in arousing and organizing, directly or indirectly, an unprecedented amount of "vigilantism" which was used to enforce the "back-to-work" movement. During the first month of the strike the four companies refused all compromise offers and broke up attempts at governmental mediation. The Inland Steel Company, however, finally left the united front of the steel companies and signed a compromise agreement with the Indiana State Labor Department early in July pending decision by the National Labor Relations Board as to whether the company had violated the Wagner Act. As the "back-to-work" movement gained momentum, the union allowed its members to return to work with the nonstrikers and began a campaign to bring about action by the National Labor Relations Board against the remaining three companies.

Early in August, 1937, one year after the beginning of the organizing campaign, the S.W.O.C. estimated its membership at approximately 370,000. It had secured contracts with about 260 steel companies covering from 380,000 to 400,000 men. The factors which made this campaign as successful as the 1919 campaign was disastrous were numerous: First was the financial support, unified direction, boldness, imagination and brilliance of strategy which the C.I.O. brought to the campaign. Second was the prestige and protection accorded to the movement by the indirect support of state and Federal Government. Third was the elimination of race and language conflicts by sixteen years of restricted immigration and mass education. Fourth was the fact that the steel industry was engaging in a concerted "sit-down" against the government by refusing to bid on government contracts under the terms of the Walsh-Healy Act. This placed the S.W.O.C. and the government squarely on the same side of the fence and swung public opinion away from the steel companies. Finally, the steel industry was experiencing an extraordinary prosperity because of the rearmament programs of most of the great nations. Wage increases were quickly passed on in prices greater than were necessitated by increased costs for labor and materials, and the industry could not afford to precipitate a strike over the question of union recognition.

Industrial unionism under the C.I.O. is well entrenched in the steel industry. The efforts of Mr. Green and Colonel Frey, leader of the extreme conservative bloc in the A.F. of L., to advance the rival claims of the Structural Steel and Iron Workers in the fabrication plants or to use company unions as a basis of operations have already proved abortive. The appearance of a crop of "independent" unions looking suspiciously like the company unions they replaced has done little to check the advance of the S.W.O.C. Nothing short of a deep business recession accompanied by disastrous strikes, the militarization of industry during war or complete political reaction is likely to dislodge the Amalgamated Association from the steel industry in the near future.

Back of steel lies coal. Anthracite coal is both a natural and a man-made monopoly. American anthracite deposits lie within a relatively small area of the state of Pennsylvania. As early as the 1890's the chief deposits in this area had come under the control of a small group of railroads which were themselves controlled by New York financial interests. A united front against coal unionism was thus presented early in its history. Bituminous mining on the contrary, is found in about two dozen states all over the country under a great variety of natural and social conditions. Until very recently it has been as violently competitive as agriculture and closely related to it in many ways.

Unionism appeared early in the 1850's under the leadership of British immigrants in both hard and soft coal areas. Organization was local in scope and industrial in form. Craft unionism never appealed to coal workers although craft unions have tried to capture organized coal workers. The depression following the Civil War broke up these early unions but they revived on a broader basis in the 1870's. Brutal frontier conditions in the relatively isolated coal towns; language and race conflicts resulting from the influx of "new" immigrants; long hours, low wages and extremely dangerous working conditions; the cheating of the miners in the weighing of coal; and excessive company charges for rent, food and clothing—these formed both the basis for the drive toward unionism and the causes of its weakness. The product of these conditions plus the introduction of Pinkerton spies by the coal railroads drove the Irish workers into secret terrorism under the Molly Maguires. Unionism in the anthracite was broken by the "revelations" [2] of the Pinkerton spies in the 1870's.

In soft coal, however, especially in Illinois and Ohio, the first signs of national unions began to appear in the 1880's. Some of these unions were gathered up and given impetus by the Knights of Labor. From the wreck of the Knights there emerged in 1890 the United Mine Workers of America. Membership increased rapidly but the depression of 1893 forced the union into a strike which ended in failure although 125,000 men answered the call. Four years of depression reduced union membership to 9,000 and the miner's condition to desperation. In 1897 a strike call of bituminous miners in the central states was almost unanimously answered. The strike was successful and resulted in the signing of an agreement covering western Pennsylvania, Indiana, Ohio and Illinois.

The union then adopted a three-fold policy consisting of, first, an effort to stabilize the central bituminous field by faithfully observing trade agreements covering whole districts; second, organizing the scattered remaining two thirds of the Southern and Western soft coal fields; and, third, unionizing the anthracite miners in order to check potential competition. In spite of the determined anti-unionism in anthracite of the same financial interests which broke the steel union at Homestead in 1892, the United Mine Workers called strikes in 1900 and 1902 and won concessions which finally resulted by 1912 in complete recognition of the union in anthracite. In the soft coal regions of the West and South the union was less successful. The isolated company towns in West Virginia and Alabama were almost impregnable to unionism. The Rockefeller interests in Colorado broke the union in the

---

[2] It has never been possible to determine accurately how much of the violence was committed by workers and how much was planted or stimulated by spies.

bloody strike of 1903. In spite of this, however, the union had by 1912 organized about 35 per cent of the coal workers in the country.

The War stabilized the coal industry on the basis of expanding demand and rising prices. The union prospered with the industry and increased its membership to about 400,000 in 1920. It did not, however, succeed in extending its power in the South. This spelled failure for the union's future. In the 1920-21 depression the bituminous industry began to disintegrate. Post-War contraction, the development of competing sources of power, extremely inefficient management, the introduction of labor-saving machinery, and the existence of favorable freight rates in the nonunion Southern field soon made bituminous mining an extremely "sick" industry from the viewpoint of both management and the union. As a consequence of operators' demands for wage reductions, a nation-wide strike was called in 1922. This resulted in the perpetuation of the wartime rates, but the settlement did not protect the operators and workers in the central field from the competition of the lower wage rates in the South. Although the union succeeded in renewing this agreement in 1924 and in increasing its membership to an all-time high of 500,000 out of 700,000 in 1925, it did so at the expense of both profits and employment in the central field.

After 1926 disintegration of both the industry and the union took its inexorable course. Small operators repudiated the 1924 agreement and slashed their wages. An important segment of the bituminous field had come under the financial control of steel, railroad and automobile companies which mined directly for their own use. These companies took the advantage presented by the weakness of the union, proclaimed an open-shop policy in the "captive mines" and thus tore from the union's grasp another area of bituminous production. The union surrendered its activities in the South but clung desperately and stubbornly to the crumbling central field. Wholesale disaffection among the rank and file, especially in the Illinois district, resulted in the exercise of autocratic disciplinary powers by the union's leaders. This was followed by the appearance of two new opposition unions. One, the National Mine Workers, was under the Communist leadership of the Trade Union Unity League but did not have an important following. The Progressive Mine Workers, however, centering in Illinois, brought the majority of the Illinois miners into its following. The leaders of the United Mine Workers dropped their advocacy of the nationalization of the industry as the solution of its troubles and adopted the fatalistic policy of allowing "natural forces" to do their work. It was expected that the inefficient mines would be driven out of existence and that superfluous miners would be forced into other occupations. Economic and social factors peculiar to the coal industry rendered this policy useless and, eventually, disastrous. Although in 1932 the union continued to pay per capita tax upon 300,000 members, it actually retained a bare 175,000.

With the announcement of the coming of the N.R.A. in 1933, however, the union's leaders began a remarkably successful campaign of reorganization. The soft coal code gave the industry a measure of temporary stability and Section 7a provided a psychological stimulus badly needed after fifteen years of court decisions which had effectively tied the union's hands in pushing its organizing work. Coal operators, led by the Frick and United States Steel interests, began forming company unions to head off the United Mine Workers. In the race which followed, the U.M.W. was victorious. A series of bitter strikes in the summer of 1933 followed by equally bitter litigation in which President Roosevelt and General Johnson took an important part finally forced the capitulation of the United States Steel interests. Wage increases, hour reductions, the checkoff and union checkweighmen [3] became general throughout the industry. The U.M.W. fought off an independent union of Anthracite Miners in Pennsylvania, reduced the Progressive Miners to relative unimportance and secured the passage of the Guffey Coal Act which set up a "little N.R.A." in the coal industry to replace the invalidated coal code.

Although general contracts covering about 90 per cent of the tonnage in both the anthracite and bituminous industries were subsequently renewed, there were distinct indications in 1936 that the steel interests might lead a counter-attack on the union early in 1937 when the time came for a new contract. After weeks of negotiation, however, and a peaceful one-day stoppage affecting about 400,000 men, a contract was secured which covered 300,000 miners in the Appalachian region. This contract was expected to form the basis for similar contracts covering about 500,000 workers. It included the thirty-five hour, five-day week and, for the first time, time and a half for overtime.

The United Mine Workers at present has about 600,000 members and is regarded as one of the most powerful unions in the world. It has supported the C.I.O. organizing drive by furnishing leadership and well over a million dollars in funds. It is headed by an extraordinarily able group of leaders including John Brophy, Philip Murray and John Lewis. The ultimate success of the union, however, would seem to depend either upon the nationalization of the coal industry or upon the development of a long range policy of union-management coöperation in closing superfluous mines, increasing managerial efficiency, developing new uses and outlets for coal, transfering men and capital to other industries, further reductions of hours and the payment of a stable annual income to mine work-

[3] Union agents whose duty is to check the findings of company agents in the weighing of coal mined under piece-rates of pay.

ers. There are indications that the ablest leaders in the industry are looking in this direction. There is a danger, however, that any policy less farsighted than this may result in a renewal of the warfare and disintegration of the 1920's.

While calling the roll of the primary industries, mention should be made of metal mining, petroleum, coke and gas, aluminum, chemicals, quarrying, cement and cereals. Metal mining unionism in the late 1890's and the early 1900's consisted of mortal combat between the Western Federation of Miners and mine interests in the Rocky Mountain region. The often told stories of the Ludlow massacres and the murder of ex-Governor Steunenberg epitomize industrial relations in the industry during this period. [4] The Western Federation gave birth to the I.W.W. in 1905, but in 1911 it reaffiliated with the A.F. of L., purged itself of syndicalism, became respectable and in 1916 changed its name to the International Union of Mine, Mill and Smelter Workers. From then until very recently it remained relatively unimportant. It experienced the revival common to other unions during the N.R.A., increased its membership from 1,500 to 15,900 in 1936 and became a charter member of the C.I.O. It is currently conducting an aggressive organizing campaign in iron, copper and gold mining, brass manufacture and tunneling operations which had brought its membership to about 45,000 in August, 1937. The A.F. of L., however, has recently declared that it will conduct a rival campaign using as a base the Tri-State Mine, Mill and Smelter Workers. This union is formed of strikebreakers and "loyal" workers who

[4] Steunenberg was murdered by Albert Horsely, alias Harry Orchard, who was apparently employed as a spy, bomber and plug-ugly by both the Western Federation of Miners and the Mine Owners' Association. In some cases it appeared that he had been employed by both sides for the same job. In the Ludlow massacre, armed forces employed by Rockefeller mining interests machine gunned and burned with oil a strikers' tent colony with the result that several men and women were shot and eleven children were burned to death under the tents, April 19, 1914.

broke a strike conducted by the Mine, Mill and Smelter Workers' International Union while it was still an A.F. of L. affiliate. Such strikebreaking unions have long been known in Europe and are called "yellow" by independent trade-union movements.

Coke and gas plants became organized for the first time during the N.R.A. period. About twenty large federal labor locals were set up for coke and gas workers which were then banded together in a National Coke and Gas Workers' Council. Efforts by A.F. of L. craft leaders to divide these federal labor locals into appropriate craft unions led to a request from the Coke and Gas Council that it be allowed to affiliate with the United Mine Workers. This proposal was adopted in August, 1936, by the U.M.W., and the Coke and Gas Department now forms an important group in the Miners' Union and the C.I.O.

After a series of early failures to organize oil workers, the Oil Field, Gas Well, and Refinery Workers' Union was chartered in 1918. It made some headway during the War period, especially in California. During this period the I.W.W. also made slight gains in the oil fields. In the 1920's, however, unionism in oil gradually broke down and by 1933 the membership of the Oil Field Union had diminished to 300. Under the N.R.A. rapid gains were registered and by 1936 the membership had reached 40,500. It is now a member of the C.I.O. and is engaged in an active organizing campaign under the Petroleum Workers' Organizing Committee. The P.W.O.C. has already made significant gains in the Southwestern oil fields and in the distributing companies of the East bringing its present membership to 100,000. In several large distributing centers company unions have come over to the P.W.O.C. and union contracts have been signed by the companies. It appears likely that the P.W.O.C. will absorb the twenty-five locals of filling-station employees which are now directly affiliated with the A.F. of L., and thus complete the vertical organization of the industry from the well to the consumer. There is a distinct possibility, however, of jurisdictional conflict with the Truck Drivers' Union at the retail end of the process. The A.F. of L., furthermore, has announced its intention of conducting a rival organizing campaign in the oil fields.

During and after the N.R.A. period the A.F. of L. set up about twenty federal labor locals in the aluminum industry. By 1937 these had a membership of 12,000 and had signed contracts covering about 16,000 workers of the 50,000 in the industry. Fearing partition among craft claimants, these locals severed their connection with the A.F. of L. and on April 12, 1937, set up a new international union, the Aluminum Workers of America. The new union then joined the C.I.O. and began an organizing campaign to extend its membership to the rest of the industry. Similar action may be expected from the 28 locals of cement workers, 20 locals of chemical workers and 36 locals of grain, feed and cereal workers which remain directly attached to the A.F. of L. at the present time. There is a possibility also that the more than 20,000 members of the Quarry Workers' Union, some of whose locals are engaged in jurisdictional conflict with craft unions, will also transfer allegiance to the C.I.O. in the near future.

Durable Goods

FINANCIALLY and industrially related to steel are the durable goods industries: automobiles, rubber, glass, electrical appliances, machinery and building. Until very recently there has been little organization of workers in any of these industries except machinery and building.

With the exception of the formation of a short-lived automobile union at the end of the War and a futile gesture of the A.F. of L. convention of 1926 toward union-management cooperation, no important organization of automobile workers existed prior to the depression. In the early spring of 1933 strikes broke out all over the face of the automobile industry. These represented a blind and spontaneous protest against unemployment, wage-cuts, speed-up and industrial espionage. They gave rise to half a dozen competing unions led by people representing almost every color in the political spectrum from bright red to black. These strikes also formed the basis for a half-hearted organizing campaign led by the A.F. of L. The automobile industry began vigorously to set up company unions wherever it was faced with independent unionism and also succeeded in incorporating the "merit clause" in its N.R.A. code and thereby fortifying its antiunion policy. The A.F. of L., however, was successful by 1934 in setting up more than 100 federal labor locals with a membership estimated at from 150,000 to 210,000.

In March, 1934, very general unrest among automobile workers over their failure to achieve substantial improvement of conditions through the N.R.A. code authorities and through mediation proceedings led to the threat of a general strike in the automobile industry. Unquestionably the majority of automobile workers at this time would have followed the lead of the organized workers in a strike action. Through the intervention of President Roosevelt the strike was averted and a "compromise" settlement was effected. The acceptance of this settlement by the A.F. of L. leaders aroused deep resentment among union members and a drift away from the A.F. of L. began. The several varieties of nonaffiliated unions gained somewhat by this defection from A.F. of L. ranks and led several partially successful strikes. The setting up of a National Council of Automobile Workers in the summer of 1934 to connect the federal labor locals did little to stem the tide of disorganization.

The San Francisco convention of the A.F. of L. in 1934 instructed the Executive Council to press its organizing campaign in the automobile industry and to allow the setting up of a national union which would include all but the skilled craftsmen. After nine months of delay a convention of automobile workers was called in August, 1935, and the United Automobile Workers came into existence. Against the vote of the Auto Workers' convention, the Executive Council of the A.F. of L. imposed upon the new union an A.F. of L. organizer as its first president. During the fall of 1935 and the early part of 1936 this officer and his immediate following completed the process of discrediting A.F. of L. leadership among automobile workers. By the autumn of 1936 the membership of the union was reported as 19,000.

In the meantime, however, the Automobile Workers had held a second convention, elected their own officers, adopted a militant organizing and strike policy and joined the C.I.O. The original strategy of the C.I.O. called for concentration first upon the steel industry and second upon its satellites. This program was carried out until December, 1936. Late in December a series of relatively spontaneous strikes broke out in automobiles. These, combined with strikes in flat glass, indicated that a complete tie-up of the automobile industry was possible. The sudden spread of stay-in strikes made the automobile situation far more important from a political and strategic point of view than the steel campaign. The stay-in strike also called for great resources in leadership, organization, finances and discipline. Both industrial and labor leaders recognized that in the General Motors strike of January, 1937, a decisive point in the history of the American labor movement had been reached. The final settlement represented both an actual and a symbolic gain of great importance to the future of organized labor. The somewhat less successful Chrysler strike and the "capitulation" of United States Steel, both of which followed the General Motors strike, were almost anticlimatic. A rapid influx of members

Pictures Inc.

Organizer Frankensteen of the Automobile Workers' Union being beaten by Ford "Service" men as union organizers attempted to distribute leaflets near the Dearborn plant.

Pictures Inc.

Although Harry Bennett, chief of the Ford "Service" men, asserted that the beating was administered by "loyal" Ford workers, the picture, as the editors of *Time* have pointed out, shows one of the "loyal" workers with a pair of handcuffs in his hip pocket.

during and immediately after these strikes brought the membership in the union to 400,000 out of approximately 500,000 in the industry. The union is now faced with the difficulty of organizing the Ford Company and of introducing the shop steward [5] method of settling grievances to an industry which has had no experience and little sympathy with it. The introduction of the shop steward system has already resulted in numerous short sit-down strikes which may be expected to continue until both management and the union have developed methods of quick and intelligent handling of the irritants and injustices characteristic of human relations in modern mass production industries.

Mr. Ford has assumed a position of open defiance of the union. The company made a bad strategic mistake, however, on May 26, by allowing company police to administer a brutal beating to prominent union organizers in the presence of press photographers and government investigators. The attack was precipitated by efforts of the organizers to distribute leaflets at the River Rouge plant. Photographers were also beaten and unsuccessful efforts were made to destroy their plates. The union is going on with a period of quiet organizing in the River Rouge and an encircling movement in scattered plants. The latter program has already brought results in California and Missouri.

In the rubber, glass and electrical appliance industry the history of unionism is almost identical with that in automobiles. Each of these industries was nonunion until the N.R.A. In each, organization progressed rapidly under the N.R.A. The unions in these industries passed through the stage of direct affiliation with the A.F. of L., set up national councils and eventually created independent national unions after unsatisfactory relationships with the A.F. of L. Each joined the C.I.O. early in the committee's

[5] Below, chap. VII, p. 218 *et seq.*

Courtesy of Union News Service

This C.I.O. cartoon indicates the original intention of the C.I.O. to supplement rather than supplant the A.F. of L. in the American labor movement.

history, began intensive organizing campaigns and rapidly increased its membership. The only important variation in this pattern was in the case of the United Electrical and Radio Workers. Although this union applied for admission to the A.F. of L., permission was refused because of a protest from the International Brotherhood of Electrical Workers. The I.B.E.W., a powerful semicraft union having, in 1936, 170,000 members almost exclusively in the building industry, created a subdepartment for production workers in the radio and electrical appliance industry. These workers are offered a "nonbeneficiary" status, which means that they pay lower dues, do not receive benefits and have one vote per local in national conventions as compared with the one vote per member of the Class A group.

Having been refused admission by the A.F. of L. the United Electrical and Radio Workers' Union joined the C.I.O. and launched a very successful organizing campaign. Its greatest accomplishment has been the securing of sole bargaining power in most of the General Electric Company's plants. It is now engaged in organizing utility workers all over the country by coöperating with the Gas and Coke Workers on one wing and the American Radio Telegraphers on the other. It is, however, faced with opposition from the International Brotherhood of Electrical Workers and from several strong company unions of a nearly independent variety. The I.B.E.W. will be forced to disregard the claims of more than a score of other A.F. of L. craft unions if it presses its organizing drive among utility and electrical appliance workers. This will place the A.F. of L. Executive Council in a position of open, but perhaps not embarrassing, self-contradiction.

The remaining important durable goods industry is building. The unions in this industry have long been the backbone of the A.F. of L. and constitute its chief remaining source of power. The sixteen unions in the Building

Trades Department of the A.F. of L. in August, 1937, had a membership of 884,300. This was almost one third of the total membership at that time. Only one of these unions, the International Brotherhood of Electrical Workers, appreciably increased its membership between 1928 and 1937. The Electrical Workers, as noted above, have accomplished this increase by branching out into fields other than building. The other unions in the building industry, with the exception of slight gains by the Structural Iron Workers and the Operating Engineers, have either lost considerable ground or barely maintained their customary per capita tax payments during this ten-year period.

The Carpenters dropped from 322,000 to 300,000 in a similar period in spite of having assumed jurisdiction over workers in the lumber, plywood, shingle, sawmill, box-wood, furniture, cooperage, and pile driving industries! These workers, to the number of about 75,000, after enjoying Class B "nonbeneficiary" status in the Carpenters' Union, increased their membership to more than 100,000 and transferred allegiance to the C.I.O. in July, 1937. In assuming jurisdiction over these fields the Carpenters' Union was not greatly disturbed by the fact that it was transgressing the jurisdictional lines of a large variety of craft unions in the A.F. of L. President Hutcheson, who led the fight against the C.I.O. in the 1935 A.F. of L. convention, has made a specialty (during his long and colorful career) of swallowing up other smaller unions. In this instance, however, the lumber and sawmill workers would not stay swallowed.

Although the building trades remain the stronghold of the A.F. of L. the power of the unions in this field is clearly declining. Between August, 1928, and August, 1937, the Building Trades Department suffered a loss of slightly more than 100,000 members. There are several reasons for this heavy reverse. In general the building industry has not experienced the revival common to other industries in the 1933-37 period. If and when a building boom begins, the union may be expected to gain somewhat. As previously pointed out, however, the building industry is becoming increasingly a matter of assembling prefabricated materials. The changes in building methods have caused the building trade unions to waste much of their strength and influence in jurisdictional conflicts. This is a continuing source of weakness which can be remedied only by a greater degree of surrender of craft autonomy among the building trades unions than appears to be likely in the near future.

The third source of weakness has been the reactionary leadership in many of the building trades unions which, when combined with the peculiar characteristics of the building industry, has led to racketeering and gangsterism, especially in New York and Chicago. The seasonal character of the industry makes the union member dependent upon the business agent of the union to provide him with a job. The business agent may, if he wishes, extract tribute from the union members in the form of "kickbacks" or "job permits" from nonunion workers. The fact that most building is done under bonded contracts calling for completion within a limited time places the contractor at the mercy of the business agent. The business agent sells the contractor protection against strikes or even against unionism. The solidity of the business agent's position is completed by his connections with local politics which come to him through public works. Favors from political bosses, police and courts come to the business agent in exchange for delivering votes on election day. The business agent may therefore play all three ends against the middle. Union workers may gain substantially from the strategic power of their business agents, but they are relatively powerless to protest if the business agent chooses to sell them down the river. The frequency with which this has occurred during the last twenty years is an important reason for the failure of the building trades to keep pace with the expansion enjoyed by the industrial unions.

Consumer's Goods

IN the consumers' goods and service industries the most important unions are those in the men's and women's clothing, textiles, brewing, shoes, printing and hat industries. Among these the International Ladies' Garment Workers' Union in women's clothing and the Amalgamated Clothing Workers in men's clothing are predominant. Both unions have long been known for their "progressive" policies, both have done much to stabilize highly competitive industries in which "sweatshops" have been familiar characteristics, both have had a profound effect on the American labor movement and both are charter members of the C.I.O.

The Amalgamated Clothing Workers originated from a split in the United Garment Workers in 1914. It was the first "dual" union to rise to a position of permanent dominance in spite of ostracism by the A.F. of L. Although it took the lead during the 1920's in pushing a policy of union-management coöperation, it also developed under able leadership an elaborate and aggressive organizing program with notable successes even in the scattered and highly competitive shirtmaking industry. In men's suits and coats, the union's business policy has centered around job control, extensive arbitration of grievances and regularization of production. This union has given aid to other struggling progressive unions and has developed an advanced program of educational and welfare work among its members. Its structure has shown a high degree of flexibility. Although it is commonly spoken of as an industrial union, its local unions are craft, mixed craft, racial and industrial in composition. It was finally admitted in 1933 to the A.F. of L. in spite of the conflicting jurisdictional claims of the United Garment Workers. Under the N.R.A. the A.C.W. rapidly regained its membership and spread out again over the whole men's clothing field with the exception of men's work clothes. This territory was allotted to the United Garment Workers. The A.C.W. took a leading part in the formation of the C.I.O. and now provides it with a "brain trust" and welcome financial contributions. The A.F. of L. has announced its intention of boycotting A.C.W. products. It is unlikely that this project can actually be carried out without unduly exposing A.F. of L. members to the elements.

The International Ladies' Garment Workers' Union appeared in 1900 as the result of a fusion of several conflicting semicraft organizations which survived the decline of the Knights of Labor. During the generation which followed, this union faced one of the most difficult organizational tasks in the American scene. Race conflicts, political factionalism, small-scale and highly competitive methods of production presented the union with a very discouraging prospect. With the exception of the major depression periods, during which both the industry and the union disintegrated, the I.L.G.W.U. has been very successful in building and rebuilding its power. Some of the union's important characteristics have been its enforcement of trade agreements covering large areas of the industry, the influence of both Socialist and Communist philosophy upon its members, its extraordinary generosity to other progressive union movements, its leadership in the field of workers' education and welfare work, and the unstinting aid which it has brought to the C.I.O. movement. In extent of organization, the union is now one of the most powerful in America. It recently reported a membership of 250,000 out of a possible total of approximately 300,000.

The dozen or more textile industries which constitute *the* textile "industry" employ over a million workers and form the largest manufacturing unit in the country.

Unionism in this industry goes well back into the nine-teenth century but has never been able to establish much more than a toe hold in the relatively skilled textile crafts. Constant technological change, geographical migration, the cultural heterogeneity of the workers, intense anti-unionism both in the South and the large-scale centers of the North, and inadequate leadership have powerfully militated against effective unionization of the industry. These conditions, however, have provided the basis for large-scale and bitterly fought strikes which have re-peatedly been the nation's cynosure. The far-flung boun-daries of the textile empire and the great difference among the separate industries which compose it have provided fertile ground for a variety of competing labor organiza-tions. Although the chartering of the United Textile Workers by the A.F. of L. in 1901 temporarily brought together the competing elements in the textile labor move-ment, it was a matter of only a few years before secession to the right and dualism to the left drove the U.T.W. into disastrous fratricidal warfare. The War period revived the fortunes of textile unionism and brought it to a peak in 1920 when the U.T.W. had a membership of 105,000 with perhaps another 50,000 in other unions. The long and al-most unbroken decline of the textile industry from 192c to 1933 provided the U.T.W. with the pyrrhic satisfac-tion of outliving its rivals, but reduced its membership to 15,000.

Under the N.R.A., textile unionism rapidly revived. The U.T.W. was reorganized by the setting up of separate departments or federations for the distinct branches of the industry. The textile code provided minimum wages upon the basis of which the union could operate. Members poured in until the union reached a peak strength of about 350,000 in the summer of 1934. The spectacular but un-successful general strike of September, 1934, broke the bubble. An intense antiunion campaign during the remainder of 1934 and 1935, acute discontent with the strike settlement and disgust with both government boards and union leadership kept the union's average paid-up membership at about 80,000 for the year 1935. In this connection, however, it must be observed that the strength of unionism in textiles, as in many other industries, has been far greater than is indicated by membership figures. The continuous flow of workers through the union and the leadership which it has provided in time of strikes have made its influence much more pervasive than paid-up membership figures suggest.

In the fall of 1935 the U.T.W. entered the C.I.O. as a charter member and during 1936 revived its organizing efforts with some success, but not until the spring of 1937 did the influence of the C.I.O. begin to be felt. In March the Textile Workers Organizing Committee, under the guidance of Sidney Hillman of the Amalgamated Clothing Workers, was set up to carry on the most comprehensive organizing campaign in American labor history. The country was divided into seven regions, elaborate technical and research services were provided, approximately 500 organizers (many of whom were college graduates) were trained and put in the field and all the elaborate publicity devices of big business were marshaled. Immediate success met the T.W.O.C.'s campaign in the North and the Middle South. Between April and July thousands of textile workers joined the union and trade agreements were signed covering many more. The crux of the campaign, however, lies in the South where localism and management's hostility to unionism remain strong. The indications are that the South can be organized, but whether it can be done without violent and armed opposition from the forces of "law and order" remains to be seen.[6]

[6] On June 15, 1937, the C.I.O. reported that 125,000 workers were covered by newly won contracts. Gains were also reported in the South in spite of antiunion violence. In October a total textile membership of 450,000 was claimed.

Among the remaining consumers' goods unions of importance are those in shoes, hats, brewing and printing. In the shoe industry, moribund leadership of the Boot and Shoe Workers (the A.F. of L. affiliate) and technological change resulted in the appearance of a variety of competing unions. In 1933 many of these were brought together in the United Shoe and Leather Workers' Union. Early in 1937 this union was merged with another, the Shoe Workers' Protective Union, to form the United Shoe Workers of America under the auspices of the C.I.O. With an initial membership of more than 30,000, the United Shoe Workers has begun an active organizing campaign in New England and the Midwest which seems likely to eclipse the rival organization of the A.F. of L. [7] In the hat industry competing organizations were brought together in 1933 under the United Hatters, Cap, and Millinery Workers. In 1935 the president of this union with a membership of 22,000 joined the C.I.O. [8] and was supported in this action by one department of the union in the 1936 convention.

The Brewery workmen have long been organized on a semi-industrial basis and have been compelled to fight the conflicting claims of the Teamsters', Engineers' and Firemen's unions. Having finally won the battle on this front the Brewery Workmen were dealt an almost mortal blow by the enactment of Prohibition. The union was able to survive only by extending its jurisdiction over flour, cereal and soft drink workers. After conducting a successful or-

[7] Early in June, 1937, the 14,000 New York City members of the Boot and Shoe Workers' Union left the national union and affiliated with the United Shoe Workers of the C.I.O. The Boot and Shoe Workers thus lost more than half of its membership at one blow.

[8] The International Fur Workers' Union, with about 30,000 members, left the A.F. of L. and joined the C.I.O. during the first week of June, 1937. An assessment of $2.00 per capita was levied for the coming year to be used for organizing purposes. The union soon scored an important success by organizing the workers in and signing a contract with the largest firm in the industry—a firm which had long been strongly antiunion.

ganizing campaign in the flour and cereal mills, the union
was promptly faced by attack from a variety of craft
unions. The A.F. of L. supported the jurisdictional claims
of these crafts and the Brewery Workmen withdrew from
the flour and cereal mill field. Since the time of this withdrawal, no organization has existed among the flour and
cereal workers except in occasional federal labor locals.
The Brewery Workmen clung to a precarious existence
in the near beer and soft drink industries until 1933. The
modification of the Volstead Act in 1933 and the subsequent repeal of the Eighteenth Amendment quickly revived the union but brought the Teamsters, Engineers, and
Firemen back to the attack. These unions were again upheld by the A.F. of L. in 1934 but the Brewers refused
to accept the dismemberment of their union. Between
1934 and 1936 the Teamsters' Union assisted in breaking
Brewers' strikes by furnishing truck drivers to breweries
where strikes were in progress and by issuing union cards
to maltsters who were not members of the Brewers' Union.
Although the Brewery Workmen remain in the A.F. of L.
the union has repeatedly declared its sympathy and may
soon cast its lot with the C.I.O.

In the printing industry unionism goes back to the beginning of the American labor movement. Of the eight
craft or semicraft unions in the field, seven remain within
the A.F. of L. These unions, the Bookbinders, Photo-
gravers, Lithographers, Pressmen, Plate Printers, Siderographers and Stereotypers, had a combined membership
in 1936 of 60,000. The president of the largest union in
the industry, the International Typographical Union, is
secretary of the C.I.O.[9] His union's 1936 membership was
greater than that of all other printing unions combined. Al-

[9] Although the Typographical was not suspended by the A.F. of L.
in either the 1936 convention or the May, 1937, conference, President
Howard of the Typographical first joined the C.I.O. as an individual and
was then supported by vote of his union's convention. The union continues to pay per capita tax, however, to the A.F. of L.

though it remains a semicraft organization, it has given the C.I.O. valuable assistance both in leadership and organizational services and has recently increased its membership to 80,000.

Transportation and Communication

IN water transportation the most important unions are the International Seamen's Union and the Longshoremen's Association. Between 1900 and 1920 the Seamen's Union, under the leadership of Andrew Furuseth, made considerable progress both in securing protective legislation for seamen and in extending its organization, but after its 1921 strike the power of the union was broken. Since 1934 it has revived in spite of the fact that its national leaders appear to have become willing instruments of the shipping interests. On the West Coast the rank and file has split away from the national officers and has come under the "militant" leadership of Harry Lundeberg. It has joined with the Longshoremen's Union and other smaller organizations in the formation of a powerful alliance, the Maritime Federation of the Pacific.

The Longshoremen on the Pacific Coast have likewise broken away from the control of their national officers and have come under the leadership of Harry Bridges. The Maritime Federation conducted the protracted shipping strikes of 1934 and 1936 and succeeded in winning and retaining the control of the hiring halls which are of crucial importance in the maintenance of a "closed" or "preferential" union shop policy in these industries. On the Gulf Coast these unions remain relatively weak. In the East the seamen, under the leadership of Joseph Curran, have broken away from the national officers. Without the support of the longshoremen they were unable, however, to secure more than minor concessions in their 1936 strike directed against the ship owners, the international union officers and the legal requirement of the continuous discharge book.

The insurgent elements in the Seamen's Union in 1937 broke away from their national officers and joined with the American Radio Telegraphists' Association in forming the National Maritime Union. This union joined the C.I.O. and rapidly won a series of short strikes and N.L.R.B. elections which awarded bargaining power to the new union on a number of shipping lines. In July, 1937, the Maritime Federation of the Pacific transferred to the C.I.O., leaving the A.F. of L. almost without members in the shipping field. The C.I.O. announced its intention of setting up one large maritime federation to cover the 300,000 workers in shipping, longshore work, fishing and shipbuilding.

On the railroads there are now twenty-one craft or semicraft unions. Of these, five are affiliated with the A.F. of L. and sixteen are not affiliated with any other organization. The nonaffiliated unions have come to be called the "railway brotherhoods" although this term is often reserved for the Big Four: the Engineers, Firemen, Conductors and Trainmen. In 1935 there were about 480,000 union workers on American railroads. Of these, about 150,000 were members of A.F. of L. unions and about 330,000 were members of nonaffiliated unions. Since 1935 membership in the railroad unions has increased appreciably as a result of the transfer of several system employees' associations to membership in the national unions. The distinguishing characteristic of the railroad unions has always been their conservatism. This has taken the form of reluctance to strike and of emphasis upon financial benefit plans. The unions' conservatism has been partly the result of the fact that the strategic position of the Brotherhoods has given them sufficient bargaining power to render strikes unnecessary, and partly the result of the constant imminence of legal regulation of labor relations in the railroad industry. In spite of their increased membership, however, the railroad unions are being forced into a defensive position by the decline of railroading in the face of competing methods of transport. Either consolidation of existing railway systems under increasingly stringent government regulation or outright nationalization of the industry appears to be inevitable. In either case railway workers are faced with displacement. If the unions are to protect their members and assist in ordering the affairs of the industry, increased participation in Federal politics and in the main stream of the labor movement are necessary conditions of success.[10]

In the electrical communication industry there are diminutive organizations whose growth would seem to depend upon the success of the C.I.O. in proselytizing the comparatively independent and successful employee associations in this field. The chief progress of the labor movement in communications has been in the unrelated field of postal service. Fourteen unions, of which only four are affiliated with the A.F. of L., operate in this area. The total membership, however, of about 235,000 is almost equally divided between the A.F. of L. and the non-affiliated unions. Like the railroad unions, the postal organizations have been rendered relatively conservative by their strategic position and by their proximity to governmental control. They have placed their chief emphasis upon the payment of financial benefits and upon the maintenance of lobbies for political protection.

A significant forecast of the future is perhaps to be found in the growing extent of organization among professional workers. In this field organizations now exist among the actors, technicians, draftsmen, musicians,

[10] In the spring of 1937 the Transport Workers' Union came into existence as a C.I.O. affiliate. It was formed from defections from three A.F. of L. groups: the Machinists, Street Railway Workers, and Teamsters, etc. It has grown very rapidly, has won several Labor Board elections and has announced that it is determined to organize "everything on wheels," and has already nearly reached this goal in Greater New York.

teachers and newspaper men. The oldest and most powerful of these is the Musicians which has been able to hold its membership of about 100,000 in spite of the mechanization of music. The Associated Actors and Artistes was seriously undermined by the depression and by new forms of amusement but is now making inroads upon the moving picture and radio entertainment industries. The American Federation of Teachers, although primarily interested in the maintenance of academic freedom, has become increasingly concerned with salary reductions and unemployment among teachers, especially in the public schools, and is already moving toward the development of political and economic bargaining power. The Newspaper Guild, with its 1937 membership of 14,000, had organized more than one third of the reporters and editorial writers in the country and has recently begun to organize office workers in the newspaper industry. The strategic importance of their alliance with the labor movement has already made itself felt in several successful strikes. The Guild is increasingly performing publicity and intelligence functions for labor and is receiving in return the active support of other organizations in strike actions. The recent decision of the Supreme Court upholding the applicability of the Wagner Act to the Associated Press has greatly increased the prestige of the Guild. In addition to the organizations named, several less pretentious organizations on a local basis have made their appearance among hospital, laboratory and other institutional attendants. Most of these organizations are federal labor locals attached directly to the A.F. of L. Only the Newspaper Guild and the Technicians' Union are affiliated with the C.I.O., although the American Federation of Teachers has declared its sympathy with the committee's objectives. [11]

In summary of the material in this chapter and in the

[11] In its August, 1937, convention, the Teachers' Union, after a bitter fight, referred the matter of C.I.O. affiliation to a vote of the membership. There were indications on several test votes that a pro-C.I.O. motion could have been carried by a very narrow margin.

appendix, it may be said, first, that the C.I.O. has successfully established itself in the extractive, power-producing
and durable goods industries. With the exception of the
coal industry this has never before been accomplished. The
importance of the achievement can scarcely be overestimated. Second, the C.I.O. is solidly entrenched in the
clothing industries and is making rapid inroads in textiles
and shoes. Third, the A.F. of L. maintains a position of
dwindling importance in the building and machine trades.
The policies and leadership of these unions are not in-
dicative of a brilliant career in the immediate future.
Fourth, there remains within the A.F. of L. a large number of small unions of a craft or semicraft variety which
will survive as long as the skills upon which they are based
persist. Fifth, in transport and communications, although
the A.F. of L. still retains a position of importance, insurgent movements among taxidrivers and workers in water
transport, street railways and busses have launched the
C.I.O. in these fields. Sixth, nonaffiliated unions remain
important on the railroads and in the postal services.
Seventh, there are signs of increasing union consciousness
among the professional,[12] clerical,[13] personal service and
agricultural workers though at present these fields remain
practically untouched. Finally, the split between the C.I.O.
and the A.F. of L. will involve important losses in unity.
These, however, will not offset either the strategic importance of the position which the C.I.O. now occupies

[12] Two A.F. of L. affiliates in the field of government service, the American Federation of State, County, and Municipal Employees, and the American Federation of Government Employees split with the A.F. of L. in the
summer of 1937 and brought several important locals into two new unions
affiliated with the C.I.O.

[13] After several years of conflict between a rank and file group and
the officers of the Retail Clerks' International Protective Association in
which the rank and file charged their officers with conniving at racketeering, the group split away in May, 1937, to form the United Retail Employees of America, affiliated with the C.I.O. An active organizing campaign
is already under way. In November, 1937, this union reported 40,000
members.

in the center of American industrial society or the renewed vigor which it has contributed to the American labor movement.[14]

[14] In addition to the members which the Machinists (A.F. of L.) lost to the Transport Workers' Union (C.I.O.), they have also recently lost 15,000 members to the United Electrical and Radio Workers. The A.F. of L. has also lost blocks of federal labor locals among optical, office and distillery workers. By November, 1937, the C.I.O. had established 48 regional and 10 subregional headquarters and secured the direct affiliation of 600 local unions.

CHAPTER VII

The Business Policies of Labor

IT has become clear during the preceding chapters that the tradition of American business and finance is one of intense opposition to organized labor. There have been business enterprises which have welcomed labor organizations. There have been others which have allowed unionism a prolonged tolerance. And there have been still others which have bowed to the inevitable and have bided their time for a favorable opportunity to turn the tables. But the great majority of industrialists have used every available means of fighting unionism to the last contestable ditch. That very inquisitive (and highly useful) Man from Mars might appropriately ask what the policies of unionism have been which have provoked such a determined and sanguinary contest. From the replies which would at once be forthcoming, he would learn, among other things, that labor organizations almost invariably press for increases in wage rates, reductions in working hours and improvement in working conditions. He would infer from the tone of the reply that these demands were inimical to the interests of management and even the workers themselves and, therefore, that the opposition of ownership to unionism was a reasonable and necessary attitude.

Not being conditioned by the prevailing beliefs in earthly managerial circles, the Man from Mars might, however, place a query after the conclusion that unionism's business policies and the interests of ownership are invariably in conflict. Being of an inquiring turn of mind, he might undertake an examination of the business policies which unions actually do pursue. If he did so he might find: First, that many of unionism's business policies provide a stability in industry which would not otherwise exist; second, that higher wage rates, shorter hours and better conditions can actually decrease costs of production; third, that in other instances improvements in these respects may come from the pocket of the consumer rather than the owner; fourth, that the monopolistic or extortionist policies of some unions bear a close resemblance to similar policies practiced in more respectable circles; fifth, that although union policies may be inimical to the interests of ownership, they are not to those of the community as a whole; and finally, that some union practices are disastrous to everybody including, in the long run, the union itself.

The business policies of unionism are focused upon the act of collective bargaining and the embodiment of the conclusions of this bargain in a contract or trade agreement. The demand for collective bargaining is based upon the assertion that in modern industry there is no bargaining at all unless workers engage in joint action. Otherwise all that happens is that the employer posts a wage scale which labor is "free" to accept or reject. Except in very small businesses the worker no longer discusses the wages or conditions of his labor with an employer. Where bargaining actually does take place, the bargaining power of the individual worker is unequal to that of the employer. This is partly because the worker's economic reserves, information of alternative opportunity and bargaining skill are likely to be less than those of his employer, but chiefly because the worker in competitive industry is the final absorbent of all of the shocks of competition. In textiles and clothing, for example, prices are likely to be determined at the retail end of the process. Large department stores agree upon prices above which they will not go in bidding for clothing and textiles. Middlemen are forced to accept these prices and in turn press down the prices which they pay to manufacturers or contractors. Manufacturers then squeeze their pay rolls by posting wage reductions which the worker is "free" to accept or reject. The worker, however, has no one to squeeze. Rejection of the offer by an individual workman is futile if there is always another who will underbid his fellow available to take his place. The weakest worker sets the wage by appearing on the scene when other workers exercise their "freedom" to reject the employer's offer. This may not be the end of the process if one employer, less efficient than the others, is forced to reduce his wages in order to remain in competition. His competitors, in order to retain their advantage, again reduce their wages and the cycle is renewed. Under these conditions, frequently characteristic of the clothing, neckware, cleaning and dyeing, laundry, textile, soft coal, minor fabricated metal and novelty industries, the workers' constitutional freedom from involuntary servitude becomes a subject for interesting philosophical speculation.

The basic business principle of unionism is the reversal of the process of competition by establishing a "standard rate" or minimum wage below which employment shall not be allowed. The minimum wage may be based upon piece rates, hourly rates or occasionally upon a monthly or yearly salary. There may be differentials above it based upon skill or other scarcity factors, length of service, or even marital status and number of children. The wage provisions of a craft union trade agreement are likely to be very simple since only one or two types of labor are involved. An industrial union contract, on the contrary, may be a very complicated document running into scores of pages providing separate wage rates for the dozens of occupations in and around a plant. As industrial unionism develops, it is likely that the spread between wage rates will be reduced by the frequently observed tendency of a minimum wage to become a maximum, and because present wage structures in some industries are meaninglessly overcomplicated.[1] This, however, is not an inevitable development. The splitting up of a large industrial local into occupational subdivisions may provide sufficient separation of interests to perpetuate wage differentials according to degrees of skill or other criteria.

The minimum wage provided in a trade agreement may apply only to one job, shop or plant, or it may apply to an entire area or industry. In industries such as building, in which there is little competition between localities, a union can successfully apply a minimum wage policy on a local basis. This is also true to a lesser extent of semi-monopoly industries, although the manager may transfer production from a high wage to a low wage area. In competitive industries it is imperative that minimum wage agreements extend over most of the industry. Otherwise the nonunion areas undercut the unionized sections and destroy the union. Until recently there have been very few industry-wide minimum wage agreements. This has partly been due to short-sighted union policy, but has chiefly resulted from the utter impossibility of organizing an entire industry at once, especially in the low-wage sections most in need of it. This is the obvious significance of the present effort of the C.I.O. to organize the textile industry upon a nation-wide basis. It is also the significance of that section of the Wagner Labor Relations Act which empowers the Board to designate a whole industry as an appropriate bargaining unit if a majority of the workers in that industry elect to be represented by a labor organization.

The minimum-wage policy of the labor movement is not based solely upon the demand that a competitive bottom shall be established for the protection of the worker. It is also recognized that the setting of minimum

[1] Different rates of pay based upon supposed differences in skill or productivity often remain in force long after changing methods of production have rendered the differentials meaningless.

wages will eliminate some workers from employment and some plants from production. The theory back of this is that if workers are not capable of earning the standard rate, they should be classed as unemployable rather than unemployed and should be cared for by appropriate social institutions: pensions for the aged, schools for the young, vocational rehabilitation for physical defectives, and custody or care for the morally and mentally deficient. It is also recognized that if the standard rate can be enforced so that a living wage for the family is provided, many of those who are displaced will no longer find it necessary to work. The grandparents may return to the rocking chair and the children to the playground. With respect to the elimination of the relatively inefficient plants, shops and mines, it is admitted that this results in temporary unemployment of both labor and capital. By driving the inefficient units out of existence, however, production is concentrated in the superior units. Their volume of output is increased, unit costs are decreased and their sales rise. The workers displaced from the inefficient plants are replaced at the higher wage rate through the expanded operations of the more efficient producers. The enforcement of a rising minimum wage becomes, therefore, a matter of driving an industry toward a higher level of efficiency. This policy is bitterly resisted by the less efficient producers, but may actually be welcomed by the more efficient.

The minimum wage policy of the labor movement is defended not only as a means of increasing the productivity of a whole industry, but also as a means of reducing costs within a particular plant. Workers' self-interest has long led them to believe that high wage rates do not necessarily mean high production costs. It is contended that high wage rates will compel more efficient organization of the plant, will increase the physical efficiency of the worker, improve his attitude toward management and thus reduce the extent of conscious and unconscious sabotage, industrial disputes and high rates of labor turnover. In all of these ways costs may be reduced more than enough to offset the increase in wage rates imposed by the union. The result may be that employment is actually greater at the high wage rate than at the previous level. Some unions have pressed this policy to the point of introducing "efficiency" systems, as in the Naumkeag Steam Cotton Co., or undertaking the complete reorganization of high cost plants in order to enable them to remain in competition while granting union conditions of employment.[2]

The enforcement of a minimum "living" wage is also defended by labor leaders even if it results in increased prices to the consumer. The contention in this instance is that although the public has to pay higher prices for textiles, clothing, safety pins, coal, and sugar beets, other hidden expenses are reduced. Low wage industries, it is held, are actually being subsidized by formal or informal public relief, wholesale theft from freight cars, fruit stands and so on, bootlegging, extortion of various sorts, prostitution, hospitalization and public health expenses attributable to malnutrition, the gradual physical deterioration of whole classes of people and the losses involved in industrial disputes. The public, as consumer, may pay more for its goods if a minimum wage is established, but the public may thereby escape the expenses of social pathology.

During the last fifteen years, American management has been greatly influenced by a "high wage philosophy" similar in most respects to the defense given by labor for its minimum wage policy. Management's "high wage philosophy," however, has in many instances been pure publicity material. In many industries it has not been accepted even as publicity material, and in still others it has been entirely inapplicable because common action among

[2] The Amalgamated Clothing Workers ran a bankrupt clothing factory in Milwaukee from 1929 to 1932.

producers has been impossible to achieve. The basic wage policy of the labor movement is to compel the adoption of standardized minimum wages as more than mere advertising and to make possible their application in competitive industries in which producers are unable and, perhaps, unwilling to apply them.

The description of union wage policy thus far has applied primarily to competitive industries. Increasingly, however, union leaders are compelled to direct their attention toward the wage problems raised by the widespread existence of partial and complete monopoly in American industry. Modified competition, running all the way from the gentleman's agreement to the almost complete monopoly of the American Aluminum Company, causes some degree of restriction of output and the maintenance of higher prices than would exist under free competition. Monopoly profits and reduced real wages are the result. This condition might be remedied by stringent governmental regulation of prices, but the labor movement has not thus far emphasized this possibility. Labor's primary policy in this respect has been an effort to recapture monopoly profits by driving wages up in the industries in which such profits appear. Until the present time the strength of the labor movement has been far from sufficient to effect the recapture of profits in the industries in which modified competition is most apparent. As its strength increases, however, it may confidently be expected that this policy will be pressed. If the prices of goods sold under modified competition are not increased equally with advances in labor costs, the interests of workers and managers come in conflict at this point, since the effect of such wage increases is to decrease monopoly profits and enlarge workers' incomes. In the recent steel wage increases, however, prices were raised by more than the amount of the wage increase. To the extent that this is the result of the drive for higher wages in monopoly and semimonopoly industries, labor will be forced to turn to politics to secure the degree of price regulation necessary to insure rising real wages.

With respect to the method of wage payment, American trade unions have no uniform policy. In some industries, such as cotton textiles, the speed of machines has been gradually increased by management without effective opposition from labor. If time rates are paid, the gains from speed-up go to ownership or perhaps to the consumer. If piece rates are used, the gains go to labor. In this type of industry, therefore, unions are likely to demand piece-rate payment. In other industries workers have had long experience with managerial policies of reducing piece rates as the workers increase their speed, with the result that the workers' income remains constant although their effort is much increased. Piece rates, under such conditions, cease to be an incentive to individual efficiency and become a refined method of exploitation. Such experience is likely to lead to a demand that straight time rates be paid, at least until the union is sufficiently strong to assure its members that reductions in piece rates will not be made if workers' incomes are sharply increased by extra effort.

The remaining wage policies of American unions deal with women's wages and overtime payments. The traditional union demand for equal pay for equal work is in part based upon abstract conceptions of justice as between men and women, but springs fundamentally from more practical considerations. If women do not receive wages equal to men for the same amount of work, employers may, by substituting women for men, undercut the standard rate for men and nullify the basic business principle of unionism. Unions' demands for time-and-a-quarter, time-and-a-half and, in rare instances, double-time for overtime rest in part upon the simple desire to increase the worker's weekly income, but also represent an attempt to force employers to regularize production sufficiently to render overtime work unnecessary. Back of this is the desire, first, to distribute work among as many people as possible; second, to protect union members as human beings from the disturbance to social relations which results from irregular hours of work.

The second major business policy of the labor movement has been to shorten hours of work. During the last hundred years American trade unions have progressively demanded first the ten-hour day, then the eight-hour day, then the forty-five- and forty-hour week, and now the thirty-five- and even thirty-hour week. Unions have worked for shorter hours both with and without compensatory wage increases. When reduction of hours has been secured without compensating wage increases, however, unions have subsequently made efforts to secure wage increases as soon as conditions were favorable. Both economic and social considerations lie back of the persistent effort to reduce the hours of labor. There is usually an assumption that the productivity of industry has increased without proportional gain to the worker; that is, that cost reductions have not been followed by wage increases or by lowered prices, with the result that profits have been increased. Under these conditions union leaders are faced with a choice of policies. They may elect to drive for price reductions so that the workers may gain in company with other consumers by the increased output of goods. They may determine to secure wage increases commensurate with the cost reduction so that the workers gain as wage receivers. Or they may decide to try for reduction of hours at the same weekly income with the result that the worker consumes no more than before but does less work because of the improvement in methods of production.

Driving down prices is usually not possible for labor leaders except through devious political channels. Increasing weekly wages without reduction of hours has been widely sponsored by labor leaders in the past. A decrease in weekly hours at the same weekly income is at present being adopted with increasing frequency as a means of alleviating technological unemployment. To the extent that labor successfully imposes this policy upon industry, the effect of technological improvements is to provide greater leisure for workers rather than lower prices for consumers or higher profits for producers. Although both lower prices for consumers and higher profits for producers may eventually result in the replacement of workers displaced by technological change, organized labor is becoming more and more conscious of the fact that this replacement may not take place at all, or may occur only after serious suffering by workers. Labor leaders are therefore adopting a policy of pressing for reductions in hours on the assumption that the certainty of greater leisure for workers is better than the possibility that workers will eventually gain as consumers through lower prices.

Another economic consideration bearing on union policy has been the belief that reduction of working hours might be a cause as well as a result of reductions in the cost of production. Workers have long felt what scientific management has begun to disclose, that more goods may actually be turned out on a forty- rather than a sixty-hour week basis, if a sufficiently long period is taken into account. Accumulated fatigue reduces speed and causes spoilage of goods, high accident rates, rapid labor turnover, tendencies toward exhausting debauches, and acute industrial unrest. All of these are expensive to management and the community. The reduction of working hours may decrease these expenses more than enough to offset proportionally higher wage rates. Each occupation in an industry has its saturation point under given conditions of production below which hours may not be reduced without decreasing output. Until this saturation point is reached, management and labor may march together. Union leaders have learned by experience, however, that intense pressure from a well-organized labor group is very often necessary to compel attention to this matter and that labor's interests may demand reduction of hours below the point which management (attending closely to its production costs) is willing to go.

Labor looks at hours not only from the viewpoint of monthly costs of production, but from the viewpoint of the lifetime cost of production. Here the question of the hours of work becomes inseparable from that of the speed of work. A nine-hour day and a high speed of work may bring both labor and management greater incomes over a ten-year period than a seven-hour day and a lesser speed of work. But the worker is interested in what happens to him at the end of the ten-year period, while management may no longer be greatly concerned with that problem. If at the end of the ten years the worker is incapable of maintaining the required speed and hours of work he is eliminated from industry and becomes in some measure a burden upon his family or his community. Unions are increasingly interested in this aspect of modern industry. They demand that the speed and hours of labor be further reduced. Management cannot be expected to concede this demand willingly if it is attending solely to its own economic interests. Unions use force to secure the reduction, however, and appeal to their community for support on the ground that the extra cost may come from the profits of ownership and management or out of the raised price of the product. If the increased cost is added to the price of the product, the community pays as consumer but is spared the expense of supporting the worker who is unable any longer to support himself. This argument is usually documented by statistics showing the falling "age deadline" in industry and the relatively high proportion of unemployment in the higher age group.

The worker and the labor leader also look at the hours of labor from a social point of view. This is often in conflict with the desires of management. In a recent strike the plant manager was vehemently protesting that a demand for a 3.30 P.M. quitting time would hamstring the company during the rush season. The strike leader's reply, "We guys wanta play golf like youse guys," expressed a viewpoint which was strictly noneconomic. It indicated a growing conviction among organized workers that labor has produced goods in mass, and now needs time in which to consume them. As this demand is presented with increasing force and grammatical accuracy, the National Association of Manufacturers may experience a twinge of nostalgia for the days before the "American Way of Life" came to include eighteen holes of golf before dinner.

After wages and hours come "conditions." Few trade agreements are signed without the inclusion of clauses referring to the circumstances under which work shall be done. It is these "conditions" which frequently arouse the bitterest opposition from management. Although increases in wages and decreases in hours may excite the hostility of management because of the effect of these changes on income, the imposition of "conditions" may stimulate even more hostility because of the effect of these regulations upon the power of management to do as it wishes with its property.

The most important traditional item under "conditions" has been the imposition of policies leading toward restriction of output. There are at least three possible motives for such policies: to restrict quantity of production in order to preserve its quality; to "make the job last" and thus extend the period of employment; and to prevent exploitation of the worker through excessive speed. Although these three motives are often blended together, it is possible to discuss them separately. The first motive, maintenance of quality, can usually be regarded as window dressing for the other two. In operations requiring skill and precision, nevertheless, workers may take a greater interest than the management in the quality of the product. The æsthetic satisfactions of craftsmanship have not been entirely destroyed by modern machinery. Labor is closer to these satisfactions than employers and is not under the same compulsions to reduce costs. Here, therefore, is a possible, but not important, source of conflict.

Back of the demand for quality output, especially in nonmechanical industries, lies the desire to make the job last by spreading it out thin. Fear of unemployment rather than laziness is the basic reason for this form of restriction. Wherever fear of unemployment is strong there are dual and opposed attitudes on the part of labor. The individualistic attitude is to seek favor with the employer by working hard, with the expectation that the most willing workers will not be laid off. The group attitude is to get together on a policy of taking it easy so that everyone's employment may last longer. "Going slow" or "ca'canny" is not necessarily a product of unionism. Frequently it is the result of a common understanding or custom among otherwise unorganized workers. The gospel spreads easily. "Take it easy, kid, you'll work yourself right out of this job." "What's the hurry, brother, there's no need to rush." "Say you, there's work enough here for all of us if we don't kill the job." This attitude has its parallel in the common pleasure attending a snowstorm because of the employment it provides, or the belief that wasteful and useless forms of industry should not be eliminated because of the unemployment which would result. Fear of unemployment permeates governmental and managerial circles as well, and results in overstaffed bureaus and the multiplication of the ranks of vice-presidents. In public policy it takes the form of make-work projects, even if these projects are socially useless.

Although fear of unemployment, rather than unionism,

lies behind labor's restriction of output, among some unions it is raised to the level of a conscious policy. Limitation of the number of bricks to be laid in one day by each worker, reduction in the size of the paintbrush to be used on union contracts, requiring the plumber to walk from his shop to his job are all familiar examples of restrictive policies. Resistance to the introduction of labor-saving machinery has also been a part of unionism's business program. These policies may be embodied in the trade agreement; they may be rules imposed by the union on its members; they may be made the subject of tacit understanding between employers and unions; or they may be informally adopted by members without action by the union.

Economists and businessmen have long protested against restriction of output as practiced by labor. They have pointed out that restriction of production increases costs and prices, reduces sales and eventually decreases employment. This argument, advanced by relatively comfortable people who are not continuously faced with the immediate prospect of destitution, has had little effect upon the practices of either organized or unorganized labor. A job in the hand has always seemed more attractive than two jobs in the future. The inexorable forward march of machinery, however, has had a profound effect upon the power of unions to enforce restrictive practices. The adoption of semiautomatic machinery, precision tools, assembly lines and minute subdivision of tasks has taken away from the individual worker the control over the speed of his work and given it to an efficiency engineer. Resistance to the introduction of labor-saving machinery has been rendered futile by the immense power back of the drive toward mechanization. Unions resisting mechanization have fallen by the wayside just as producers opposing new methods have lost the race. Other unions have successfully made arrangements for the gradual introduction of labor-displacing machinery and for the payment of dismissal wages to the workers who have been eliminated. In the occupations, however, in which the worker still retains some individual control over the speed of his work, it may be expected that both the organized and unorganized will discount the uncertainties of the future by extending the certainties of the present. This may involve the progressive decline of the unions in these areas until they can provide security for their members in other ways.

In the mass production industries in which the dozen or more major industrial unions now operate, restriction of output to make the worker's job last tends to pass over into restriction of output to make the worker's life last. This point has already been discussed in connection with unions' demands for reduction of hours. With the expansion of a union to the extent of covering a whole industry comes a breadth of vision on the part of the union leader which makes unlikely the adoption of policies based upon the make-work doctrine. This same breadth of vision, however, forces the union leader to consider the working lifetime of the union's members rather than the length of a particular job. The great power of industrial unionism also places the efficiency engineer within the control of the union. The result may frequently be, as previously pointed out, that unions demand a reduction in the speed of production (even if it results in increased costs and prices) in order to extend the working lifetime of the union's members. The union justifies this policy on the ground that in the long run relief and other disguised expenses of the public will be reduced and the higher price of the product thus need not cause a decrease in sales and employment. The community, therefore, rather than the individual worker, is forced to face the problem in its long-run aspects. The major industrial unions, in the industries in which the speed-up has proceeded so far that it has become a subject for popular moving picture presentation, are therefore insisting that the speed of production be regulated either by the trade agreement or by conference between union leaders and company engineers.

Insistence on regulation of the speed of production is an interference with the traditional prerogatives of management which is likely to be especially irritating in the industries to which unionism is a stranger. It represents an encroachment upon the control over property which may not, in the long run, decrease the income from property, but which may be stiffly resisted because of the involved transfer of power from managers to union leaders. It is, nevertheless, an encroachment which will be insisted upon with increasing determination as the power of industrial unionism advances.

Additional matters often contained in a trade agreement come under the head of "job control." These include restrictions upon the right of the employer to hire and fire, provisions for seniority in promotions and layoffs, rest periods, safe and sanitary working conditions and joint control of shop discipline and the settlement of grievances. In all these respects a union's demands represent encroachments upon the absolute power of the management which may not affect income, but which cut across traditional concepts of property rights. It is perfectly possible that the owner's income may actually be increased by putting these matters within the control of the union. Employers may, nevertheless, resist with great determination any union policy which limits the power flowing from the ownership or management of the means of production.

Restrictions upon the right to hire and fire are primarily organizing rather than business policies. Restriction may take the form of an agreement to give union members preference in hiring, or to hire none but union members. When restrictions are placed upon the employer's right to discharge, the chief object is to prevent the employer from weakening the union by weeding out its members. As employers gradually come to accept the presence of unions in their plants, this aspect of the matter becomes less important. Emphasis then shifts to the protection of workers from arbitrary action by foremen and others. It is often arranged that the worker shall have the right to appeal for review to the union and to higher management authorities. In some cases provision is made for the regular use of outside arbitration.

Unions have very generally adopted the principle that those workers with the longest period of employment in an industry should be the last to be laid off, the first to be taken on, and should have preference over others with equal ability in the granting of promotion. From the viewpoint of abstract justice, there is perhaps no reason why seniority, rather than marital status, number of children or the color of the hair should be adopted as the criterion of judgment. What is more important than abstract justice is that there be a generally understood rule by which the game is played. Many employers have long since adopted this rule, except where great differences in ability make it inapplicable. Upon this point, therefore, there should be no quarrel between unions and management. Nevertheless, some companies which publicly announce the adoption of the seniority principle as a basis for wage increases have actually avoided the application of this principle by transferring workers from one shop to another, or by discharging and rehiring them with the result that senior workers become "new" workers as far as eligibility for wage increases is concerned. The very rapid rate of labor turnover in Midwestern industrial areas is in part explained by the wholesale evasion of seniority policies by nonunion industries. The task of the union is to enforce the actual application of the seniority principle and make it more than a publicity stunt.

Most modern trade agreements contain some provision for the orderly settlement of grievances through the "shop steward" system. In each shop or appropriate production

Courtesy of Union News Service

"The Business Policies of Labor"

unit the union elects a steward to whom grievances are reported. The steward then takes up the matter with the proper authority and an effort to secure an amicable settlement is made. Many such grievances are relatively trivial in nature but become important sources of unrest if they are allowed to accumulate. It is usually provided that every possible means of arbitration be exhausted before resort is had to strike action. In the automobile industry, since the settlement of the General Motors strike, there have been numerous short sit-downs or walk-outs in spite of the no-strike agreement. This has been the result, in large part, of the unfamiliarity of both workers and management with the shop steward system. If intelligent self-interest is pursued by both sides, increasing experience with this system may easily dispose of the majority of petty industrial injustices, irritations and their consequent wastes.

In almost all the matters included under the head of job control, there is no logical reason why management, in pursuing its own economic interests, should not protect the worker as adequately as a union. The expense of dealing intelligently with hiring and firing, promotions and layoffs, discipline and the disposition of grievances is much less in the long run than the expenses of failing to deal adequately with these matters. Nevertheless, American management, with relatively few exceptions, has failed to realize its opportunities in this respect. Management has thus far been primarily concerned with the mechanical aspects of production, and with sales and financial policies to the exclusion of the problem of human relations in industry. When management has faced the question of human relations it has done so through personnel management devices and through employee representation schemes. Personnel management is still considered something of a paternalistic luxury to be dispensed with in times of depression, or, like employee representation, to be perverted into a coercive agent of management. Employee representation, instead of being confined to its legitimate function as a reliable and dignified channel of communication between management and workers in matters of mutual interest, has usually been disguised as a collective bargaining agency although, as previously indicated, it has no bargaining power until it develops the attributes of independent unionism. This has resulted in destroying the confidence of workers and, to a large extent, of the public in any personnel or representation device sponsored by management. Even when management is honest and intelligent in its industrial relations, however, there are inherent defects in placing the control over these affairs in the hands of employees of the company. Company-paid employee representatives may feel impelled to minimize the grievances presented to them and fail to press the workers' claims as forcefully as is necessary for complete elimination of the source of trouble. Personnel managers, feeling that their job depends upon soft-pedaling trouble, may elect to cover up the sources of disturbance rather than to remove the causes. Evidence in support of the existence of this tendency may be found in the genuine astonishment and bitterness displayed by some of the higher executives in industry when faced by strikes or other disturbances in their plants. Frequently these executives, as well as being preoccupied with other things, have been prevented from learning the real state of affairs by the muffling activities of their own personnel officers.[3]

On the other hand, the self-interest of the union's stewards compels them to press grievance claims as forcefully as possible. Sources of trouble are thereby promptly

[3] In this connection the following sentence from a letter by a tear gas salesman to his company is interesting. "The Buick wanted this material [$170.00 worth of tear gas equipment] delivered personally *to their plant protection department to circumvent the receiving department*, so I took it up myself Wednesday." (Author's italics.) The author has also witnessed the sincere amazement and disbelief of a prominent industrialist when told that his company had recently bought a large shipment of tear gas.

aired and strong pressure for action applied. No mechanical engineer would think of muffling a continuous screech emitted by a valuable piece of machinery. He not only applies oil to eliminate the cause of the screech, but he develops instruments of stethoscopic precision to anticipate causes of trouble. He does this because the company owns the machinery and its loss is obviously expensive. When human machinery begins to protest, company unions smother its manifestations and personnel managers, in fear for their jobs, report that all is well. Sooner or later an expensive explosion takes place, and the higher executives are disturbed or infuriated. The task of a union is to magnify the irritations of human relations in industry as a microscope magnifies the imperfections of a cylinder. The self-interest of workers and their own representatives can be counted upon as a better loud-speaker in this respect than the remote good will of company executives. As long as management continues to regard unions as "professional troublemakers," trouble in industry will persist. When unions come to be regarded as magnifiers, and therefore as anticipators of trouble, this source of conflict in industry may be removed. There is a distinct possibility, of course, that labor's stewards will escape from the control of their consituencies and will pursue their self-interest along lines already perfected by some personnel managers, many tear gas salesmen, most spy agencies and all other racketeering sellers of "protection." [4] It is also possible that management may itself develop superior stethoscopes for industrial trouble than unionism provides. When and where either of these developments takes place, unionism will have lost one of its business functions and, therefore, one of its most powerful appeals to the industrial worker.

---

[4] There have been occasional instances in which union leaders, in return for favors from the management, have used their power to suppress manifestations of unrest among workers. Unionism may thus be perverted, just as personnel management has frequently been used for the suppression of unrest rather than the removal of its causes.

The major items likely to appear in a trade agreement are, therefore, the imposition of a minimum wage over as large an area of the industry as possible; the setting up of wage differentials upon the basis of seniority, experience, skill or other scarcity factors; equal pay for equal work without regard to sex; overtime rates for overtime work; shorter hours, and rest periods; restriction of output to preserve quality, spread the work, or prevent exploitation of the worker through excessive speed; and job control in hiring and firing, promotions, layoffs, shop discipline and the handling of grievances.

The actual process of reaching an agreement may be preceded by a strike. It may come as the culmination of a peaceful organizing campaign. Or it may be simply the renewal of an old agreement which has expired. In some unions bargaining is carried on by a very few representatives of the union who have had power to act conferred upon them. In others, elaborate systems of representation are devised for the preservation of democracy in the bargaining process, and the agreement must be referred to union members before acceptance is assured. When large numbers representing both sides are present the actual details of the contract must be worked out by a series of subcommittees constantly referring back to the larger group for authority to proceed. Modern unions make a practice of coming to bargaining conferences prepared with a wealth of detail about every aspect of the industry's ability to meet the union's demands.

The primary purpose of the written document itself is to act as a memorandum in order that misunderstandings shall not arise. Trade agreements are nowadays considered enforceable in the courts upon both parties to the agreement. Recent spectacular examples of the enforceability of trade agreements are provided by the case of the Dyer's Federation in northern New Jersey upon whose 20,000 members individual injunctions were served enjoining the union from going on strike in violation of a trade agreement; and by the case of a New York City employer who was compelled by a court order to resume production in New York City after he had violated a trade agreement binding him to remain within the five-cent fare limit. The primary purpose of a trade agreement is not, however, to compel either employers or unions by court action to abide by their word against their will. Even if courts do uphold trade agreements, it is difficult to produce goods efficiently in the atmosphere of conflict which court enforcements engender. When employer and union have passed through the area of bitter conflict, the agreement becomes of importance chiefly as a memorandum. Refusal to sign an agreement, therefore, is likely to be an indication that attitudes of conflict remain predominant and that the party refusing to sign is biding its time for a renewal of hostilities, or, as in the case of the 1937 steel strike, is using this refusal as a means of provoking hostilities.

There is another form of union business activity which usually falls somewhat outside the field of the trade agreement. This activity is the limitation, rather than the expansion, of union membership. It is, therefore, the antithesis of the ordinary organizing policies of unionism. It may be achieved through trade agreements which limit the number of apprentices employed in a given production unit, but it is more likely to be accomplished by the adoption of a "closed-union" policy in conjunction with the closed shop. In this respect the closed shop ceases to be an organizing device designed to compel nonunion workers to support union policies, and becomes a method of limiting employment to those workers fortunate enough to be in the union at the time of the adoption of the closed-union policy.

Of the 160 or so national unions in existence, 46 impose admission requirements which may be used to curtail the supply of labor in their trades. These requirements, covering about 1,100,000 union members, all refer to the degree of skill necessary for admission to the unions in question. Twenty-two unions, covering 584,000 members, require journeyman status before union membership is allowed. Among these the Carpenters, Painters, Plumbers, and Typographical Workers account for more than four fifths of the total. Ten unions, covering 387,000 workers, require experience varying from thirty days to two years. Among these unions the Electrical Workers and the Railroad Conductors, Clerks, and Firemen account for more than nine tenths of the total. Eight unions, covering 125,000 members, require an examination or demonstration of competence. The Bricklayers, Sheet Metal Workers, and Stage Employees account for five sixths of the total membership in this group. Six unions, covering 13,-800 members, require some form of governmental license. From a survey of the requirements of these unions, some conclusions follow: First, not more than one fifth of the present membership of organized labor is affected by membership requirements laid down by the national unions. No important industrial union is included in this group. Second, these requirements are imposed in occupations calling for a considerable degree of skill or responsibility. Third, if taken literally, none of the restrictions are out of accord with the degree of skill required in the trade in question.

These admission requirements of the national unions may not, however, be taken at their face value. There is nothing to prevent the local unions from interpreting these restrictions so severely as to form a barrier to entrance far more formidable than can be required to provide necessary skill. In addition, there is usually nothing to prevent the local unions from setting up further obstacles to membership in the form of high initiation fees or dues, or simply by "closing" the union's "books." When these practices are used, motives other than the assurance of necessary skill are clearly dominant. Some unions refuse to take on additional members until those already in the union are fully employed. Many locals of the Amalgamated Clothing Workers, for example, have adopted this policy along with innumerable locals in the craft union group. The explanation offered by local union officers is that they wish to make sure that those who have already paid dues for some time have preference in employment, and that they see no justice in taking the dues of new members if there is no possibility of their securing jobs.

The honesty of this explanation depends largely upon the wages and hours which the union has established in the shop or plant in question. If the conditions established can be justified by the union as providing a competitive bottom to the industry, as actually decreasing labor costs, as passing on to the consumer costs he would otherwise bear in a disguised form, or as extraction of monopoly profits from the employer, then the explanation given for this form of membership restriction may be precisely that offered by the local union officer. The suspicion is strong, however, that there are behind this form of exclusion motives other than those stated. Unions wishing to avoid this suspicion might easily do so by adopting a regulation that members of longer standing receive preference in employment and that if other workers actually want to join the union and pay the fees in spite of their poor chances of employment, there is nothing to prevent them.

The usual motive behind a policy of exclusion is one of reaping the advantages of monopoly. It is extremely difficult to draw a sharp line between monopolistic union policies, and those which are designed to stabilize industry, reduce long-run labor costs, or pass on to the consumer costs which the public would otherwise bear in other forms. As indicated above, the stabilization of an industry or the setting of a minimum living wage is very likely to result in the displacement of some workers. This is also a characteristic result of monopolistic policies. The two programs tend to shade imperceptibly into each other. At some point in this shading of policies, however, it becomes obvious enough that the objective of a union is the establishment of so great a degree of scarcity of labor of a particular type that a few workers gain at the expense of others.

The pursuit of clearly monopolistic policies by unions takes a variety of forms. Closing of the books and the setting of fantastically high initiation fees combined with the closed shop establish a monopoly which makes possible the exaction of high wage rates. The high wages may come out of the pocket of a monopoly producer but they are likely to come from the consumer in the form of higher prices. If prices are increased, the purchase of goods or services decreases (unless the demand is absolutely inelastic) and eventually unemployment of workers in the industry results. Nonunion workers suffer at the expense of the union workers. The consumer suffers either from decreased purchase of the goods in question or from decreased purchase of other goods.

There is little to distinguish this policy, as far as its effect upon the nonunion worker and the consumer is concerned, from burning Brazilian coffee, dumping bananas in the Gulf of Mexico, plowing under cotton and restricting the output of copper. In some instances, the monopoly becomes a two-sided affair in which the union and the employer collaborate in restricting employment and output at the expense of the consumer. In others, the union limits its membership to the number which can be employed at the established rate during the slack season and then issues "work-permits" to nonmembers during the rush season. The cost of work-permits amounts to a wage reduction for the nonunion members. The proceeds from this wage reduction redound to the advantage of the union members or their business agent rather than to the employer.

The long-run effects of monopolistic practices are likely to be more disastrous to the monopolist when practiced by labor than when practiced by management. The essence of monopoly is that the few gain at the expense of the many. The owners of the means of production, being relatively few, may successfully extort from the many. Labor, however, can exact only limited gains from the relatively few owners in modern society. Its chief hope lies in expansion rather than contraction of production. Obviously, organized labor as a whole cannot resort to monopolistic practices without extorting primarily from itself. Even in particular trades, the long-run effect of restriction of union membership is to drive the nonunion workers into competition with those in the union and thus provide the basis for ultimate disintegration of the organization. There is evidence that the decline in the power of the building trades unions has resulted from the adoption of restriction rather than expansion as a membership policy. There is little likelihood that the power of these unions will be restored until this policy, among others, is abandoned. It goes almost without saying that restriction of membership by the large industrial unions would be suicidal, that the whole basis of the drive toward industrial unionism is to move away from this exclusiveness and that, as the area occupied by both mass production and industrial unionism increases, the policy of membership exclusion will become even less important than it now is in the program of the labor movement.

From this summary survey of the business policies of unionism some conclusions may be drawn: First, the basic policy of unionism in competitive industries is the introducton of a minimum wage which protects the worker from becoming the butt of the competitive process, introduces an element of stability into the business, is likely to eliminate high cost producers and concentrate production in the more efficient units, may or may not displace workers from the industry, and renders the relatively unfit workers individually unemployable. Efficient employers may welcome this aspect of unionism if they attend only to their economic interests. Inefficient employers bitterly contest unionism on identical grounds. Second, the increases in wages, reductions in working hours and improvement of working conditions which unions demand may actually decrease rather than increase unit costs of production by raising the efficiency of the worker himself and by removing the causes of many disguised costs of production. The interests of workers, producers and the community are identical in this matter. Employers, however, are often led to this conclusion only after force applied by unions has demonstrated its accuracy. Employer resistance has therefore sprung from nonlogical sources, but has frequently been nonetheless determined. Third, the costs of meeting unionism's demands may actually be passed on to the consumer. In these instances the producers may not suffer from acquiescence in union policies, but the consumer has to pay more for his goods. The increased costs of goods, however, may be more than offset in the long run by the elimination of the sources of social pathology and its attendant expenses. Fourth, in the industries in which monopoly or modified competition prevails, labor's business program takes the form of an effort to recapture through higher wages and shorter hours the semimonopoly profits of ownership and management. In these instances the interests of labor and ownership are at odds, but the community may gain through the broader distribution of the proceeds of industry. Fifth, some unions themselves engage in monopolistic practices through restriction of output and membership. This is in part a response to fear of unemployment or excessive speed, but beyond a certain point becomes indistinguish-able from the restrictive program of some producers. Organized labor as a whole suffers from these policies and even particular labor groups find them eventually disastrous. Purely monopolistic policies become less important as industrial unionism advances. Finally, almost all union business policies encroach upon the traditional powers of ownership and management. For this reason managers often resist unionism even though the income to management and ownership may not be reduced by union policies. Conservative unionism, therefore, contains revolutionary implications in that it transfers power from ownership to labor and from management to the leaders of labor. It also directs the loyalties of workers toward a new set of social symbols. These loyalties are not exclusively founded upon matters of wages, hours and working conditions. Unions also minister to the worker's desire for security and dignity through welfare and educational programs which will be discussed in the following chapter.

CHAPTER VIII

The Benefit and Welfare Policies of Unionism

WHEN the New England mill girls of the 1840's discovered that the factory system cut them off from a way of life which they cherished, they established Sewing Circles and Mutual Improvement Societies in the factory boardinghouses. When early industrialism added insecurity to poverty, workers organized Burial Societies to exorcise the specter of the potter's field. When the Knights of Labor discovered in a Brooklyn carpet factory that "the demoralization of young women . . . [was] one of the shocking results of modern industry," they led a strike "for the protection of [the girls'] honor against the assaults of the villains in charge of the factory."

A union leader, traveling through North Carolina three years after a disastrous strike, was recognized by a group of former union members. They begged her to take them for a picnic, relight their old campfire, lead them in workers' songs and revive the stories of former struggles. An organizer, standing in front of a steel-fenced factory with doors like a county jail, accosts worker No. 2,301 who has just been released from the assembly line, and says "Come on, pal, join the union and hold your head up. You'll feel like you're a free man. We'll kick the lousy spies the hell outa here. You belong, *brother*, we're for you." A group of girls in a clock factory hear that the union can keep the foreman from bursting unexpectedly into the women's restroom and soliciting their favors after hours. . . . "Jeeze, kids, let's join. We can tell them bums where to head in."

The tune of *My Bonnie Lies Over the Ocean* is wafted from the windows of the Rotary Room in the Middlesex

Hotel and on a near-by picket line the same tune acts as a vehicle for "Soo-oop, soo-oop, they gave me a bow-wol of soo-oo-oop!" In one classroom of the local college a member of the economics department tells a group of bankers that their business has become a profession and that service, in the long run, means profits. In another room in the same building, a younger member of the department tells a group of union leaders that their courage and altruism will bear fruit in a better society. Up on the hill the Junior Debs are having a contract bridge game, while across the railroad tracks Local 613 is putting on a square dance and "*somebody* spiked the punch." Three girls in the Y. W. C. A. Industrial Girls' Club have been to a summer school for workers. They know the initials of several unions by heart and can rattle off A.C.W., I.L.G.W.U., U.T.W. and T.W.O.C. with *savoir-faire*. In the back room of a union bakery, one old-timer says to another, "Do you remember the time in the winter of '19 when the flatfeet had us cornered in the angle by the river and we let them charge us and ducked at the last minute and they all fell in. Jeeze, that was funny. They couldn't decide whether to climb ashore or to swim after their hats which was floating downstream at a dollar and a half apiece."

THE rise of modern industry has brought with it great changes in social institutions, symbols, loyalties and beliefs. The unequal rate of change in different parts of the country, the lag of social institutions behind economic change, and the tardiness with which beliefs conform to changing institutions make this development one of immense complexity. Institutions and beliefs are in a constant state of delayed adjustment to evolving methods of production. The labor movement is an example of this complex adjustment to developing economic life. When the worker loses the ownership of his tools and becomes an infinitesimal fraction of a vast economic mechanism, he not only loses his influence over the wages and conditions of his labor, but he also surrenders some of his security and his personal dignity. When small-scale agriculture is replaced by large-scale industry, the husking bee, the Grange, the general store and the town meeting cease to be adequate forms for the expression of gregarious, recreational and political inclinations. When economic life becomes monotonous, or isolated and brutalized, new forms of emotional expression thrust themselves forward. New loyalties, new slogans, new legends, new forms of literary expression and new codes of ethics emerge from the old.

The labor movement has faced the problem of economic insecurity primarily through its efforts to raise wages, shorten hours, and increase the worker's control over the conditions and tenure of his job. Very early in its development, however, organized labor concerned itself with the provision of financial benefits for union members. Benefits for strikes, lockouts and discharge for union activity are obviously related to the wage and hour program of unionism. Benefits at death or for funeral expenses, old age, sickness and disability, however, represent a response to the need for group action in fields outside the wage relationship in industry. The financial benefit program of the labor movement gradually increased in elaborateness during the nineteenth century until practically all contingencies had been touched, however inadequately. In the 1920's labor's security policies expanded still further and came to include labor banking, credit unions, charitable institutions and coöperative enterprises. There was, in fact, a certain amount of very loose talk about the possibility that labor might provide security for itself by capturing the credit resources of the nation through the investment of its savings and its benefit reserves.

In some respects the history of union benefit and banking policies during the 1920's parallels the history of company welfare policies. Business offered profit-sharing, employee stock-ownership and publicity to the effect that the conflict between capital and labor might be resolved by having every worker become a capitalist through individual purchase of stock. Not until late in the depression did either capital or labor surrender these dreams. The programs of both business and labor were window trimmings to the essential wage relationship. But both programs appealed to the worker's desire for security and for a fuller participation in economic and social life. The depression liquidated the benefit program of labor and the welfare program of business as far as the realities of social insecurity were concerned.

Business, however, shows signs of reviving interest in profit-sharing as a substitute for wage increases, and the wealthier unions have clung to their benefit policies. At the present time fifty-four national unions make some provision for the death of members. The benefits paid are usually just sufficient to cover funeral expenses. Twenty-one unions make payments frankly designed for mortuary costs. Eighteen unions carry life insurance policies for the benefit of contributing members. Seventeen provide sickness benefits and an equal number make payments for total disability. Seven unions maintain homes for aged or tubercular members. Five give accident compensation; two insure their members' tools; and one, the Siderographers, a diminutive union with one hundred members, provides unemployment insurance. In addition to these programs, the locals in many national unions have their own benefit and relief policies, some of which are more elaborate than those of the nationals. [1]

[1] During the year 1935 the national and international unions in the A.F. of L. and their constituent locals paid the following amounts in benefits: death, $12,650,302; old age, $3,684,954; disability, $3,379,275; unemployment, $3,356,276; sickness, $1,047,010; miscellaneous, $1,190,786. Although these sums appear large as absolute amounts, they are very small in relation to the total membership of the A.F. of L. A large part of the payments indicated as unemployment benefits is probably remission of membership dues during unemployment. A.F. of L. Convention *Proceedings,* 1936, p. 64.

Because the leaders of the A.F. of L. shared the prevailing beliefs of the 1920's as thoroughly as any other element in that society, and because the unions feared to lose the advertising value of their benefit programs, organized labor determinedly opposed the assumption by government of the financial burdens of social insecurity. Although the Amalgamated Clothing Workers, then outside the A.F. of L., was the only large union which had faced the question of unemployment insurance, the annual conventions of the A.F. of L. repeatedly went on record in opposition to a government "dole." In 1932, when the volume of unemployment was many times larger than the entire membership of the A.F. of L., the convention finally recorded itself in favor of state unemployment insurance. Having moved from individual to group action in their search for economic security, American labor leaders have finally concluded that even the most powerful unions or businesses are impotent in the face of old-age dependence, industrial accidents, sickness and unemployment. On the whole, this has also been the conclusion of American business, although both unions and business may cling to their own programs as added attractions to workers' loyalties.

The transfer to the Federal and state governments of the problem of social security will, however, compel both business and labor to participate more actively in political affairs. Business will be interested in preventing further encroachments upon its income through increased taxation. Labor will be interested in developing the adequacy of the social security program and in transferring its cost, as far as possible, to the higher incomes. The area of collective action by labor will have been widened to conform to the vastness and the complexity of the conditions which determine labor's security.

Labor's power, as well as its security, is closely connected with the wage relationship. As in the case of security, however, labor's power and dignity may be extended in ways which are not directly related to the wage and hour contract. Through the labor movement the worker is offered a sense of personal power which industry in effect denies him. Industry is autocratic, immense, remote and often arbitrary. The worker is told that there is plenty of room for good men at the top. As long as economic and social conditions actually do offer opportunities for advance or escape the worker may find solace in the hope that as an individual he may move up, away, or back to his native habitat. When he finds himself finally penned within the narrow limits of an inadequate income, mocked by the certainty or suspicion that spies, stool pigeons, black lists, a week-end brawl and a dependent old age are the boundaries of his earthly existence, the conviction may be born that personal power and dignity can come only from joining in concerted action with others who have similar economic and social interests.

If man is an incurable political animal, part of the drive toward unionism springs from this fact. Democracy in an agricultural society can be achieved in the annual town meeting. When industry cuts across the political boundaries of towns, counties, states and even nations, the agricultural forms of political organization become meaningless. Unionism represents a reorientation of the forms of democracy toward the new facts of economic life. In thousands of union halls all over the country one may witness on almost any week-day night the open discussion of all sorts of economic and social issues, the expert manipulation of parliamentary procedure either as an assistance or an obstacle to action, the sonorous delight of people hearing themselves talk, the boredom of those who listen, the difficulties of maintaining order ("Will the Sergeant-at-Arms throw out the two brothers in the back row?"), the spectacle of a steam roller flattening out a righteous opposition—every characteristic, in short, of democracy at its best and its worst.

If a union organizer tells a worker to sign up because then he will feel that he "belongs," any tough-minded worker will reply, "Belong to what?" The only final answer to this question is, "Come on in and see." Because the labor movement is in a formative state, experience still remains by far the best teacher. If the labor movement continues to extend its boundaries, simplify its practices and define its objectives with greater clarity, it may become possible to give workers short courses of instruction so that they will know what they are joining. Until these developments take place, however, the best way to find out about the labor movement is to look at it from the inside. Nevertheless, organized labor has begun to develop methods of instruction which are a short cut to the knowledge based on experience. "Workers' education" programs in this country have had a formal existence for sixteen years. The basic purpose of this program is to inform the worker about the structure, methods, objectives and traditions of the labor movement; to indicate the changing group interests of the worker in an evolving industrial society; and to provide training and an outlet for the expression of literary, dramatic and artistic work based upon workers' experiences.

In its simplest form workers' education consists of the discussions, arguments, parliamentary wrangles and resolutions which compose the subject matter of trade-union meetings. Comparisons of wage rates and shop practices in different parts of the industry, the passing of a resolution condemning the continued imprisonment of Tom Mooney, an argument over the feasibility of affiliating with the state federation of labor, and the quick-witted motion to refer to committee, make up an evening's program of considerable educational value. Slightly above this level is the presentation of outside speakers who address the union meeting on any and all subjects, sometimes appropriate but often otherwise. In many communities all over the country, ministers, college and high-school teachers, Christian Association and community-center leaders have become interested in the labor movement and have assisted in setting up workers' classes or speakers' bureaus. Occasionally, in the larger centers, these classes develop into "workers' colleges" or "workers' schools" with several separate classes and teachers. In 1921 the Workers' Education Bureau was organized as a fraternal affiliate of the A.F. of L. to coördinate the activities of these classes, provide them with materials and guidance. Several unions, among which the International Ladies' Garment Workers' is by far the most important, operate their own educational services and carry on extension work among their constituent locals. Many of the new large C.I.O. local unions are taking on educational directors and services. Under the F.E.R.A. and the W.P.A. adult education programs, special programs for workers' education were launched and in some communities have been remarkably successful. The most formal educational machinery in the labor movement is that provided by the residential and semi-residential labor colleges. Among these Brookwood College at Katonah, New York; Commonwealth College at Mena, Arkansas; the Highland Folk School at Monteagle, Tennessee; and the Affiliated Schools for Workers with headquarters in New York City are the most important. In addition to these there are the schools maintained by labor political parties: the Rand School (Socialist) and the Workers' School (Communist), both in New York City.

The labor colleges are supported by scholarships from trade unions, contributions from sympathizers, gifts from interested unions and the physical work of the students who attend. Brookwood, the most ambitious of the labor colleges, has both a winter and a summer session and carries on extension services. Commonwealth, which has experienced powerful political and economic opposition, concerns itself to a considerable extent with the problem of the Southern sharecroppers. The Affiliated Schools conducts summer schools for women workers at Bryn Mawr College and at movable points in the South, a coeducational summer school at the University of Wisconsin and a summer school for office workers in New York City. Brookwood, the Affiliated Schools, the Workers' Education Bureau, and the Educational Department of the I.L.G.W.U. all provide textbook material in pamphlet form for use throughout the labor movement.

Workers' education differs from adult education in general in that it is directly related to the worker's status as a wage earner. Although it may be "cultural," in the sense that it encompasses the field of literature and the arts, it surveys these fields from the wage earner's point of view. Since it centers around the group interests of wage workers, it concerns itself with everything from the practical mechanics of strike action to the recent developments in the content of the novel. Typical courses in a labor school are Strike and Organizing Tactics; The Economics of Wages and Hours; Labor Publicity; Trade Union History; Parliamentary Procedure; Labor Law; Labor and Government; Labor Dramatics; Labor Literature; and (occasionally) Labor and the Arts. Effective labor teachers are difficult to find. College teachers suffer from their incomprehensible vocabularies or, in some instances, their embittered radicalism. Rarely do workers themselves possess the breadth of information and background necessary. Ministers often carry over a missionary attitude and vocabulary which is not identical with the missionary aspects of either the labor movement or modern business. The field of workers' education, however, is constantly expanding and has recently attracted a large number of capable teachers and organizers. The workers' education movement has already made an indelible impression upon the methods, the language and the ideology of organized labor's leaders.

The labor movement, both inside and outside its schools, is also developing its own methods of expression in novels, biographies, plays and poems. Workers' experience in this respect is both appreciative and creative. In the labor schools and in progressive union headquarters may be found shelves loaded with well-thumbed copies of *Studs Lonigan, The Foundry, The Shadow Before, Tobacco Road, A World to Win, You Can't Sleep Here, Proletarian Literature in the United States, Strike, Death Ship, Gathering Storm, Some American People, Somebody in Boots*, and scores of other recent novels written by or about workers and farmers. Labor students are encouraged to write their own essays, poems and plays. The table of contents of a recent issue of one of the labor college magazines lists the following titles, among others: "Housing," "Buttons," "Night Shift," "The New York Elevator Strike," "I Hunt for a Job," "My First Arrest," "On the Picket Line," "The Boss," "Sold Out." Among the poems written by girl workers at the school, one is a little ridiculous:

> *I know now why a tree and I*
> *Seem so much akin.*
> *The same stuff runs in both of us;*
> *We're sisters under the skin.*

One is a little false:

> *Some women have gems of the finest cut,*
> *Others wear the cheapest glass;*
> *I found the most beautiful of them all*
> *Shining one morning in the grass.*

And one is offered to the reader's judgment as typical of many others:

The clang, clang, clang of the noisy loom,
The swish, swish, swish of the sweeper's broom,
I close my eyes, I think, I can't.
All I hear is the ceaseless chant
Of whirring wheels and flying spindles.
I listen awhile, then within me kindles
A hatred for all that my eye can see,
I stop and think, why must this be?

In many unions, as well as in the schools, extensive use is made of labor dramatics. Scores of short plays written by or for workers have been produced in union halls during the last three or four years. Some are simple attempts to personalize abstract issues such as the company union, the Supreme Court and the "kept" press. Others are symbolic tableaux or pantomime. Still others are rhythmic or mass dances expressing moods and aspects of workers' lives: the assembly line, quitting time or the strike. Remarkably effective results have been achieved with limited funds and materials.

A large body of workers' songs has already grown up. For many of its songs the labor movement is indebted to its song writer, Joe Hill, who was shot by a firing squad in the Utah penitentiary. He was convicted of murder after an indictment and trial which many people consider one of the classic "frameups" of United States labor history. Like many high-school, college, Rotary Club, and Boy Scout songs, workers' songs are often set to tunes which have long since become popular in other connections. "Solidarity" (The Battle Hymn of the Republic), "Soup Song" (My Bonnie Lies Over the Ocean) "Hallelujah, I'm a Bum!" (Revive Us Again), "The Picket Line" (Polly-wolly-doodle), "We Are Building a Strong Union" (We Are Climbing Jacob's Ladder), "To Labor" (My Maryland) are examples of this. Many songs, however, are directly associated with the labor movement. Among the better known are "Hold the Fort," "March of the Hungry Men," ".Whirlwinds of Danger," "Bread and Roses," "Not One Cent," "Casey Jones" and "I'm Labor." In recent strikes, "Solidarity," "Hold the Fort" and "The Picket Line" have frequently been sung. Selections from these songs follow:

HOLD THE FORT

(chorus)

Hold the fort for we are coming
Union men, be strong;
Side by side we battle onward
Victory will come.

SOLIDARITY

(Tune: The Battle Hymn of the Republic)

When the union's inspiration through the worker's blood
*   shall run,*
There can be no power greater anywhere beneath the sun.
Yet what force on earth is weaker than the feeble strength
*   of one*
But the Union makes us strong.

(chorus)

Solidarity forever!
Solidarity forever!
Solidarity forever!
For the Union makes us strong.

THE PICKET LINE

(Tune: Polly-Wolly-Doodle)

The Union is the place for me
The place for working men
Who want some time to sing and play
And money we can spend.

(chorus)

On the line, on the line, on the picket, picket line,
We'll win our fight, our fight for the right
On the picket, picket line.

Within recent years trade-union leaders have become increasingly conscious of the union's functions as a center for the community and recreational life of its members. In urban centers progressive union leaders have felt that they must compete with other forms of diversion and amusement which attract workers away from the labor movement. In isolated communities unions have frequently become the natural agency for the expression of recreational inclinations. The leaders of progressive national unions now urge their local union officers to establish clean, attractive headquarters in respectable sections of the community and, as far as funds permit, to equip these headquarters with restrooms, game rooms, dance halls, restaurant facilities, libraries and even moving picture projectors and screens. Many of the more ambitious locals in urban centers already encourage the interest of their members by holding dances, card parties, banquets or beer parties. In isolated communities, straw rides, field days, baseball games and square dances are favorite forms of union activity. In some localities the union hall has become the veritable center of community life, just as the Grange Hall still retains this function in agricultural sections of the country. In a few instances the Grange Hall has actually been taken over by unions which have developed in decentralized industries. In all of these respects, as previously indicated, the union finds itself in competition not only with modern commercialized recreation but with the welfare policies of the employer. If unions continue to increase in strength it will in part be both cause and result of their success in developing a program of satisfying workers' desires for recreational life and community activity.

Although unionism is fundamentally a response to the emergence of a wage relationship and the decline in the status of the individual worker in industry, it has other powers and other appeals. The labor movement has with

varying success responded to the worker's desire for security, dignity, decency, participation in democratic affairs
and a form of education which interprets his position to
him. It provides techniques for the control of his destiny
and means for the expression of artistic, recreational and
communal inclinations. Where business, government,
public or endowed schools, the church, Christian Associations and territorial organization of democracy are sufficient to satisfy the desires of workers in these respects,
unionism may rest content with its strictly economic
functions. Elsewhere, as the power of unions develops, the
labor movement may become a new way of life as well as
a bargaining institution.

CHAPTER IX

Union Finances, Administration and Leadership

THROUGHOUT the entire history of American unionism there has been a continuous trend toward the centralization of power within the labor movement. This trend is observable in other aspects of modern society. In governmental affairs power is moving from the states toward the Federal Government. Within the Federal Government itself, there may be observed a drift away from the theoretical separation of powers toward a consolidation of control in the hands of the executive. In the operation of the means of production, the rise of the modern corporation is transferring control from a large body of owners to a small group of managers and financiers. All these developments are intimately related to the growing integration and interdependence of the processes of production.

Among existing national unions there is great variety in the actual allocation of power to their component parts. Many unions have local joint boards, district councils, occupational departments and other subdivisions, as well as the national and local organizations. The local joint boards may be composed of two or more local unions in the same vicinity, all locals covering the same type of occupation as, for example, in the case of the Carpenters; or they may be made up of several locals each of which contain the members of different occupations in the industry. In the International Ladies' Garment Workers' Union, for example, there are separate locals in some communities for the cloakmakers, dressmakers, designers and embroidery workers. The joint board in each of these communities is made up of the representatives from each occupational local. Above the joint boards come the territorial organizations usually based upon state lines. The Carpenters and Textile Workers have state councils or federations, while the Miners have district councils whose jurisdiction is determined by county as well as state lines. Some unions have national occupational subdivisions in addition to those already mentioned. The United Textile Workers is made up of federations of Hosiery Workers, Dyers and Finishers, Silk Workers, Woolen and Worsted Workers as well as the directly affiliated cotton textile locals.

Authority is variously distributed among the component parts of the national organizations. In some unions the subdivisions have a purely nominal existence, in others the locals have powers which dwarf those of the national. In still others the subdivisions of the national unions have dissimilar powers among themselves. In the United Textile Workers the Hosiery Federation enjoys almost complete autonomy, while other federations remain fully dependent upon the national union. In the United Mine Workers, District No. 12 in Illinois, for historical and personal reasons, has asserted an unusual amount of independence as compared with other districts.

The actual allocation of power within the national unions has been affected by a variety of factors including historical accidents and the force of particular personalities, but the primary determinant has been the economic structure of the industry in which the union operates. Where great disparities of conditions exist, as among the separate textile industries, years of experimentation have forced the union to decentralize power among the branches of the industry. Where competition among several producing centers of the same industry has been very active, the unions have been forced to centralize power in the hands of one national office. When the common interests of the several occupations within an industry have been very close, control over the various occupations has gradually been vested in a single agency. The condition of any national union or of the labor movement as a whole at a given time represents a compromise between an original condition of separatism on the one hand and the integrating forces of economic life on the other.

The methods by which the centralization of power has been accomplished within the national unions have been the transfer of the control of the purse from the local to the national union, the elaboration of "machine" or "boss" methods, and the eventual recognition of these developments by constitutional changes. The financial policies of the early unions consisted simply of the collection of *membership dues* and the use of these funds for benefits, strike relief, organizing costs, officers' wages and overhead expenses. With the setting up of coördinating agencies, the national officers began to press for extensions of their financial powers. This resulted in the adoption of the device known as the *per capita tax*. Under this system, the local unions are required to pay to the national office a fixed amount per member every month or quarter of a year. The locals are usually left free to charge whatever they wish in membership dues, but the dues must obviously be sufficient to pay the per capita tax to the national as well as the expenses of the local. Many nationals have eventually recognized this situation by fixing the minimum dues which the locals must charge. This policy has often been accompanied by constant pressure from the national officers for an increase in the per capita tax. The result has necessarily been a transfer of powers and functions from the local to the national unions.

There are several methods by which the national unions compel the locals to pay taxes upon their full membership. The first is the threat of suspension or expulsion of locals which fail to comply with constitutional per capita tax provisions. A second method is the denial of insurance or strike benefits and other services to local unions which are in arrears. A third method is the granting of representation in national conventions or referenda upon the basis of per capita tax payments. Some national unions also carry in their national headquarters card records of the individual members of the locals and thereby provide themselves with a check upon the membership declarations of the locals.

When there are coördinating agencies between the locals and the nationals, these agencies may also receive a share of the dues collected from the membership. A rough index of the power of the constituent bodies of the national unions is provided by the distribution of funds among these bodies. It may be found, for example, that the average dues collected by the locals of a given union are one dollar and fifty cents a month from each member. Of this amount, five cents may be paid to the local joint board, five cents to the state or district council, twenty cents to the national occupational department, and fifty cents to the national union office, leaving seventy cents per member per month in the hands of the local unions.

With respect to the amount of money actually collected from union members, no accurate estimate is possible. Since the national unions do not usually prescribe the membership dues of their locals, there is great diversity within each national union. In the large industrial unions which now cover about half of the total union membership in the country the average dues of the local unions run from one to two dollars a month. Of this amount, from thirty-five cents to a dollar may be collected by the national union in per capita tax depending upon the distribution of powers and services within the union. In the craft and semicraft unions of the higher paid workers, both the dues and the per capita tax may be very much larger, especially if either the local or the national union provides an elaborate system of financial benefits for its members.

Second in importance to membership dues and per

capita tax as a method of raising funds is the use of assessments. Many national unions prefer to avoid this method as far as possible because of the expense and difficulty of collection and because assessments are often permitted to the national officers only when authorized by conventions or referenda. The necessity for appealing to a convention or a referendum limits the power of the national officers since the purposes for which the funds are to be used have to be explained and justified. The frequent use of assessments by a union may be taken as a rough indication that power within the union remains decentralized. Exceptions to this, however, are found in unions which have empowered their executive councils to impose assessments and collect them through the checkoff. Under these conditions, the assessment becomes a powerful instrument in the hands of the national officers. The United Mine Workers raised approximately a million dollars by this method in January and February, 1937, for use in the steel and automobile organizing campaigns.

The third method used by national unions in raising money is by the collection of initiation and charter fees. The charter fees are relatively unimportant. They are usually no more than sufficient to pay the costs of the charter, record books, seals and installation expenses. The initiation fees are primarily designed to pay the expenses of securing new members. They are usually about equal to one month's membership dues, and are divided between the local and the national unions in about the same proportion as the membership dues. During intensive organizing campaigns either the initiation fee or the first month's dues are sometmes cancelled in order to reduce the initial expense to new locals. With respect to membership dues and initiation fees, local unions often make a practice of charging according to the wage rates in the separate occupational groups within the union. Occasionally the national unions also vary the per capita tax in a similar manner. Both dues and per capita tax are frequently remitted in the case of unemployed members. As pointed out in the section on union business policies, some local unions charge fantastically high initiation fees. This is a method of excluding new members, however, rather than of raising money.

The primary expenses of national unions, in order of usual importance, are for carrying on strikes, paying financial benefits, conducting organizing activities, overhead expenses of national and district offices and the salaries of national officers. Strike expenses have already been discussed. It may be pointed out, however, that the disbursement of strike relief by the national office places great power in its hands. National unions almost invariably lay down conditions upon which strike aid will be granted to the locals. Whenever the national union has secured any degree of power, it insists that strikes shall not be called by the locals until the national office has had opportunity to investigate and, if possible, to arbitrate or settle the dispute. If locals refuse to abide by these conditions, they may not only be denied financial or other support, but may also be suspended or expelled from the national union. The national union, furthermore, may cut off the local from outside sources of support by persuading the A.F. of L. (and soon, perhaps, the C.I.O.) to close the channels of the city central unions and state federations.

The disbursement of financial benefits by the national union to the members of the locals gives the national union the same power over the locals that company welfare programs give to the employer over his workers. In both cases, the benefits are usually granted only if certain conditions are fulfilled. The company may refuse to pay old-age pensions to its members if they go on strike. The union may refuse to pay benefits to its members if they do not obey a strike call issued by the union. Financial benefits are therefore not only an organizing device and a miniature social security program, but also a method of increasing the power of the national office over its constituent parts. To the extent that the state and Federal governments take over the security program of business and labor, both sides will be forced to attempt to control the conditions under which government grants are made. Business, for example, insists that unemployment benefits should not be paid to workers who are on strike. Labor insists that the fact of destitution, rather than its cause, is the primary condition upon which relief should be granted.

To the extent that the national unions assume the functions and pay the expenses of organizing campaigns, power is given to the central office. In most of the important unions the national offices have long since taken over the active work of organization. Strong local unions occasionally supplement the work of the national organizers by providing their own facilities for local use. In the main, however, it is the district and national offices to which the organizers are attached, and it is from the national treasury that their salaries and expenses are paid. By granting or denying organizing facilities, therefore, the national office may effectively discipline its locals.

The overhead expenses of the national offices are becoming increasingly important. In the past they have not been a relatively large item except in the small struggling unions. In the vicinity of Union Square in New York City there are many headquarters of national unions in dingy surroundings, with overcrowded rooms, antique business equipment and meager secretarial forces. In recent years, however, unions have begun to take over the methods of big business. Headquarters in New York, Washington, Pittsburgh, Detroit, Akron, Chicago and Indianapolis have been modernized or moved into new quarters. Business equipment is much in evidence. Elaborate statistical and accounting facilities have been installed and attractive stenographers are employed. [1] In spite of the increase in office expenses of the larger unions, however, it is probable that the overhead expense per union member has actually decreased because of the increased membership in these unions.

With respect to the financial accounts and reports of national unions, there are a number of parallels between union policies and those of business. Although accounts usually exist in both cases, they are frequently inadequate. There are at least two reasons for this. The first is that unions, as well as business, have grown up like Topsy. In the early stages of a union or a business the men in charge are likely to carry in their heads most of the details of their affairs, or to use the simplest kind of records. As the organizations expand, it may not occur to the leaders to alter their methods of record to correspond to changed conditions. Frequently it is not until a major error, defalcation, or death of a key individual takes place that the organization is shocked into recognizing the inadequacy of its accounts and reports. The second reason is that both business and labor have reasons for concealing the internal state of their affairs from the general public. Businessmen conceal their financial affairs from their competitors, their workers and their customers. This is in the best business tradition. In the interest of their own members, labor leaders may wish to conceal the union's financial weakness

[1] In connection with the stenographers, an interesting development is taking place. Under the stimulus of the N.R.A., bookkeepers, stenographers, and accountants began to organize in federal labor locals. Many of those who took the lead in the formation of these locals were employees at local and national union headquarters. On May 30, 1937, at a convention attended by representatives from sixteen cities, it was decided to withdraw from the A.F. of L. and form a new national union affiliated with the C.I.O. A.F. of L. officials will now find themselves at the mercy of C.I.O. stenographers! The new organization has a membership of approximately 10,000 and is now conducting an active organizing campaign under C.I.O. auspices. It has adopted the title: United Office and Professional Workers of America. Recently the United Automobile Workers acceded to demands presented by the Office Workers' Union on behalf of office workers in the automobile union's headquarters.

from employers. In a poker game people don't wave their cards.

It may also be that corporate managers are unwilling to allow their shareholders or the government to know what has been going on. The corporation's internal records may be excellent, while those to which the public has access are impressive but not illuminating. Similarly, a labor leader may be unwilling to account to his membership for the whereabouts of funds which they have paid in. Very much the same methods of milking the outsiders for the benefit of the insiders are open to the labor leader that have been practiced by corporate managers, with the exception that labor leaders cannot literally sell short the shares of their organization, run the union into the ground and then cover the short sales at reduced prices!

As far as the national unions are concerned, the financial reports and responsibility of union leaders are equal to those of the average corporate manager. Almost all national unions publish annual reports showing income broken down into per capita tax, assessments, initiation fees, charter fees, sale of periodicals, sale of labels and gifts; expenses broken down into strike relief, financial benefits, organizing expenses, officers' salaries and expense accounts, and office expenses; balances carried over from the preceding period, balances carried forward, and the nature and whereabouts of the investment of these balances. These accounts are certified by public accountants, surveyed by the auditors appointed at the national convention, and are frequently available to the public in the union periodical as well as in the convention proceedings. National unions usually require that officers who handle funds make all payments by check and give evidence of financial responsibility. The A.F. of L. publishes its financial reports in the annual convention proceedings which are available in most college libraries. The C.I.O. is now in the process of regularizing its financial procedures. Some of the national unions issue financial reports on a monthly or quarterly basis which are models of detail and intelligibility. The reports of the Typographical Union are especially noteworthy in this respect. Others contain little but general verbal statements which are practically meaningless.

The policy of local unions, on the other hand, is much more variable. Many national unions require that their locals make financial reports to the national officers at regular intervals and that the books of the local unions be made available at all times for inspection by superior officers. In other national unions, the locals have almost complete autonomy and adopt all sorts of practices from full public statement to complete denial of information even to the members of the local. In the latter instances, union officers have frequently laid themselves open to well-founded suspicion of defalcation of funds. As a result of long and occasionally bitter experience in this matter, national unions have come more or less universally to require at least that the local officers be bonded by responsible companies.

On the whole the American labor movement is probably no worse, perhaps better, than American business in the matter of financial reports and responsibility. If the labor movement continues to grow in scope, if power continues to be centralized in the hands of the national officers, and if the conflict aspects of unionism become less important, it may be expected that methods of accounting and reporting financial affairs will become more uniform, comprehensive and intelligible. Unions may also drop their antipathy toward reporting their financial affairs to governmental agencies. If this is not construed to mean that unions should be required to incorporate,[2] the labor movement will have little to lose by such publicity. The

[2] As noted in chap. III, pages 79-81, the advocacy of incorporation of unions is an antiunion device. Publicity can be secured without incorporation.

use of labor spies has become so general in American industry that when unions have attempted to maintain secrecy, employers have often known more about the union's financial condition than the union's members. Several amusing instances are on record in which employers have furnished to union officers copies of spies' reports dealing with the financial state of the union. Occasionally the spies' reports have been more intelligible than the union's records themselves. On the other hand, weak unions which have concealed their financial condition may actually gain by fuller publicity since secrecy breeds suspicion, and suspicion is a condition of weakness.

A clear distinction must be drawn, however, between financial reports and membership *figures*, on the one hand, and membership *lists* on the other. As long as employers pursue antiunion policies, unions are forced in self-protection to guard the names of their members against black lists. It may be expected that unions will view with extreme suspicion any legislative proposal requiring disclosure of members' names. Many of the recent bills introduced to state legislatures by antiunion interests contain the possibility of such a disclosure while directing primary attention toward the question of financial reports and responsibility.

During the life of the American labor movement, the leaders of labor have been more or less continuously under fire from employers, on the one hand, and the radical opposition, on the other, for "autocracy," "bureaucracy," "treachery" and "racketeering." To a considerable extent these charges may be regarded simply as epithets which form part of the ammunition of conflict. As in the case of political mud-slinging, those who make the charges frequently do not believe them and wonder whether anyone else will. It may also be observed that those who live in glass houses should not throw stones. Nevertheless, these accusations deserve examination.

The charges "autocracy" and "bureaucracy" are difficult to separate. The specific content of each merges into the other. Taken together, "autocracy" and "bureaucracy" in the labor movement mean that union officers have centralized their power by driving up the per capita tax, suspending or expelling locals or whole districts, denying financial benefits or services to opposition elements, failing to call meetings and conventions and using other methods of machine control such as the packing of conventions and committees, abuse of the presiding officer's power to recognize speakers from the floor, arbitrary rulings from the chair, overriding *viva voce* votes, denying credentials to opposition elements, bartering positions and favors for votes, physical expulsion of delegates from the convention floor and so on.

Innumerable examples of these practices can be culled from recent union history. The Carpenters, for example, in 1937 had their first convention since 1929. The A.F. of L. Executive Council suspended the C.I.O. unions *before* the 1936 convention and assured itself of being upheld by refusing to grant the suspended unions the right to vote. The May 24, 1937, conference of the A.F. of L. which took the final step of expelling C.I.O. affiliates from state federations and central labor bodies eliminated all opposition to this action by failing to invite delegates from the state federations, central labor councils and federal labor locals since a majority of these bodies was not in favor of such action. During the period of disintegration of the United Mine Workers in the 'twenties, illustrations of almost every method of autocratic and bureaucratic control were provided by the John L. Lewis machine. To quote a recent *Fortune* article: "Two rebels named McCarty and Manley . . . got into a convention in Scranton in 1923. Lewis introduced them as 'industrial buzzards' . . . 'I want to warn you against these carrion birds.' The convention seethed while the Chair marked oratorical time.

'I now ask,' he wound up in a thunderous calm, 'that you remove your carcasses without the door.' McCarty and Manley were given a quick bum's rush to the courthouse yard and there beaten up." [3]

An honest and intelligent labor leader faced with these charges might reply that he admitted the whole thing; that running a labor union is not a Sunday-school picnic any more than business or city politics is; and that in the labor movement there are special reasons which sometimes make autocracy inevitable. In antiunion industries trade unions are primarily fighting organizations. They are faced by an opponent who has autocratic control over the means of production and who is usually only remotely responsible to his shareholders. Fighting organizations must be disciplined and must act as a unit if they are to be effective. No one would think of consulting the ordinary privates in an army as to the proper tactics for a major battle. Secondly, in a highly competitive industry a union cannot long exist unless it preserves uniform standards of wages and hours over the whole industry. This means that the officers must be given or must assume power to enforce a common policy. Third, there is usually no criticism of autocratic policies from the rank and file until things begin to go badly. Democracy is all very well, but somebody has to do the work. Union members are frequently apathetic, would rather go to bed or to the movies than attend union meetings. The union leader is forced to build up a machine to carry on the essential functions of the organization. Then when something goes wrong, everybody turns up at the union meeting and complains about the high-handed manner in which things have been done. Fourth, the opposition elements never practice, when they secure power, what they preach while in opposition. They find that things look different on the inside; that if they are going to produce results they too have to play favorites

[3] *Fortune*, Oct., 1936, p. 156.

and use the iron claw as well as the silk glove. Fifth, a good deal of the machinery of democracy is cumbrous, expensive and not really democratic. People don't pay much attention to referenda. Even if they did, the holding of a referendum is such a lengthy process that the time for action is over before the returns come in. Conventions are expensive. The initiative and recall are infrequently used even where adequate provision for them is made. The election of committees from the floor of a convention is a time-wasting process which usually results in choosing the same people the national officers would have appointed. Unless the presiding officer runs a large national convention with a high hand and with everything mapped out ahead of time, bedlam is the only possible result.

If the union leader were asked in what respect the control of labor by a union autocrat is superior to the control of labor by a business autocrat, he would reply that in the long run the labor leader is responsible to labor. He can hold his job only if he produces results. If he does not come through with wages, hours and "conditions," he will either lose his job or the union will disintegrate. The business autocrat, on the other hand, is ultimately responsible to the owners. Workers cannot remove him from power. He may then depress the condition of the worker while enjoying the applause and the continued support of the owner. To this it must be added that a large degree of democracy does exist in most unions, that antiunionism has exaggerated the problem of centralization of power, that extended experience with unionism on the part of the worker advances the possibilities and actualities of democracy, and that the rise of the workers' education movement carries with it a developing understanding of the methods of leadership control and induces a healthy skepticism toward those in power.

The importance from the worker's viewpoint of preserving and extending democratic control within the labor movement increases rather than decreases with the rise of industrial unionism. Labor sympathizers are currently inclined to believe that because the unions of the skilled craftsmen are plutocratic with respect to the rest of the labor movement they are therefore internally autocratic. There is no necessary relation between these two phenomena. As a matter of fact, the relatively small groups of better educated and better-to-do craft unionists have been able to develop and maintain a high degree of democracy within their own unions. In the huge industrial unions, on the contrary, with their masses of relatively new recruits many of whom are new to industry itself, the problem of preserving a semblance of democratic control may become acute. Although the influx of masses of workers to the labor movement has obviously revived and invigorated it, it does not follow that the internal life of the movement will necessarily remain democratic. Large mobs are often easier to control than small groups. If the membership of the new large industrial unions is to be retained, it will be necessary to break up the huge industrial locals into subordinate special interest groups according to shop, occupation, residence or language. These groups must be small enough to permit active discussion of separate interests and participation in the affairs of the union by all who wish to do so. It will also be necessary to emphasize the education of the new members with respect to the requirements of discipline as well as the need for active criticism.

There is no question here of returning to the separatism of craft unions as long as the scope of centralized power is equal to the scope of the problem involved. The control over the jurisdiction of groups within the local must rest finally with the officers of the local. The control over the jurisdiction of locals must rest with the district or national officers. The final authority over the jurisdiction of national unions must rest with a body which is superior to the national unions, such as the A.F. of L. or the C.I.O. It does not matter much to the labor movement whether rayon workers are organized in a textile union or in a chemical workers' union. It is of the greatest importance to the labor movement that there be an authority with the power to render final decision.[4] Similarly, the questions of local dues, time of meetings, educational and entertainment programs and the discussion of candidates for office may be taken up by the subordinate groups of the local unions, but it is imperative that the final drawing up of trade agreements shall rest with officers whose power is coterminous with that of the employer. In competitive industries, the final authority over wage agreements cannot be delegated to anyone but the national officers without danger of inducing the disintegration of the union. A high degree of centralization of power over business policies, jurisdiction and other matters of general concern is not incompatible with great freedom of criticism, freedom to depose or recall superior officers, and to deal with local affairs.

Other elements in the charge of "bureaucracy" are that the officers become remote from the rank and file, that they perpetuate themselves in power long after they have ceased adequately to represent the interests of the workers, and that they pay themselves very large salaries and expense accounts. To the first charge the average labor leader would agree, but would hold that this is inevitable. When a union member rises in the scale of union officialdom he ceases to be a worker. If the union is still in the fighting stage the officer becomes, in effect, a general with military

---

[4] It is becoming apparent that the holding of elections by the National Labor Relations and National Mediation Boards to determine the union which the workers want to represent them is actually a method of settling jurisdictional conflicts by democratic action. Although the Board cannot enforce its decision except by requiring the employer to deal with the majority group, the prestige of the Boards has been sufficient to prevent defeated unions from protesting the decisions by strike action.

powers. If the union has passed into the stage of quiet bargaining based upon the consciousness of economic power, the leader becomes a businessman selling labor under the most favorable conditions he can secure for his members. Even while the union is in its fighting stage, the leader is remote from his followers. He may lead strikes, he may be put in jail, he may lead mass meetings and he may work at his task for eighteen hours a day. But he has risen above the mass. He has left his bench or tools. He travels, lives in hotels, wears better clothes, talks with reporters, businessmen, politicians and social leaders, and he develops a vested interest in these perquisites which he is reluctant to surrender. After the union has become a bargaining rather than a fighting organization, all of these aspects of the leader's life are further emphasized. He sits at a desk instead of on a platform. He deals with statistics of wages, hours, accident rates and labor turnover instead of strike strategies and tactics. He talks quietly, moves sedately, smokes good cigars and experiences increasing difficulty in rising from his swivel chair. Occasionally he rebels against his sedentary existence by going back to the soapbox or by a personal appearance on the picket line, but for the most part his emotional catharsis takes the form of endless reminiscences.

It may perhaps be conceded that this is an inevitable development in any social institution; that the same phenomenon may be observed in business, in the schools and colleges, in government and in the hierarchy of the church. The question of leaders' remoteness from the rank and file tends to pass over into the question of the length of time that the leader holds power, and the degree of remoteness from his followers that he establishes.

Labor leaders have shown an exceptional capacity to maintain themselves in office. In justifying themselves they modestly maintain that good leadership is a rare phenomenon, that experience in office is the best teacher and that a rapid turnover of leaders destroys the values of experience and training in office. This contention is familiar in most social and political institutions. So, also, is the opposite contention that extended tenure carries with it the twin dangers of tyranny and fatty degeneracy.

In the labor movement the problem raised by this conflict of principles is especially acute. The business leader may sell out, retire and go to Florida or California to die; or he may be eased upstairs to the chairmanship of the Board at a nominal salary of $75,000. When political leaders pass out of active political life they open a law firm in Washington or are appointed to the bench. In many colleges the permanent tenure of full professors is cut short at the age of sixty-eight by compulsory retirement to an *emeritus* status and the income of pension funds. The labor leader, however, must die with his boots on, and the process is often pathetic. Business does not want the retired labor leader because he no longer has anything to sell. Government agencies hold out a few plums, but there is no reason for being enthusiastic about having labor departments and boards become the boneyard of the labor movement. Union members themselves say, "The old man has softening of the brain so bad he's afraid to blow his nose, but you can't turn the old war horse out to die."

There are several devices which the labor movement might adopt to meet this problem. Experience has commended them to other social institutions. It is essential to make a distinction between the officers performing relatively routine technical tasks on the one hand and the policy-making, political leaders on the other. The first group should be selected by appointment based upon examination. The second group should be elected. After two terms of a stated length, elective union officers should be required to retire for at least one term before becoming eligible for reelection. This may be unwise in particular instances of officers of extraordinary ability, but circumstances do make the man. Leadership abilities are developed through rotation of officers. Paucity of union leadership has resulted partly from the fact that relatively few have had an opportunity to develop and to demonstrate their leadership capacities. Technical workers might also be retired at an arbitrary age limit. Unions should provide pensions for both their technical and political retired leaders. The costs of such a pension system would be slight compared to the expenses of incompetence and senility. The more cruel aspects of compulsory retirement to a pensioner's status may be softened by the adoption of the usual devices: the presentation of badges, ribbons, engraved testimonials, farewell dinners and a formal title as Honorary Fourth Vice-President.

The degree of the officer's remoteness from the rank and file is to some extent determined by the size of his salary and expense accounts. The question of officers' salaries presents particular difficulties in the labor movement. One principle which has been espoused by radical and progressive elements is that the officer should be paid no more than the best-paid worker in the occupation or industry. The contention is that under such conditions, the officer's living standards remain similar to those of the workers he represents, that he will therefore retain a better understanding of the viewpoint of his constituency. The assumption is that the union can depend upon the missionary spirit to keep him honest in spite of the temptations presented by his low salary and his opportunity to graft on the side. The second principle is that the salaries of officers should be high enough to attract the best available men and keep them from succumbing to the many temptations which present themselves to union leaders. The feeling is that union members like to have their representatives dress well, put up at good hotels, be able to hand out good cigars and radiate an air of easy affluence. It is also contended that even though low-paid union officers may not sell out through the acceptance of bribes and graft, if they are able men they are constantly faced with tempting offers from business and political enterprises. The usual criticism of this position is that money breeds a love of money and that it is therefore safer to depend upon class and group loyalty rather than large salaries; and that the overstuffed and bejeweled atmosphere of an A.F. of L. convention does not make a good impression upon the general public, since the public's sympathy with labor rests chiefly upon the idea that labor is the underdog.

Actually, the whole question of the salaries of labor leaders has been much exaggerated by antiunion publicity. Most of such publicity originates with people who are themselves embarrassed by the publication of their own incomes. Local union officers are paid very little. Ten dollars a week to the president, executive secretary or business agent of a local for his part-time work after hours is a fair estimate of the average amount paid. In locals which are large enough to afford a full-time business agent, the salary may run from two to four thousand dollars a year, depending upon a great variety of factors. The business agent may, of course, also receive immense sums in graft, but this is a somewhat different question and must be discussed in another connection. National union officers' salaries run from $1,000 or less to $20,000 a year. The small struggling unions or the unions with decentralized power may have only one full-time national officer with little more than an expense account. A middle-sized union such as the United Textile Workers, with 100,000 members, pays its president $3,750, its secretary-treasurer $3,300, and its vice-presidents, $2,860 and "all legitimate expenses." The Typographical Union (smaller but wealthier than the U.T.W.) pays its president $7,500. The president of the largest union in the country, John L. Lewis of the United Mine Workers, receives $12,000 and expenses, but accepts no extra pay for his work as chairman of the C.I.O. The president of the A.F. of L. receives a salary of $12,000 a year and in 1936 was granted $7,347.61 for expenses. The secretary-treasurer of the A.F. of L. receives a salary of $10,000 a year and in 1936 was paid $1,235.02 for expenses.[5] Standards for justifying or condemning the size of these salaries from the viewpoint of labor or the public are entirely lacking. There is no open market for labor leaders in which the supply and the demand are equalized by the movement of price. It becomes a question of taste, and the determinants of good taste in this matter are very complex.

The padding of expense accounts is an old American custom (and probably Chinese, Spanish and Lithuanian as well). Only the large and wealthy unions, however, can afford this luxury. Many unions fix the expense account at a certain number of dollars a day or week and allow it only for time actually spent on the road. Union leaders who enjoy large expense accounts may actually live very simply in the bosom of their family. Luxurious hotel suites leased by union officers (when such establishments exist outside the imagination of antiunion publicity agents) are charged up to advertising. Union members, like corporate stockholders, are likely to conclude (accurately or otherwise) that this is all right as long as it brings home the bacon.

The remaining important charges against union leaders are "treachery" and "racketeering." With respect to treachery, the specific items usually advanced are that union leaders have "sold out" or "thrown" strikes to employers, that they have broken the strikes of other unions, and that they become oversympathetic with the employer's

[5] Mr. Tobin of the Truck Drivers receives $20,000; Mr. Hillman of the Clothing Workers receives $7,500; Mr. Dubinsky of the Garment Workers receives $10,000. The officers of the new unions in automobiles, glass, rubber and radios receive between $3,000 and $4,000 a year. The major compensations of labor leadership are power, prestige and satisfied altruism.

point of view and act as the agent of the employer in coercing workers to accept trade agreements injurious to them. A labor leader who knew the history of American unionism would admit that all these things have frequently come to pass. He would then suggest that in many instances these acts have been committed by *agents provocateurs* who have been planted in the union by antiunion employers. And he would conclude with a discussion of the actual situation in which union officers find themselves when forced to make a decision in the face of a strike which is going badly, an industry which is declining or "dualism" and lack of discipline in the ranks of organized labor in his field.

As has been observed in an earlier chapter, the successful conduct of a strike and the negotiations which bring it to a close are very complex affairs. No one but an old hand at the game can realize how many variables are involved, how many snap decisions have to be made and how frequent are the opportunities for mistake. To the worker, however, these complexities are likely to be obscured by the immediacy of his own personal plight. The failure of a strike, whether due to honest mistakes by the leader or the magnitude of the task involved, is very likely to be put down to the "treachery" of the union officers. Even when the strike is not entirely lost, the worker may be disgusted by the paucity of the gains and brand the settlement a "sell-out," although it may actually represent the balance of forces at the time. Charges of "treachery" under these conditions are likely to be emphasized if the strike leader has carried on negotiations secretly with the employer, if the leader does not submit the settlement to the workers for final ratification, and especially if the leader covers his retreat by asserting that the outcome of the strike represents a "moral victory." Secret negotiations, under ordinary circumstances should be severely avoided. The dangers attending their use are great. Sometimes, however, relations between the subordinate officers or leaders on both sides may be so embittered that a public conference between them is either impossible or futile. Under these circumstances, secret conferences between the most important leader on each side may be the only possible method of reaching an agreement. This was true of the negotiations between John Lewis and Myron Taylor of United States Steel which resulted in the peaceful acceptance by the company of the S.W.O.C. as bargaining agent for its members. The secrecy of the negotiations and the fact that they were carried on by only two very able leaders made possible the avoidance of an explosion in a situation loaded with dynamite. If Lewis had secured less than he did from these conferences, there would have been cries of "traitor." As it was, the labor movement cut another notch in Mr. Lewis' totem pole. The labor movement has had its share of treacherous leadership, but some distinctions must be made between making the best of a bad situation or using bad judgment in a good situation, on the one hand, and actions which are treacherous both in motive and consequences, on the other.

Cries of "treachery" have also arisen in connection with the active breaking of strikes by union leaders. There are three general types of cases involved. The first is the situation in which a strike leader, having won the demands of his own group, calls off the strike before the demands of other unions striking against the same employer have been met. Examples of this type of strikebreaking can be cited from the earliest days of the labor movement to the present time. In 1879 the secretary of the Fall River Mulespinners called off a strike on the basis of gains for the spinners and nothing for the weavers. The weavers remained out for some time, but their strike was effectively broken. The weavers' comment on this affair was that the Mulespinners' secretary was a "crawling lickspittle." They added:

> *Treachery to treachery*
> *Bust to bust*
> *If the mill czars won't have you*
> *The devil must.*

In May, 1937, one group of Hollywood film strikers (the actors) settled with the company before the other crafts had secured their demands. There was immediate talk of "treachery" and of boycotting the films made by the leaders of the Actors' Guild. Whether this is treachery or not depends upon the standards of judgment which are brought to bear. From the viewpoint of the labor movement as a whole such a policy is treachery of the worst sort since, in the long run, it makes possible a policy of "divide and conquer" by employers. From the immediate viewpoint of the craft group whose interests the leader is paid to serve, however, the return to work represents good horse sense. The conclusion that it is treachery assumes a condition of labor solidarity which in many places and at many times has been nonexistent. Industrial unionism will go a long way toward eliminating strikebreaking of this sort, since the rise of industrial unionism indicates a growing consciousness of workers' common interests.

The second form of union strikebreaking occurs when union leaders attempt to enforce discipline upon any one of the component parts of the union. National leaders often refuse strike permission to a local because the union's funds are inadequate, because the national officers are convinced that the grievance can be peacefully settled, or for other reasons, good, bad and dubious. For similar reasons, the national officers may call off the strike of a local. In either case, locals occasionally persist in carrying on with the strike. The question becomes that of determining whether or not the union's officers can maintain the discipline which is necessary to preserve a fighting and bargaining organization. The decision as to the nature and the degree of discipline required to maintain an organization can be rendered only in the light of the exact circumstances of each particular case. The making of such a decision requires the coolest and most acute kind of calculation. In a situation of this sort, calculation is likely to be swept away by emotion. The result is that disciplinary action is resorted to when it is unnecessary, or that the measures taken are more extreme than required by the case. Cries of "treachery" fill the air.

Suppose, for example, that an employer in plant A wishes to break an agreement. Against the terms of the contract he places spies in the union and foments a strike during the slack season. The union leader in the meantime is engaged in the delicate business of negotiating an agreement with another more important employer, B, who is wavering on the point of acceptance and who is impressed with the union's record for faithful observance of agreements. The leader tries and fails to get his members in plant A back to work. He argues, shuts off strike relief, closes up outside relief channels and finally suspends or expels the local, but without result. The spies are posing as progressives or militants who condemn the "reactionary" leader for "selling out." Employer B tells the leader that he is fed up with the leader's inability to enforce contracts. Should the leader transfer union members from other areas to plant A, break the strike and save his skin with employer B?

Or, suppose, on the other hand, that 90 per cent of a union's membership has become thoroughly convinced that their leaders are lining their own pockets with graft from the employers' association in return for signing contracts which are much less favorable than the strength of the union will warrant. Insurgent leaders, supported by two thirds of the union's membership, declare a strike against the renewal of an unfavorable contract. Should the "legitimate" union leaders provide the employers with strikebreakers in the name of sanctity of contract?

The third form of union strikebreaking occurs when there is dualism in the organization of a given field. Suppose that two unions exist in a given industry. The leaders in each union believe in the essential soundness of their respective positions. One set of leaders believes that the opposing union is riddled with spies and has long since "sold out" to the "bosses." The other set believes that the first union is filled with *agents provocateurs*, Bolsheviks and foreign secret service agents. Each is convinced that to allow the other to become dominant is to invite the suicide of the labor movement. They declare war and resort to its implements, one of which is breaking each other's strikes. The A.F. of L. has successively fought the Knights of Labor and the I.W.W. in these terms. There are indications that the conflict between the A.F. of L. and the C.I.O. may soon provide examples of "dual" unions breaking each other's strikes in transport, in the maritime industries, in electrical work and perhaps even in mining and clothing. This situation is easier to explain than to justify from the long run viewpoint of the labor movement.

The description of the business policies of labor in a previous chapter suggests that the complexity of the economic problems faced by the union leader may frequently lay him open to charges of "treachery." In setting a minimum wage in an industry, the leader is in something of a dilemma. If he places the wage at a point high enough to do any good to his members, the relatively inefficient firms may be eliminated. The resultant unemployment may be only temporary but may cause a good deal of suffering for which the leader takes the blame. If he sets the wage at a point which will enable all firms to remain in business, he is damned for "selling out."

The leader may become convinced that if the union will accept a wage reduction, the expanded employment which will follow will result in an increase in the total of wage payments to the members. He knows, however, that if he tries to force the wage cut upon the union the opposition will attack him for his "treachery." On the other hand, if he does not put through the wage reduction, he is convinced that many of his own members, in desperation, will begin undercutting the union rate by "kicking back" part of their wages to their employers. This will eventually destroy the union.

Suppose that a leader has been unable to organize the workers in an important section of the country and consequently the wage rates there are lower than in the organized area. The industry is gradually moving out from under the union's control. Should the leader force a wage reduction upon his members which will place the organized section upon an equal competitive footing with the unorganized area? If he does, he will put a powerful weapon in the hands of both the opposition in his union and the nonunion employers. Each will say, "He can't do any better for the union workers than the nonunion." If he does not, he faces the certainty that his organization will crumble away. At one time or another this has been the situation in cotton textiles, soft coal and hosiery. The leaders in the unions in each of these fields have been faced with charges of "rule or ruin tactics," "treachery," "machine control," and "personal ambition at the expense of the long-suffering worker."

The final charge which has frequently been directed against union leaders is "graft and racketeering." "Graft" is separable from "racketeering," although in common parlance the two tend to run together. "Graft" usually refers to such items as padded expense accounts, petty peculation or large-scale defalcation, the selling of supplies to the union by the officers at exorbitant prices, the receipt by union officers of favors (political, social and monetary) from employers in return for concessions, and the establishment by union leaders of business concerns (such as building supplies) from which employers are compelled to purchase the materials upon which the union members work. Some of these practices injure the union's members, others do not. One of the most fantastic cases of attemped graft of this sort was described in a recent racket trial in New York. A labor "leader," Jules Martin (who was also an employer and a gangster), attempted to arrange the fusion of an A.F. of L. local of restaurant workers with a Communist local of food workers. The bargain which he is alleged to have offered the Communist local was that it would receive the support of the stronger A.F. of L. national union if, in return, the Communist leaders would use their "influence" with the Soviet government to persuade it to purchase from Martin the automobiles which he manufactured from second-hand parts!

Graft of this sort is a familiar aspect of business, banking and political life as well as of the labor movement. This, of course, does not help matters much. It indicates, however, that graft is not a peculiar attribute of the labor movement. The amount of graft in any social institution, including the labor movement, depends upon the opportunities which are afforded for it and the controls which can be developed by the many over the few. The controls are mechanical, political and ethical. Standardized accounts, frequent financial reports, bonding of officers and examination of their expense accounts, bankbooks and income tax reports are the mechanical checks upon graft which are available to the corporate shareholder, the church member and the taxpayer, as well as to the union member. The political controls are all those which constitute the essentials of democracy. Freedom of discussion and criticism, frequent meetings, question periods, removing the officer from the chair during the discussion of affairs in which he is involved, appeal from the local to the national officers, appeal to other institutions such as the newspapers, impartial investigators, the courts, the district attorney, the legislature and governmental boards. The ethical controls are those group moral codes which bind together the leader and the follower whether the institution is a management-controlled corporation or a leader-controlled union. The only final answer to the problem of graft is the aggressive development and use by union members of these mechanical, political and ethical controls.

The dividing line between "graft" and "racketeering" is difficult to establish. The phrase "labor racketeering" however, is usually used in connection with extortion from union members. There are two varieties of this in the labor movement. The first is that in which the union leader extorts from either the members or the employer or both more than is returned to the worker in the form of improved conditions. Examples of this have already been given: The labor leader may sell "protection" against strikes to the employer in exchange for lump sum payments to the union officer; the worker is compelled to "kickback" to the leader part of his wages in exchange for "job protection"; the union leader and the employer combine forces to terrorize competitors and extract from the consumer and the worker. Illustrations of all these forms of racketeering can be supplied in the building trades', moving picture operators', and musicians' unions, among others.

The second type of labor racketeering is that in which outside gangsters, either with or without the acquiescence of the union leaders, "take over" a trade union and operate it for their own benefit by means of violence and terrorism. This is a somewhat newer development, but probably antedates the adoption of Prohibition. It has been expanded since the repeal of the Eighteenth Amendment by the transfer of the bootleg gangsters to other fields. It

attacks business and unionism alike and concentrates upon
the weaker enterprises in both fields. Occasionally professional gangsters have been invited into unions to throw out
racketeering labor leaders. Al Capone is reported to have
been the Good Samaritan in this respect on a number of
occasions in Chicago. The Good Samaritan has his price,
of course, which takes the form of continued control of
the union, but at marked-down rates. In other instances
gangsters have secured entrance by terrorizing the union
leaders into handing over the funds or the control of funds.
Sometimes the leaders get a cut of the proceeds for being
easily "persuaded" that discretion is the better part of
valor. On other occasions the union leaders have fought
back with determination and great courage and subsequently have been "bumped off," "taken for a ride,"
"rubbed out," or "put in a bag." New York restaurants,
Brooklyn painters and Chicago cleaners and dyers have
been recent victims of this kind of labor racketeering.

In several instances (the Retail Clerks' International
Protective Association, for one), there has been abundant
evidence that the national officers have been fully aware
of the domination of their locals by racketeering interests
and have done nothing about it. This has even been true
of the A.F. of L. Executive Council. For example, in
Labor and Modern Industrial Society, Professor Norman
Ware gives a vivid description of the effort of a courageous
old-time labor man, Steve Sumner, at the 1933 convention
of the A.F. of L., to compel the convention to undertake
a housecleaning campaign. Sumner told a good many
stories, cited individuals, and said that he could point out
some interesting characters on the floor of the convention.
All he asked was that the Executive Council get busy and
help throw out the racketeers. He was suppressed and his
remarks were expunged from the published convention
proceedings.

There are two reasons for this attitude on the part of

the higher labor officials. The first is that, in some instances, the higher officials are themselves involved. The second is the familiar attitude of "hush-hush" adopted by the leaders of many large social institutions. "Don't tell the people that some banks are corruptly managed, because the whole banking system will collapse." "Don't let it get out that some priests or clergymen are immoral because the people will lose their religion." "Don't let the students hear that faculties are torn by internal strife, part of which is selfish and stupid, because students will lose their respect for education." "Keep it quiet, men." "Let's not wash our dirty linen in public." The point is, of course, that the dirty linen isn't washed at all. It is waved from the house-tops by unsympathetic contestants for power. The point at which stupidity in this matter ends and treachery begins is a somewhat metaphysical question.

The caliber of the leadership of any social institution has a double relationship to the growth or decline of the institution. Leaders influence the development of the institution, but the movement creates the leaders. Under the domination of restrictive craft policies and subject to the conservative conditions of the 'twenties organized labor was a declining institution. This was due partly to inferior leadership, but the inferior leadership was basically a reflection of the economic and social conditions which led to the decline of the movement as a whole. The crisis of the depression, its corrosive effects upon other social institutions, the realignment of political forces and the smashing of many of the important social beliefs gave new life to the labor movement. Old leaders and policies have been discredited both in the labor movement and in business. Labor, however, has gained in relation to business. Opportunities for leadership in the labor field have increased more than in business. The labor movement is developing new and better leaders from its midst and is attracting from the outside others who, a few years ago, might have gone into business. It is already drawing upon the colleges, the law schools, the scientific schools and the government services for its organizers and its technicians. Some of these recruits will move from technical to political functions within the labor movement and rise to posts of national leadership. Others will affect the policies of the national leaders through their own work in the quieter fields of research and technical service. Ultimately the quality of leadership as well as its policies are profoundly influenced by the vitality of the labor movement and the nature of the basic economic and social conditions from which it springs.

CHAPTER X

The Labor Movement and Political Action

THE labor movement has an internal political life of its own. Most of the aspects of city, state and Federal political action can be duplicated within it. There are the same two-party or multiple-party systems which tend to coalesce around the group in power, on the one hand, and around the opposition, on the other. There are the same theoretical separations of power among executive, legislative and judicial groups. There are the same machine methods of control which cut across these separations of power. There are platforms, promises, elections, disputes over the method of representation, rotten boroughs, distinctions between state and constitutional law, watchers at the polls, appeals to home, mother and the flag, stumping tours, prearranged demonstrations and so on.

There are two important distinctions, however, between the political life of the labor movement and that of cities, states and the nation. The first is that the labor movement is organized along strictly economic lines cutting across the boundaries of cities, states and nations, while the older forms of political action are organized on a territorial basis cutting across the boundaries of industry. The second difference is that the older political symbols have much greater prestige than those of the labor movement. The lieutenant governor of Pennsylvania is a more powerful person than the secretary-treasurer of the United Mine Workers, even though the same individual occupies both offices. For these two reasons there is a constant tendency in the labor movement (as well as in business) to move toward political action through the instruments of the city, state and nation. By this means the power of the labor movement may be broadened and deepened.

There are very specific reasons for labor's interest in the political machinery of the state; they may be roughly classified as economic and civic. First among economic questions are those which deal with wages, hours and "conditions." While it is true that the control of these matters is the primary reason for the existence of unionism as an economic organization, there are circumstances in which it is nearly impossible for unionism to exercise control. There are "sweatshop" industries which can be organized only with extreme difficulty, if at all. Organized labor's interest in these industries is more than humanitarian. The low wages, long hours and inferior conditions prevailing in one industry tend to undercut the conditions established by unions elsewhere. When unions have succeeded in organizing the "sweatshop" trades, it has been very difficult to enforce union standards. The prestige of the labor movement has been less than sufficient to compel obedience to trade agreements, and the power of the labor movement has not been great enough to prevent the migration of these industries from union to nonunion areas. Unions, therefore, are impelled to make use of the machinery and prestige of the state to establish minimum wage and maximum hour laws and to secure legislation dealing with accidents, industrial disease, fatigue and sanitation. The territorial organization of the state makes possible the enforcement of minimum standards in nonunion industries if the power of unions in other industries is sufficient to secure regulatory legislation. The improved condition of the regulated industries may eventually prepare them for organization by unions. The power of unionism is thus enhanced by an interacting relationship between economic and political activity.

Second in importance among the economic objectives of labor politics is regulation of the labor of women, chil-

dren and convicts. Women and children are often difficult
to organize. And for other reasons unionism thus far has
not been spectacularly successful in the jails and peni-
tentiaries! Here again, organized labor's interest is more
than humanitarian. The employment standards of women,
children and convicts tend to undercut those established
by organized labor. Long experience has taught the labor
movement that it has much to gain by acting through the
machinery of the state in an effort to regulate women's
labor, abolish child labor and limit the sale of convict-
made goods. If or when organized labor succeeds in establishing regulation of these three forms of substandard
labor, it finds that its power within its own field has been
enhanced.

The third economic objective in labor's political program is the provision of social security. Few students of
the contemporary scene can continue to persuade themselves that the problem of social security remains within
the scope of private charity, business welfare policies or
trade union benefits. Unemployment, old-age dependence,
industrial accidents, inadequate provision for community
health and inferior housing are social diseases, most of
which have been aggravated by the development of modern industry. Individuals, organized charity, business and
unionism may all contribute toward the palliation and, to
some extent, the prevention of these diseases. But, in the
last analysis, no agency short of the Federal Government
is sufficiently comprehensive in its coverage of the resources of the nation to deal effectively with them.

Although organized labor has only recently committed
itself to this point of view, it may be expected to take the
lead in urging the expansion of the social security program
of the state and Federal governments. Again, this will not
be because the leaders of organized labor are any more
intelligent, farseeing or altruistic than other social leaders.
It will be because the constituency of the labor leader feels

the impact of social insecurity with far greater force than the higher income groups in society. It is true that mass unemployment, social ill-health, slums and old-age dependence do affect the income, the peace of mind and the stability of owning, managing and professional groups. But the effect of these forces on their incomes is more remote than the effect on workers' incomes. It is relatively easy for the people who live on the hill to close their eyes to what happens on the other side of the tracks. And as for political stability, "*Après moi, le déluge*" and "It can't happen here" have long been opposite but satisfying attitudes toward the specter of the future. In the matter of social security, therefore, there is, or appears to be, a conflict of interests between the "upper" classes on the one hand, and the lower income workers on the other. The nature of the problem makes it almost inevitable that this conflict, apparent or otherwise, will be carried into the political field.

There is an even more specific reason for organized labor's interest in questions of social security. Suppose that a powerful union in the soft coal industry should attempt to coöperate with an association of mine operators in improving the condition of the workers by regularizing production, closing the high-cost mines, eliminating crosshauling and introducing labor-saving machinery. All these policies would almost inevitably result in the displacement of labor. No union leader could afford to push these policies before his constituency if it were apparent that the result would be to force some of his members into destitution. His action might easily turn out to be political suicide. Most union leaders would prefer to hang grimly on to the control of labor in a dying industry than to risk the perquisites of office in a heroic attempt to revive the industry. The result of such a situation would almost certainly be the eventual failure of coöperation in production and a renewal of warfare over a declining monetary income. If, on the other hand, the leader could point to the provision of adequate unemployment relief and the existence of a nation-wide network of employment exchanges and vocational training schools which would facilitate the absorption of the younger workers in other industries, it might become a political possibility within the union to push through the measures upon which the health of the soft coal industry depends.

A fourth objective in labor's political program lies in the field of price control. Wage increases are of little use to labor in the long run if each wage increase is offset, or more than offset, by price increases. As indicated in the chapter on business policies, wherever modified competition prevails, with the result that profits are larger than necessary to induce capital and enterprise to enter the industry, there is a mathematical possibility that wages can be increased without equal price increases. The result is simply that more of the income of the industry goes to labor and less to ownership and management. There is here a definite conflict of economic interests in which the outcome is determined by the relative power of the two groups.

Labor is not likely to move directly into the field of price regulation (i.e., by imposing price controls in the trade agreement). One reason for this is that the traditions of the labor movement are against it. A more important reason is that each separate union is likely to concentrate upon its gains to workers as wage earners and forget the losses to other workers as consumers. The A.F. of L. or the C.I.O. might, of course, become so comprehensive that they could and would be as concerned with the price as with the wage aspects of production. Long before this happened, however, the labor movement would be likely to turn toward the existing, and more comprehensive, machinery of the state as a means of price regulation.

Management also is likely to look toward the government for price regulation. It is quite conceivable that the income of ownership and management would be increased by a general policy of low prices and high wages resulting in expanding production. Unless common action can be secured, however, the tendency among managers is to "let somebody else do it." Long before common action among all managers could be secured, management, like labor, would probably turn to the government for enforcement. It is much more likely, however, that labor rather than management will press for governmental regulation of prices. Again, this is not because of superior intelligence or good will on the part of labor leaders. It is because labor, being on the lower end of the income scale, suffers more than owners and managers from high prices; and because owners, being relatively few in number, may gain from the restrictive practices of monopoly, while labor as a whole can only lose.

Labor's political drive toward adequate social insurance will inevitably raise a fifth important political objective: increased taxation of incomes and inheritances. Assumption by the Federal Government of the burden of social insurance will not increase the total costs of providing for the unemployed, the ill and the aged. These costs already exist and are borne by society through private charity, family support, and local, state and Federal Government relief. When relief is inadequate, the costs of social insecurity assume the form of gradual deterioration of the quality of the population through undernourishment, disease, crime, racketeering and social unrest. Many of these costs may be computed in dollars and cents. Others are general and diffused, but are nonetheless a real burden upon society. The assumption of this burden by the Federal Government may, however, change the distribution of these costs, depending upon the method by which the government raises the funds to defray the expenses of social insurance. The present tendency is to place the burden

upon the lower income groups in the form of taxes upon
pay rolls and wages likely to be borne by the worker both
as producer and as consumer. These taxes are not in accord with the principle of ability to pay. Organized labor
will be moved to political action in order to transfer as
much of the burden of social insurance as possible from
the lower to the higher income groups by the adoption of
higher and more steeply progressive income taxes, the closing of loopholes in present income tax laws, and the
elimination of wage and pay-roll taxes. This program
would arouse determined political opposition, although
many employers would be glad to escape the administrative
burden of collecting the present social security taxes.

Any attempt through union-management coöperation,
or by unions acting alone, to regularize competitive industries and improve their efficiency, or to eliminate the
restrictive policies of monopoly through price regulation,
seriously raises the question of government ownership.
"Property" or "ownership" has traditionally meant that
the person or institution having legal title to useful material things is thereby granted two fundamental rights:
income from and *control* over those things. During the
last one hundred years the status of private property in
the means of production has been profoundly modified.
This modification has been the result of the development
of three important institutions: the modern corporation,
government regulation and the labor movement. The great
bulk of modern manufacturing, commerce and transportation is carried on under the corporate form of organization.
With few exceptions, in the large modern corporation
there is an effective separation of ownership from control.
The shareholders who "own" the enterprise, no longer
have much, if anything, to say about how it shall be run
or how its income shall be distributed. The diffusion of
corporate ownership has made it a relatively public affair,
while the concentration of control in the hands of a

limited number of managers remains private. Legally, technically and ethically the management is responsible to the owners. Actually, within very wide limits, the management may do as it pleases with the owner's "property." This represents a change in the concept of private property which is of fundamental importance.

In the second place, throughout the same period, private property has been subjected to gradual encroachments by governmental agencies through regulation; and taxation. Wage, hour and accident compensation laws; price regulations; antitrust acts; pure food and drug acts and taxation represent infringements upon both the control of, and the income from, the means of production. This development has probably not altered the status of the property owner as profoundly as has the rise of the corporation. The two processes, however, are intimately related. Regulation and taxation represent in part an effort by interested groups to recapture through governmental machinery the powers they have lost to corporation management. This effort has met with intense resistance chiefly from the financial and managerial interests which have come to dominate the modern corporation. The success of government regulation and the extent of its application have been limited by this resistance and by the absence of organized pressure groups sufficiently powerful to secure the extension and enforcement of regulation. Nevertheless, both regulation and taxation have made advances in limiting the power and the income of ownership and management.

In the third place, the rise of the labor movement has curtailed the powers and affected the income of ownership and management. This development has obviously been limited as compared with the rise of the modern corporation and of government regulation, yet every advance made by the labor movement represents an encroachment upon the traditional powers of both ownership and management. Although labor leaders and managers or owners usually do not state the nature of their conflict in theoretical terms, the fact is that as unionism develops, private ownership of the means of production declines.

The sum of these changes is that it is no longer possible to point accurately to the locus of "property" or "ownership" rights in capital equipment. The legal title to property has been diffused by the sale of corporate shares, while the control of property has been concentrated in the hands of financiers and managers. At the same time, the powers of management have been restricted by organized consumers, investors and labor, operating either directly upon management, or indirectly through the regulative and taxing machinery of government. This suggests that "property" is evolving toward a status in which the *title* to property is "public," in the sense that shares of stock are widely diffused, and in which *control* is "public" because of the powers wrested from management by organized groups acting through government. This process of increasing diffusion of private titles to property and increasing "public" regulation of corporate management may be pushed to such a point that the only distinction between the final result and outright "public ownership" would be a question of symbols.

In facing the question of the control over the operation and income of the means of production, therefore, the labor movement has at least four logical alternative methods of action plus any number of possible combinations of these four. Current usage suggests "syndicalism," "guild socialism," "state capitalism" and "state socialism" as descriptions of these courses of action. Organized labor, either with or without the willing coöperation of managers, may face the question of coördinating, regularizing and increasing the efficiency of competitive industry, regulating the prices and increasing the output of monopolistic industry directly, by means of its own economic power and the terms of the trade agreement. It is far from impossible to conceive of a union as powerful as the United Mine Workers employing its own technicians, planners and organizers to undertake the regularization of the soft coal industry. It is also quite possible that even though efficiency were greatly increased and costs reduced the union would at the same time increase wages and shorten hours so drastically that income ceased to flow to the owners. Once the workers had secured both complete control and the entire income of the industry, "syndicalism," or a condition of worker-ownership would have been established.

Long before any one union could carry out such a program, however, it would encounter the insuperable difficulty now faced by the present managers of industry, that is, the necessity for coördinating one industry with all others. In a completely integrated economic society, no single industry can operate in a vacuum. The planning of the soft coal industry would necessitate the planning of its relationship to such existing industries as oil, coke and gas, steel, coal tar by-products and hydroelectric power, as well as the development of new industries for the absorption of workers displaced from the coal industry. Unions and management would be driven to make use of the coördinating machinery of the Federal Government in the development of nation-wide planning of production and distribution. Such a program would require a vast extension of the powers of government over the regulation of wages, hours, prices, capital allocation and so on. Unionism might, of course, become so complete that it could set up its own coördinating agency. Such a condition would be roughly what is described by the English phrase "guild socialism." Long before unionism grew sufficiently powerful to establish its own coordinating agency, however, it would be likely to make use of the existing machinery and the traditional symbols of government. "Syndicalism" would therefore become "state capitalism."

The advance of government planning and regulation of industry, even though pushed by a powerful labor movement, might be blocked by determined opposition from the managers of large corporations and the owners of small enterprises. When two groups find themselves in opposition, the "rights" of both sides tend to be stated as absolutes. Owners (and managers ostensibly acting for the owners) base their opposition to interference by labor or government upon the traditional right of the owner to control his property and the income from it. Since this "right" is stated as an absolute, it is likely to be met with an equally absolute and opposed concept: government ownership. The mechanics of the transfer from private to government ownership might take the form of the exchange of cash or government bonds for the common stock of corporations.[1] Or it might take the form of outright expropriation by government of the title to the means of production. The difference between the gradual encroachment of government regulation and the forthright declaration of government ownership is a difference of degree rather than of kind, since both programs refer to the abrogation of the two essentials of private property: the rights to its control and its income. The first, however, would be called "state capitalism" while the second is labeled "state socialism."

The question as to whether government regulation or government ownership would be the final outcome of the political program of a powerful labor movement is likely to be determined by the relation between the need for and the opposition to public planning and control of economic life. When both the need and the opposition are great, the conflict is likely to move into the state of setting up absolutely opposed concepts of a symbolic nature from which (if organized labor won) government ownership

[1] All theoretical right to the control of industry would therefore pass to the government since stocks alone carry voting power. The government bonds or cash issued in this way might be recovered through income and inheritance taxation.

would emerge. In other situations, formal title to property may remain in private hands, but with control shared in varying degree among owners, managers, labor and government. It might also be predicted that the question as to whether government ownership comes about by compensation or expropriation depends upon the relation between the need for and the opposition to government ownership. Outright expropriation is likely to take place only when extreme bitterness or prolonged physical violence has developed between the opposed contestants for power.

In summary, it may be said that both the "economic" and the "political" programs of organized labor constitute an encroachment upon the traditional concept of private property. The difference between the two programs is that in the first, the labor movement limits its objectives to those which can be secured through collective bargaining and strikes organized along industrial lines. The results of this program are recorded in the trade agreement. In the second, organized labor makes use of the territorial organization of political life to extend or enforce its gains in industrial areas which are not readily susceptible to direct union control. The results of this program are recorded in state and Federal law.

There is no logical point at which labor's leaders may stop. Even conservative craft union leaders who vigorously defend the "present economic and social system" do not allow this slogan to prevent them from pressing for higher wages, the prohibition of child labor and the strict regulation of railroad and utility rates. Each of these is an encroachment upon those "rights" of private property which constitute a symbolic cornerstone of "the present economic and social system." Conservative union leaders also denounce anyone who opposes the "present form of government" or attempts to set up "an invisible government." And yet the labor movement, if not an "invisible government," is a new form of political life which, like the employer's associations, frequently comes into conflict with, controls, or supersedes the territorial organization of political expression.

The regulation of wages, hours, women's labor and child labor and the provision of social security necessitate increased industrial efficiency and the regulation of monopoly prices. Increased efficiency can be achieved to only a limited extent without coördination and planning of industry. The effective regulation of monopoly prices is unlikely without the use of the power and prestige of the machinery of government. Resistance to such planning or regulation leads to the destruction of the symbols of private property and the substitution of the concept of government ownership. Resistance to government ownership may be the catalytic agent which turns compensation into confiscation.

In addition to the economic objectives, there are civic or social objectives in labor's political program. These may be dealt with more briefly. Labor is interested in the preservation of such civic "rights" as freedom of speech, assembly and the press, equal justice under the law, extension of the suffrage, and the development of the "rights" of collective action: the strike, picket and boycott. Labor is of course also interested in preventing the abrogation of any of these "rights" by the law, the militia, professional strikebreakers or spies. On the other hand, groups opposed to the rise of organized labor attempt to deny these rights as far as possible since without them labor is shorn of its power.

The methods used by both sides in this conflict have been surveyed in earlier chapters. Two matters of some importance may be pointed out, however, in this connection. The first is that in the struggle over civil rigths, although both sides appeal to abstract principles as justification for their part in the struggle, these abstract principles are relatively unimportant. In the long history of group struggles for power, the rising or attacking group is forced to make much of the traditional "liberties." The dominant or defending group, by the same token, is driven to deny what it terms the "license" of the attacking group. The degree of suppression of civil liberties by the dominant group is a rough index of the weakness of the group. A powerful social group in the prime of its powers can afford to allow full freedom of criticism or even of organized opposition. A declining social group, or the leadership of a social institution which has been weakened by its failure to meet the requirements of its epoch, turns toward repression of criticism or opposition.

The second matter of importance in this connection is that, although organized labor may to some extent preserve civil rights through direct action, its interests also lie in acting through the existing forms of government. Organized labor may conduct its own free speech fights, as the I.W.W. did, by sending platoons of workers to speak from soapboxes, submit to arrest, fill the jails to overflowing and break the "gag laws" of repressive communities. It may develop its own press, enforce its right to assembly by physical defiance of police opposition, conduct mass picket lines or flying squadrons armed with crude implements against opposing forces, beat up professional strikebreakers and vigilantes and throw out spies. Again, however, as in the case of its economic objectives, the machinery of government is available to the labor movement for the preservation and extension of civil rights.

Labor is therefore interested in electing local, state and national officials who will not use deputies, police, militia or the Federal Army as active strikebreakers. It is interested in legislating professional spy and strikebreaking agencies out of existence, asserting the legal right to collective bargaining, legally prohibiting the use of the more subtle antiunion devices, prosecuting the leaders of secret terrorist societies like the Black Legion and the Ku Klux Klan, resisting compulsory arbitration, the compulsory incorporation of unions and consequent publication of their membership lists and so on. In all these respects, political action may be more effective than direct action since, first, the power of strong unions in some industries may be extended through the territorial machinery of government over areas in which unions have no power, and, second, the symbols and implements of the state carry more prestige and power than those of unionism.

For all these reasons, therefore, unions are impelled, whether consciously or not, toward political action outside their own economic spheres. Throughout its entire history the American labor movement has engaged in political activity directed toward some or all of these ends. The political effectiveness of the labor movement, however, has been limited by its economic weakness. It is only within recent months that organized labor has indicated a conscious inclination to enter the lists as an important and independent political force.

The major political policy of the American labor movement has consisted of electing "friends" and defeating "enemies" of the labor movement and of using the familiar lobbying tactics of minority groups in local and national governments. The agencies through which lobbying activities are carried on are the city central unions, the state federations and the executive offices of the A.F. of L. in Washington. The officers of and delegates to the city centrals draw the attention of local union members to matters of interest to organized labor in local politics; indicate individuals to be supported in local elections; and bring their personal and organizational pressure to bear upon town or city officials and boards. The state federations set up offices in or near the state capital and employ officers and lawyers to draw up bills in which labor is interested or to scrutinize bills introduced by antilabor interests. The state federations also arrange to have labor represented at legislative committee hearings and to bring pressure to bear upon legislators through personal contact or communications from union members. In all respects these lobbying activities of the city centrals and state federations exactly parallel the work of local and state employers' associations, except that the funds available for the work of the labor lobbies are relatively limited.

The officers of the A.F. of L. act as Washington lobbyists and also employ lawyers and committeemen to carry on tasks similar to those of the state federations. The expenses of the A.F. of L. in this connection during 1936 (including the salaries and traveling expenses of lobbyists) were $15,242.33. This was a relatively modest sum for an organization representing about 4,000,000 people. The Railroad Brotherhoods and several important national unions also employ Washington lobbyists. It is impossible to estimate the success of this method of influencing legislation. The A.F. of L. itself publishes a twenty-nine page pamphlet in which it lists its legislative achievements during the last thirty-one years. It claims the credit for having secured the passage of two hundred and seventy-four "remedial" laws and prevented the passage of "hundreds" of antilabor bills. There is no question but that the influence of the state federations and the Washington lobbies has been important. It cannot be denied, however, that the activities of many organizations other than the A.F. of L. have played a large part in the "success" of the A.F. of L.'s bipartisan program. It must also be pointed out that a great many of the acts passed and bills defeated have been relatively trivial ones dealing with employment conditions in government industry or under government contracts.

Among the more important acts, all or part of which have been supported by labor lobbies, are the Clayton Act of 1914, the two antichild labor acts of 1916 and 1919, the introduction of the resolution calling for the passage of a child labor amendment to the Constitution in 1924, the prevention of Senate confirmation of the appointment of Judge Parker to the Supreme Court in 1930, the Norris-LaGuardia Anti-Injunction Act of 1932, Section 7a of the N.I.R.A. in 1933, the Wagner Labor Relations Act and the Byrnes Act which limits the interstate transportation of strikebreakers.

Although the A.F. of L. and the Railroad Brotherhoods have for fifty years adhered to their bipartisan policy, they have been almost continuously under attack from progressive elements in the labor movement for their failure to undertake independent political action. It has been repeatedly pointed out that very little has actually been won, that independent political action is an indication and source of the strength of a labor movement, that the "capitalist" parties really do not pay much attention to labor's demands, that there is frequently little or nothing to distinguish the personnel or the principles of the major parties and that labor is, therefore, left without any real choice when it goes to the polls. It has also been argued that the attempt to shift labor's interest back and forth from one party to another has dulled the interest of workers in state and Federal politics.

Although many labor leaders have agreed with these criticisms, there has been little agreement upon alternative policies. There are adherents of a policy of attempting to work through and capture one of the existing major parties. Others propose the setting up of a third party. Still others advocate a farmer-labor party. Some believe in a strictly independent labor party; and there are those who will have nothing but revolutionary political activity.

In favor of operating through an existing major party it is argued that the name and tradition of the older parties carry weight a new party would lack. Since the direct primary system is generally used in the United States, anyone may enter the field in search of nomination on an old-party ticket. Having captured the nomination, labor candidates would be assured of the support of many who vote a "straight" ticket regardless of candidates and the principles for which they stand. To this is added the fact that the absence of proportional representation in the United States makes it very difficult for a new party to place any candidates in office. A new labor party might actually poll 10,000,000 or more votes without electing anyone as long as legislators are selected on the basis of single member districts and majority rule.

In answer to these arguments it is urged that existing party machinery is controlled by political bosses and small armies of ward heelers with ample funds and the promise of patronage at their disposal. The funds come primarily from business groups antipathetic to labor's aims. Participation in an old-party primary would mean, furthermore, that labor would fall heir to the discredit attached to the name of the older party. The Democratic party, for example, is said to be controlled by "reactionary" interests in the South and by "corrupt" political machines in the cities of the North. From the beginning, therefore, labor candidates would be compromised by their political bedfellows. The rapid rise of the Republican party in the 1860's indicates that old political symbols and loyalties, if backed with a strong emotional appeal, can be transferred by a sufficiently powerful economic group.

If labor organizes a new party, it remains to be decided whether it shall be merely a "third" party, a farmer-labor party, a "pure" labor party or a revolutionary party. A third party has the advantage of having objectives sufficiently vague to attract many adherents outside the organized labor movement. This, however, is in fact its primary danger. The more diverse the economic and social elements attracted to a political movement, the more difficult it becomes to state the program of the movement. Mass support may be gained, but only at the cost of losing the precise economic and civic objectives which constitute labor's reasons for venturing into politics. A third party would suffer from the major defect of all merely territorial forms of political organization, which is that so many conflicting economic interests are represented that it becomes impossible to assume a clear-cut stand on any economic issue. Such parties are reduced at worst to flag waving, baby kissing, red baiting and indiscriminate cursing of the international bankers, droughts and anything which is not Nordic, Protestant and blond. At best they achieve gains which may be less than those which unions can establish through strictly economic activity. They carry with them the very grave danger to the labor movement that in the confusion of objectives, labor's leaders may be distracted or bribed into the betrayal of labor by opposed economic interests. The trail of labor politics in both Europe and America is well posted with the political skeletons of labor "leaders" who stepped from the beaten path laid down by the clear economic interests of their constituencies.

Repelled by this prospect, many of labor's political theoreticians swing to the opposite extreme. A "revolutionary" program is outlined which is not designed to secure the support even of organized labor, let alone the support of liberals, progressives and labor sympathizers. A revolutionary party, during a period of relative social stability, does not expect mass support. Its functions are primarily organizational and educative. Its membership is closely scrutinized and, after admission, is bound to abide by party discipline. It operates upon the "fractional" system, that is, its members are directed to enter existing economic and social organizations and attempt to influence them into the acceptance of policies decided upon at meetings of the revolutionary party. It sets up ultimate objectives which are frequently stated as slogans or in otherwise symbolic terms as, for example, "the overthrow of the capitalist system," "the establishment of a coöperative commonwealth," "production for use and not for profit" or "collective ownership of the means of production." It may nominate candidates for political office but the nominees publicly admit (a rare political phenomenon) that they do not expect to win. Its purposes in entering political contests are to use this opportunity for educational work and to provide itself with a ballotbox index of popular feeling. By organizing, educating and maintaining its integrity it expects to become the natural leader of a mass movement during a period of social crisis in which old loyalties are shattered, social behavior is in flux, and an informed, disciplined and confident organization may assume and retain power.

Between these extremes there remain two possibilities: a farmer-labor party and a strictly labor party. Those who urge farmer-labor political action point to the fact that there is a good deal of identity of economic interest between farmers and workers. Both have a common antagonism toward banker control of industry and agriculture (through land mortgages), overcharging of consumers by middlemen, and the "irresponsible" power of insurance companies over farmers (through mortgages) and over workers (through the "industrial insurance racket"). It is pointed out that the farmers themselves have a tradition of protest against the *status quo* quite as old and as important in American history as that of the workers. It is further urged that the prosperity of farmers rests increasingly upon the existence of a large domestic market for their produce and that this can exist only with well-paid and fully-employed industrial and white-collar workers. Conversely, full-time employment and high wages depend upon a broad agricultural market for industrial products which can be provided only by prosperous farmers. The supporters of farmer-labor political action point out, moreover, that many farmers are really wage workers or share-croppers employed by corporate or absentee owners. Finally, most farmers and workers hate and fear war and any form of "Fascism" which denies to the common people their basic civil liberties. It is urged that war, if not nation-wide Fascism, is imminent and that these must be fought as quickly and upon as broad a political front as possible. Such a front can be provided only by joint farmer-labor action directed toward a minimum program.

There are many politically minded leaders and members of the labor movement, however, who are unable to accept this position. They point out that the bulk of the farmers are really small employers interested in high prices for their products and in low costs of production. High prices of foodstuffs injure the workers as consumers and low costs injure the workers as wage earners either in agriculture or in the industries which manufacture farm equipment and supplies. This condition has traditionally led the farmers to favor inflation, because during a period of rising prices wages lag behind other prices. The same reason has led organized labor to oppose inflationary policies. The farmer's tradition of protest, of which much is made by farmer-labor party adherents, has usually taken the form of demands for inflationary policies like "green-backism" and "free silver." The prosperity of both farmers and workers cannot be brought about by reciprocal pushing up of each others prices. It can result only from a more effective organization of both the agricultural and industrial means of production. It is asserted that such organization can be accomplished only by a degree of centralization of power over economic life extremely distasteful to the individualistically-minded farmer. Coördinated economic control is immediately branded "socialistic" by farmers who constitute the last stronghold of small-scale enterprise. Finally, farmers form one of the most important groups from which "Fascist" movements are recruited. The most brutal suppression of industrial labor's attempts to organize has occurred in rural areas. Vigilantes, lynching parties, the Ku Klux Klan and proto-Fascist political organizations such as those of ex-Governor Talmadge of Georgia and the late Senator Long contain large elements of poverty-stricken farmers whose economic sufferings make them willing antilabor tools of dominant economic interests. The coöperation of such groups is to be secured only through the sacrifice of labor's real political objectives.

From these criticisms of joint farmer-labor political action it would follow that participation in independent labor politics should be strictly limited to organized workers, whether industrial or white collar. The objectives of such a labor party would necessarily be confined to those which bore an immediate relationship to the economic program of unionism. The party would content itself with the modest position of holding the balance of power between other larger parties, and thereby secure concessions which would reënforce its gains upon the economic front. It would expand only as unionism expanded, as a result both of direct advance on the industrial front and the protection of this position through political gains. Its leaders would remain under strict union control. Its funds would be derived from union dues. It would make no attempt to assume governmental responsibility until it became evident that it could do so without compromising the integrity of its position as the guarantor of the economic interests of wageworkers.

There is a tendency in labor political circles to argue in terms of absolutes the relative merits of various political programs. "It must be a revolutionary party, or none at all." "Farmer-labor politics is the only thing." "Bipartisan politics are suicidal." "What we really need is a new third party." The correct form of political organization, on the contrary, can be determined only by reference to the exact

social and economic conditions of a period. If a labor party
is to have mass support, its objectives cannot deviate far
from the objectives and ideologies of the mass. But in
generalizing its objectives sufficiently to capture the mass,
a labor party surrenders much if not most of what is valuable in its own specific political program. Whether labor
should make this surrender in order to enter the political
field depends upon the exigencies of the situation. If the
period is such that complete political reaction appears
imminent (so complete that all the power of the state will
be thrown against labor's ability to organize on the economic front), then labor is justified in throwing its weight
into an existing party as the lesser of two evils, [2] or organizing a new party on the broadest possible basis. This
would be true even if many of the elements in the party
had divergent economic interests, as long as it could be
held together for the attainment of the main objectives.
Such a tactic, however, should be undertaken only if the
situation is as threatening as described, since working
through an existing party or initiating a mass "third" party
involves all the dangers described above.

At the other extreme, if it appears that a period of
social crisis is at hand (such as that existing in Russia in
the summer of 1917), then a revolutionary party is prag-
matically justified in refusing to coöperate with any political group which does not advocate the transfer of all
power to the representatives of labor. But if the situation
is any less crucial than this, a revolutionary party can justify its existence only if it coöperates with existing labor
organizations in sharpening labor's political consciousness
and perfecting its economic organization. Any other
policy reduces a revolutionary party to a debating society.

If (between these extremes) it appears that labor can-

[2] This was the position taken by labor's Nonpartisan League, the American Labor party and (indirectly) the Communist party in the election
campaign of 1936.

not attain much-desired political ends without the support of farmers, then a labor party must be prepared to make concessions even at some risk to its own control. This risk should be assumed, however, only if it can effectively be demonstrated that the dangers of failing to undertake joint farmer-labor action are so great as to justify the necessary compromises.

The great difficulty of accurately balancing the dangers of the different forms of political action against the necessities of a particular situation is the source of perennial controversy within the labor movement, as a correct alternative to the traditional policy of the A.F. of L. is sought. The number of economic and social variables to be accounted for is so great that analogies from American or European history offer little guidance. Consequently the political policies of the American labor movement have for a generation remained almost immobile.

The local labor parties of the early 1800's were destroyed by depression, internal factionalism and inexperienced leadership. A revival of interest in independent labor policies after the Civil War was stopped by the decline of the unions on which the movement was based. The victory of the A.F. of L. over the Knights of Labor, and the personality of Samuel Gompers stamped "nonpartisan" political policies upon the labor movement. Independent labor politics became "radical" politics. The Socialist Labor party, the Socialist party and the Communist party [3] have divided this field among themselves without ever receiving mass support. They have functioned chiefly as organizing and educational institutions.

Immediately after the Armistice a rash of farmer-labor parties broke out in the Northwest. These parties were brought together in the Nonpartisan League, and in the election of 1920 became important political factors in

[3] Founded in 1876, 1901 and 1919, respectively.

Minnesota, Idaho, Montana and North Dakota in spite of opposition by the A.F. of L. In 1922 the Conference for Progressive Political Action was formed under the leadership of the railroad unions, farmers' and progressive organizations. It entered the 1924 political campaign with Senator LaFollette (the elder) as its candidate for President. The A.F. of L. endorsed him as a candidate but did not identify itself with the movement. LaFollette received 4,800,000 votes (one sixth of the total votes cast), but the labor movement withdrew its support of the C.P.P.A. shortly afterward and the movement passed out of existence. Only the Farmer-Labor party of Minnesota survived this period.

With the profound revival which stirred the labor movement after 1933, a new interest in independent labor politics arose. Farmer-labor parties appeared in Connecticut, New Jersey, Massachusetts, Ohio and elsewhere. Several powerful unions in the A.F. of L. combined to form a bloc committed to independent political action. This group was supported by many city centrals and state federations. The Minnesota Farmer-Labor party grew in influence and the LaFollete wing of the Republican party in Wisconsin broke away to form the Progressive party. In the 1935 convention of the A.F. of L., thirteen resolutions calling for the formation of an independent labor or farmer-labor party were introduced by unions representing about 500,000 members. In the summer of 1936 several leaders of the C.I.O. set up Labor's Nonpartisan League with the intention of mobilizing the labor vote for President Roosevelt. Large sums donated from union treasuries were devoted to active campaigning for President Roosevelt by the League. In New York State an affiliate of the League, the American Labor party, raised an average of twenty-six cents apiece from 320,000 people for the campaign and polled about 300,000 votes on its own ticket for President Roosevelt and Governor Lehman. It is currently expected that Labor's Nonpartisan League will place its own candidates in the field in 1940.[4]

There are definite indications that independent labor action may become a powerful political force within a relatively short period. Restricted immigration, universal public schooling, the radio, the movies and the automobile have removed many of the cultural conflicts which have long been obstacles to common political action among workers. The appearance of a large nucleus of politically-minded workers within the C.I.O. unions provides a basis for action. The high degree of centralization of power assumed by the Federal Government has increased the possibilities of political activity by minimizing the economic diversities resulting from the variations of state law. And the appearance of distinct lines of cleavage in both the major parties indicates declining loyalties to party labels.

It remains to be determined, however, what form a new party shall take. The indications at present are that the membership of a new party should be solidly grounded in trade-union membership. Sharecroppers and farm wageworkers, white-collar workers and professionals who have developed their own economic organizations should be admitted to party membership upon the same basis as industrial and craft workers. Organizations of the unemployed and of farmers might be admitted upon a federated basis which did not threaten the ultimate control of the organized workers. Local, state and national conventions and standing committees would be necessary to insure democratic control over leaders and policies. The leaders

[4] Shortly after the 1936 elections the Nonpartisan League became almost exclusively an adjunct of the C.I.O. During the 1937 steel strike coolness developed between the C.I.O. and President Roosevelt over the failure of the Federal administration to take positive action against the steel companies for alleged violation of the Byrnes Act and the Firearms Act. This coolness increased the likelihood of independent labor policies in 1938 and 1940.

should come from within the labor movement itself and be absolutely subject to party discipline in major issues.

If such a party is to maintain its integrity, its finances must be provided by contributions from the membership itself. Large contributions from interested outsiders should not be accepted. Long experience indicates that such contributions place a political organization within the control of the contributors. Party dues can be collected through the unions themselves. Majority rule within a union may be used to bind the members to contribute on a per capita basis to party funds. If, within a given union, there are strenuous objections to majority rule in this connection, individual members may escape their obligation by giving written notice of their objection to union officers.[5] By providing that the money be raised from the membership itself, rank and file control and interest are heightened.

The platform of a labor party should be limited and specific. Vague generalizations are unnecessary when appeal is being made to the economic and civic interests of a limited number of social groups. Such phrases as "Congress shall legislate prosperity," "We pledge ourselves to the fundamental liberties of our forefathers," "The unemployed must be liquidated," "The joys of the hearthstone and the vine-covered cottage must be preserved," are soporifics designed to close the eyes of a constituency to the fact that the divergence of economic interests represented in the party makes impossible a clear-cut statement of objectives. If labor cannot state its policies specifically, the effort and very real dangers involved in entering the political arena are not worth the possible gains. A precise

[5] This method of raising political funds was endorsed by English law from 1913 to 1927. It was called "contracting out." In the Trades Disputes Act of 1927, however, a series of repressive clauses was included by the antilabor conservative government. One of these clauses substituted "contracting in" for "contracting out," i.e., union officers must secure written permission from each member before political contributions could be made on the members' account. This was a serious blow to the British Labor party.

and limited political platform, on the other hand, makes possible the education of union membership through a discussion of the issues, and also facilitates the subjection of political leaders to union and party discipline.

The specific planks in a labor platform for the immediate future might be: Federal minimum wage and maximum hour legislation; the elimination of child labor; Federal (rather than state) unemployment insurance with extensive contribution from general treasury funds provided by increased progressive taxation of incomes and inheritances; direct contributions from the general treasury toward old-age annuities; resistance to *compulsory* arbitration of industrial disputes; [6] an expanded Federal housing program, a nation-wide network of employment exchanges, the development of regional planning centering in hydro-electric power projects, and (possibly) the nationalization of banking, railroads and such "sick" industries as soft coal.

State platforms might include more stringent enforcement of factory regulations, opposition to compulsory incorporation of unions, limitation of the use of the injunction by state courts in labor disputes, the limitation of the use of state police and militia as strikebreaking agencies, the complete elimination of professional spy and strike-breaking agencies, and the setting up of "little Wagner Acts" in each state to deal with industries operating in intrastate commerce.

[6] All labor movements have strenuously resisted any effort to impose *compulsory* arbitration upon trade unions. Their position has been that since the policies and attitudes of state are profoundly influenced by employer interests, compulsory arbitration shears labor of its ultimate power, the right to strike. Unions do submit, however, to voluntary arbitration with compulsory findings, that is, they agree to abide by the award of the arbitrators. Compulsory arbitration was one of the weapons used in destroying the labor movement in Germany and Italy. If compulsory state arbitration were adopted in this country, the political contest between employers and workers would become much more acute. Conflicting economic interests would be raised from the industrial to the political level.

Local political activities would be directed chiefly toward the election of officials and boards from a union slate.

Such a program, explicitly outlined in sample bills, might easily attract a nucleus of a million organized workers. The program itself and the announcement of solid support from half a dozen such unions as the mine, garment, clothing, textile, steel and automobile workers would attract the votes of many others both inside and outside the labor movement. It would be surprising if such a party could not poll five million votes in its first national campaign, elect several representatives to Congress, influence state legislatures and control many well-organized local centers.

On the other hand, a page from American history suggests that the opposition to a labor party would be even more intense than to unionism. Many of the planks in a labor platform would curtail the powers and incomes of dominant owning, managing and banking interests. This, of course, is also true of the strictly economic program of the labor movement. But the venture of labor into independent politics would broaden and deepen the real or apparent conflicts of group interests. Far more would be at stake in a political conflict between labor and other groups than the patronage, honors and salaries which have been fought over by two parties whose economic positions have been difficult to distinguish. Even the 1896 Bryan campaign and the 1936 Roosevelt campaign would presumably become relatively mild affairs.

The press might be expected to be somewhat more unanimous in its antilabor position than it was in its anti-Roosevelt position in 1936. The experience of Upton Sinclair in California suggests that the movies, churches and schools would be used to broadcast calumnies of labor candidates. "Bolshevism," "anarchism," "free love," "polygamy," "nationalization of the children" would be authoritatively established as the goals of the labor movement. Bombs would be noted in labor candidates' pockets. Wire hair and red beards along with physical deficiencies would be attributed to those who assumed the leadership of labor politics. "The grass will grow in the streets." "The banks will close." "Factories will be unable to operate." "We will be forced off (or on) the gold standard." "The national honor is at stake." "Let's keep Stalin out of the White House."

Bribes (monetary, social and liquid) would flow. Ballot boxes would be stuffed, recounts demanded, strong arm squads would beat up the voters—all on a grander scale than usual. Old parties would adopt labor planks, voters would be disfranchised, opposition parties (heavily financed) would appear, and labor parties would experience difficulty in getting on the ballot. If labor candidates were elected, the "social lobby" would go to work. Flattery, dinner parties, honorary chairmanships and an occasional kiss from the American equivalent of a duchess would be bestowed upon labor's political leaders. Finally, peerages not being available, "good" labor politicians who proved that they were not "dangerous" and that they "thought things through" would be rewarded by a seat in the Supreme Court, a Kentucky colonelcy or a position on the board of a life insurance company.

The question must again be raised, therefore, as to whether independent political action by labor is worth while. The answer remains, as previously indicated, that both the certain dangers and the possible gains of political action are greater than those of economic action. The difference is simply one of degree rather than of kind. Within the labor movement there are the same difficulties that there are in the broader political sphere, in attracting and retaining the interest and loyalty of members; securing the full discussion of important issues; developing competent leadership; struggling against calumny, misrepresentation or the honestly conflicting economic interests of other groups; and maintaining the control of the rank and file over their leaders. But at the same time political action through the machinery of the state carries with it the possibility of considerably greater gains. If the American labor movement turns to independent political action it will be both a consequence and a cause of its rising confidence, discipline and power on the economic front.

CHAPTER XI

The Labor Movement in an Evolving Society

INSOFAR as direct judgments have been passed, in preceding chapters, upon the policies of unionism and business, these judgments have been given from a pragmatic viewpoint. Do certain policies help the institution in question to sustain and improve its position? If so, the institution, whether union or management, should adopt the policy in question. Otherwise, it should not. Inevitably, however, in an analysis of this sort, implied judgments are rendered which assume the existence of standards higher than the success or failure of a particular group involved in social conflict. Most ordinary human beings refuse to regard the society in which they live as a congeries of conflicting groups each one of which is right if it wins and wrong if it loses. The concept of the well-being of society as a whole constantly asserts itself as being a criterion of judgment superior to the success of any particular group within the community. This belief is so strong that it almost invariably forms part of the ammunition of conflict. Few antiunionists are so "realistic" as to announce publicly that they are determined to defeat a union regardless of the effect upon the rest of society. And few union leaders publish the fact that they will maintain a tight little monoply in their trade regardless of the effect upon other workers, the employer and the community. Both groups appeal to the community as a whole for support of their respective policies as being in the interest of social well-being.

Any examination of the concept of social well-being, however, suggests that it is more likely to be a sentiment than an exact criterion of judgment. There are distinctions to be made between *quantity* and *quality* of welfare and each must be compared with the other. If there were agreement upon these matters, there would be disagreement as to the most effective method of attaining the desired end. In the face of these difficulties, it is tempting to resort to the idea that "natural laws" of human behavior will take care of everthing, and that it is unnecessary to apply intelligence to the guidance of human affairs. To some, "natural law" means the law of supply and demand. To others, it means the law of dialectical materialism. To a few, it means the law of group adjustment or survival.

Granted that each of these "laws," if defined with sufficient precision, contains elements of truth, there remains the implication that the task of the social scientist is merely to observe these laws in operation and to report from time to time that all is well simply because the laws are keeping up to schedule. If the supply of building labor or copper roofing is restricted and the demand remains constant, their prices will rise. This is a feather in the cap of the law of supply and demand, but it does not help the housing situation. Private ownership of the means of production has been in large part responsible for the immense advance in methods of production, but this advance is undermining the institution of private property. An illustration of the law of dialectical materialism is thus provided from which theoreticians may gain some satisfaction, but it does not put bread in the mouths of the unemployed. The labor movement itself is an example of group adjustment to changed conditions, but in this struggle for group survival intense suffering has been experienced both within and without the labor movement. Common sense demands that the laws of human behavior be used for the attainment of social well-being.

If natural laws are to be used, the end toward which they are directed must be defined. There must also be a means of applying natural laws toward this end. Before an engineer can apply his knowledge of physics, he must know whether the bridge he is to build should be designed to stand forever or to fall down periodically in order to provide employment. The doctor who is about to apply his knowledge of biochemistry must know whether he is supposed to return the patient to the bosom of his family, or whether the family is primarily interested in the life insurance policy. If engineering techniques are to be applied at all, there must be social institutions like private capitalism or public works to bring about their application. If use is to be made of biochemistry, society must be organized to provide private medical practice, public hospitals or health insurance. Can there be any agreement about the objectives toward which the social sciences should be directed? If so, what knowledge and what instruments for the achievement of these objectives are available?

In 1776 Adam Smith declared that the "wealth of nations" was the proper objective of economic science and that such wealth could best be secured by the pursuit of individual self-interest. A few thousand miles away, in the same year, a group of patriots asserted that "life, liberty, and the pursuit of happiness" were the proper objectives of political science and that these ends could best be served by a democracy organized upon territorial lines. Are these declarations still satisfactory? Are wealth, life, liberty and happiness objectives which can be defined with the precision the scientist demands? Are the pursuit of individual self-interest and the territorial organization of democracy adequate mechanisms for their attainment?

At the risk of treading upon valuable sentiments, it may be asserted that "life," "liberty," "happiness" are not concepts sufficiently measurable to be of great usefulness. Much more concise is the statement that the objective of both the physical and social sciences is *to maximize the production and distribution of goods and services*. It may be admitted that distinctions must be made between the quantity and quality of goods and, particularly, of services.

It may also be admitted that the question of the proportions in which goods should be distributed between various social groups is for the moment left open. It may finally be admitted that such a materialistic objective appears to have left out of account such intangible values as individual liberty, leisure and human dignity.

Suppose it is conceded that the objective of the applied sciences is to maximize the production of goods and services. What social instruments are available for the application of the knowledge and techniques provided by the sciences? Business, government and the labor movement suggest themselves.

Business, as a social institution, is founded upon the precept that the pursuit of self-interest by the individual enterpriser will automatically minister to the well-being of the investor, the consumer and the worker, as well as to the enterpriser himself. If the hand of every individual is set against that of every other in the process of competition, the investor's money will be well cared for and paid a "fair" rate of return. Consumers will receive low-priced and high quality goods. Workers will receive the best possible wages and conditions.

In spite of the immense accomplishments of free private enterprise, few social scientists accept this as an accurate description of modern business. Competition has been modified or eliminated altogether by the group action of businessmen. Small-scale production has given way to large. This has separated ownership from control and further facilitated the development of modified competition or monopoly. In the absence of competition, self-interest leads to restriction of output and the raising of prices. This places the consumer at the mercy of the producer both as to the quality and the quantity of goods. The separation of ownership from control reduces the investor to dependence upon the good will of the manager. It is fortunate for the investor that the managers do not always pursue their self-interest. The immense size, remoteness and impersonality of producing units reduces the individual worker to impotence. Where competition still prevails, as in agriculture and the soft coal, garment, shirt, necktie, cleaning and dyeing industries, instability, "sweatshops," wastes and "cutthroat competition" are the result. In addition to producing goods, modern business also produces chronic unemployment, avoidable industrial accidents, disease and unrest, old-age dependence, business cycles and fantastic inequalities in the distribution of the national income. No eulogies of the achievements of business can offset the roll call of industrial pathologies.

As the general and technical education of businessmen becomes more advanced, will there not develop a more informed understanding of self-interest which will lead businessmen to eliminate the sources of many of these pathologies? Unemployment, accidents, disease and unrest are expensive to the owner or manager. Low wages and long hours may lead to high rather than low labor costs. Mass production depends upon mass consumption and therefore upon high wages and low prices. Milking the investor dries up the sources of capital supply. Exploiting the consumer destroys the market. The wastes of fraudulent advertising eventually become apparent. Inequality in the distribution of income diverts purchasing power from mass-produced goods toward luxuries. Price rigidities lead to depression with its consequent business losses. [1]

Much of this is fully apparent to many business leaders. Developments in cost accounting and the advances being made in the study of human relations in industry indicate that there are great improvements possible in the condition of labor with consequent reductions in labor costs. Some types of unemployment are preventable. Many sources of accidents and disease can be eliminated. Huge

[1] For an able exposition of this hypothesis see Paul Douglas, *Controlling Depressions* (Norton, New York, 1935).

financial expenses result from industrial disputes which can frequently be avoided by the exercise of patience, tact and some understanding of the human aspects of the labor force. High labor turnover is a silent expression of labor discontent and at the same time an expense to management which can be reduced, with a net gain to both parties, by improved working conditions and wages. Many business-men in their own interest condemn fraudulent or mislead-ing advertising.

There are limits, however, to the extent to which even the intelligent pursuit of self-interest by individual busi-nessmen can remove the disorders of industry. Many of the expenses of industrial pathology can be transferred from the individual businessman to the community. The unemployed and the victims of accidents and disease must be supported by the family or other larger social groups. Inadequate wages can be supplemented by public relief. The costs of this relief and of hospitalization resulting from diseases induced by undernourishment can be and are transferred to the lower income groups through sales taxes, "head" taxes and property taxes. [2] The slow deteri-oration of the quality of population through undernourish-ment, pauperism and crime is a diffused expense which can be overlooked by the individual businessman. Fortu-nately, altruism and community ethics modify individual self-interest to such an extent that some of the more anti-social aspects of business life are softened.

Furthermore, many of the industrial pathologies are completely out of the control of the individual business-man. Business cycles, mass unemployment, the regulariza-tion of competitive industry, the extravagant wastes of

[2] The costs of old age assistance in Connecticut are paid by a three-dollar "head" tax upon all persons between the ages of twenty and sixty regardless of income, unless pauperism can be proved. Even W.P.A. workers in some instances have had difficulty in avoiding the payment of this tax. It is generally agreed by most economists that taxes on rented houses are shifted to the tenants (except in declining communities).

advertising, the maintenance of a high general level of wages, the enforcement of standards of quality are problems which the businessman may recognize but with which he is nearly powerless to deal as an individual. [3]

Should not businessmen organize to cope with these problems? This, of course, is what has long since happened. Through gentlemen's agreements, employers' and trade associations, businessmen's clubs, pools, trusts, holding companies, interlocking directorates and mergers, business has organized to deal with group interests. Group self-interest may in many respects be more nearly in accord with the interests of the whole community than individual self-interest. Discussion of business policies is an educational procedure which enlightens the participants. The leaders raise the followers. "Business ethics" are developed, a part of which is actually in the interest of the community as a whole. Competitive industries may be regularized by agreements upon competitive practices. The financial instruments of monopoly make possible the coördination of control necessary to handle the problems which lie beyond the scope of the individual small-scale producer.

The advantages of coördinated control, however, are being won at the cost of monopolistic restrictions of output. The same business associations and corporate instruments which make possible the regularization of industry and the elimination of wastes also enable owners and managers to extract monopoly gains by limiting output and increasing prices at the expense of the rest of the community. The question must be raised, however, whether the self-interest of owners really leads in the direction of restriction of output. It has been estimated that in 1929 there were between four and seven million corporate sharehold-

ers in American industry. This does not include the several
million partnerships and individual proprietorships in the
industries which remain characteristically competitive.
Does not the self-interest of these millions of owners and
their dependents lead in the direction of expanding output
and lowered prices? In framing a reply, two very important facts must be considered. First, the bulk of corporate
ownership is concentrated in the hands of a much smaller
number of people than is suggested by the figures above.
In 1929, for example, 73.7 per cent of all corporate dividends was received by 597,000 persons with incomes of
$5,000 or more. [4] The interests of this relatively small
group, which undoubtedly owns considerably more than
half the nation's corporate wealth, clearly lead in the direction of monopoly gains at the expense of the rest of the
community. Second, the control of corporate policy is
actually concentrated in the hands of a still smaller group
than that which receives the bulk of corporate income.
The studies of Messrs. Berle and Means have established
beyond all reasonable doubt that in the typical large
corporation there is now a wide separation between the
ownership of stock and the control of the corporation. In
many instances this divorce has become so complete that
the management is in effect a self-perpetuating body which
can be dislodged by the owners only under extraordinary
circumstances. It thus becomes possible not only for a
small group of owners to exploit the community as a
whole, but for a still smaller group of managers to exploit
the owners themselves.

Consider what happens in the annual stockholders'
meeting of a large corporation whose scores of thousands
of owners are scattered over the entire country. In the interests of business tradition, the meeting is held in Hobo-
ken, Jersey City or Wilmington. The managers appear in

[4] A. A. Berle, and G. C. Means, *The Modern Corporation and Private
Property* (Macmillan, New York, 1934), p. 60.

person and line up behind a long table near the wall of a barren room. A hundred or more shareholders with an average of thirty shares apiece are seated on benches and undertaker's chairs. Two stockholders have come all the way from California. Their train fare has cost them more than the value of their stock. They are "troublemakers." Twenty other dubious characters have appeared because it is warm and dry in the hall and there is a rumor that coffee and doughnuts will be served as usual at the conclusion of the meeting.

The meeting begins. The president, in the course of an able address, says that the employee bonus plan is working very well and that the country appears to be returning to a sound economic foundation. The "troublemakers" rise and begin to heckle. They point out that the four million dollars distributed under the "employee" bonus plan were actually divided among the president, several vice-presidents, a number of supervisors and foremen and two manual workers with twenty-year service records. They label the "employee" bonus plan as one of several devices by which the managers are "milking" the stockholders. They demand to be told why the company is buying some of its supplies at excessive prices from concerns in which certain officers of the corporation have heavy investments. They protest against the retirement of the president on a salary of $100,000 a year. They suggest $20,000 as a more reasonable figure. They talk a long time. The newspaper reporters recognize them as "radicals" from a college in the Far West. The officers of the company are polite, but their smiles take on a frozen aspect. Eventually there is a call for the question on a vote of "No Confidence" in the management. Three thousand shares vote "Aye." The officers produce proxies for four million shares all of which vote "Nay." The motion is declared lost, the officers leave the hall and the dubious characters move toward the coffee and doughnuts. Under conditions comparable to these, can the owners control their managers?

It can probably be maintained, however, that the restrictive policies of finance management cannot be pushed to an extreme without injuring the position of the managers themselves. Raising prices, depressing wages and milking the "outside" shareholders limit the market for goods and cause unemployment. Depressions and unemployment are expensive even to the people at the top. Mass misery undermines the stability of the society in which managers and financiers enjoy a favored position. The decline of economic opportunity consequent upon restrictive policies is part cause of the rise of racketeering and bootlegging. Racketeers prey upon the wealthy and the prominent. Bootlegging destroys respect for property rights and undercuts the prices established by the legitimate producers.[5] The wealthy are forced through taxation to support some of the unemployed. This is regarded by either timid or farsighted business leaders as a kind of "revolt insurance." Public works, some of which are of dubious social value, have to be financed in order to provide work for others among the unemployed. Little private armies have to be hired to keep the gangsters at bay. Militia must be paid and equipped to disperse the semimilitary formations of striking workers. Hostile minority political

[5] In the anthracite regions of Pennsylvania, for example, the maintenance of relatively rigid prices during and after the depression resulted in such a sharp drop in the output of coal and the employment of miners that the mine workers began digging the coal themselves from the outcropping veins. Beginning as a relatively informal procedure, this bootlegging soon became organized on a big scale. Coal now moves into the markets from these bootlegging operations in such volume as seriously to undercut the prices established by the legitimate producers. The feeling that "God put this coal here to be used" has permeated the coal communities so thoroughly that legal agencies refuse to take action against the bootleggers. Two state administrations, one Republican and one Democratic, have closed their eyes to the situation. In effect, there is developing in these regions of Pennsylvania a new organization of community life centering around a reversion to primitive methods of production. The mine owners have made a half-hearted attempt to meet the situation by filling the bootleg coal holes with tear and nausea gas, but when their plans for this were brought to light by the LaFollette Committee the effort was called off. The coal operators are therefore losing both income and power as an indirect result of monopoly policies.

movements such as those of Governor Talmadge of Georgia and the late Senator Huey Long of Louisiana require large financial contributions to be kept in the safe column. Large sums must be spent for "education" and propaganda. In all of these ways, the wealthy are driven by a sort of "natural law" to provide employment, distribute income and thus make possible the purchase of goods and services. The question must be raised, however, whether "revolt insurance," "make-work" programs, payments to armed guards, militia and political leaders, "protection" from racketeers, ransoms to kidnapers, and the development of organized bootlegging are really scientific methods of distributing income, goods and services. Appearances are distinctly against these methods of organizing production and distribution and yet they constitute the important checks upon the restrictive policies of monopoly.

But are these developments the only check upon monopolistic restrictions? The machinery of government immediately suggests itself as a social institution which can be employed to regulate industry for the welfare of the whole community. Why not allow industry to become even more completely integrated than it now is in order to make possible the application of improved techniques and the elimination of competitive wastes, and then parallel this development by subjecting industry to an increasing degree of governmental regulation? This regulation would consist, for the most part, of control of prices, interest rates and wages. These would be adjusted to each other in such a way as to insure that the greatest possible production of goods and services would result; that is, prices would be lowered and wages increased or hours shortened, as fast as improvements in the methods of production made this possible. Interest rates would be kept just high enough to attract new capital into industry. Profits would be unnecessary since the government would assume all risk and incentives could be provided as at present in large enterprises: through piece rates, bonuses, hope of promotion, fear of losing the job and professional interest in doing good work. By means of heavy income and inheritance taxation the inequalities of wealth and income might be reduced and funds provided for the extension of social insurance, community housing, education, recreation and other free public services.

But the machinery of government and the civil servants and elected officials who operate it do not exist in a social vacuum. They are the focal point around which conflicting economic interests resolve themselves. The more extensive the regulatory functions of government, the more determined becomes the struggle for the control of governmental machinery. The effort to control public utility rates has long since resulted in many areas in what is called the "corruption" of government. Lincoln Steffens and other "muckrakers" laid bare the anatomy of this process for all to see. Lincoln Steffens disliked the moral connotation of the word corruption. He pointed out that if self-interest is the dominating motive of business, and if self-interest leads in the direction of limiting output and raising prices, any effort to regulate business compels business to regulate government. Beginning with the cities, Steffens traced this trail of corruption up through the states to the Federal Government itself. Finding that the process was so nearly universal, he concluded that it is not immorality of government agents which causes corruption, but that the effort to put "more government into business" forces business to take over the government. Business may not always succeed in taking over the government because it is opposed by other more powerful economic interests like organized consumers, workers and farmers. But the self-interest of business men frequently compels them to make the effort. The government thus becomes the arena of a struggle for political power to control economic affairs.

If business wins, the government is said to be "corrupt." If labor or the farmer wins, the government is said to have bowed to a demand for "class legislation." In some states there are "labor" governors. In others, the governors are the "tools of reactionary interests."

If conflicting economic group interests are inevitable, it may be asked whether it is not better that these conflicts be resolved at the political level rather than with the economic weapons of the lockout, the stay-in, gentlemen's agreements and the buyer's strike. To a considerable extent it would be better. When problems are generalized, many apparent conflicts disappear. The manufacturer may come to applaud the unemployment insurance benefits which stablize his market, although he fought against them bitterly when they were first proposed. The employer may welcome the Labor Board which settles the jurisdictional disputes from which he has suffered for years, although at first he was willing to pour out thousands of dollars in a political campaign to defeat candidates committed to the establishment of such a board. Scores of other similar examples might be given. There remains the fundamental question, however, as to whether political life organized upon a territorial basis can adequately clarify and express the problems of economic life. How can a political representative stand for election from a constituency which, because its limits are geographic, includes a great variety of both real and apparent conflicts of economic interest? He may not enjoy kissing babies in public, but what alternative has he when to do anything else will bring down upon his head the wrath of one or more groups in his constituency?

If political life is to express the needs, attitudes and aspirations of all the economic groups in the society, people must organize around their most important economic interests. Within this economic organization, political life takes place and its product, in the form of policies or demands, may then be enforced directly on the economic front or raised to the level of the political life of the whole community.

The most important economic interests in modern society, other than those of the finance-manager and corporate shareholder which have already been discussed, are the consumer, the farmer-owner, the "small" businessman, and the industrial, white-collar, agricultural and professional wageworkers. If each of these groups were organized around its economic self-interest, which group might be expected to evolve a program most likely to contribute to the well-being of society as a whole?

One would be inclined to suggest that the interests of the largest economic group would be most nearly identical with those of the community. The largest is obviously the consumers since everyone falls within this category. There, indeed, is the rub. Everyone is a consumer, but he is also a worker, a farmer, a financier, a shareholder, a coupon clipper or a grocer with intense interests in his producer status. No matter how completely society is organized as consumers, the conflicts of producer interests remain.

There are very good reasons why consumers should organize to protect themselves against extortionate prices, shoddy goods and the wastes of competitive selling. Consumers' organizations may take the form of advisory services such as Consumers' Research and Consumers' Union or local cooperative stores controlled by the consumers. When the coöperative store movement reaches a high stage of development, as in England and Sweden, the local stores may be bound together in regional or national wholesale societies which in turn develop their own factories, farms and mines. Democratic control is assured by the election of delegates from the local societies to regional or national boards which in turn select business managers and determine general policies. In both England and Sweden local and wholesale coöperative societies have accomplished remarkable results in protecting and advancing the interests of consumers.

Such consumers' organizations probably represent economic democracy at its best, but it is a democracy suffering from the same limitations which beset the territorial organization of economic life. Observe the kind of thing that happens in a local consumers' association meeting. Mr. Brown (who is a liberal sympathizer with organized labor) rises and says, "Mr. Chairman, I understand that the last shipment of perfume we received came from a plant in which sweatshop conditions prevail. I protest against this. I believe that our manager should be instructed not to buy from any source which does not pay good wages and provide the best conditions of labor." Before he is seated, another member pops up and says, "That's right, now I don't care about perfume because I work in a clothing factory myself, but I protest against the long hours and bad conditions that we have in our factory. You all know it's a Coöp concern. The foremen are screwing down our wages and speeding us up and the place reeks with grievances, but what can we do about it? The super tells us that he has to meet the price set by the wholesale society, and the wholesale officers say that the national board insists that prices be kept down. I move that our delegate be instructed to insist that the clothing workers be allowed to form a union and handle their grievances in an orderly manner." The motion is seconded. Eight people are on their feet clamoring to be recognized. Mr. Smith (who is a retired broker living on the dividends of steel and automobile stock) succeeds in being recognized. He says, "Mr. Chairman, this is a consumers' coöperative, not the C.I.O. I joined this organization to get good goods at low prices. If you become concerned with pushing up wages either prices must go up or dividends down. I'm against both. I'm against this motion." Mr. Blalok has the floor. "Mr. Chairman, I'm a steel worker, and they've got us back on the nine-hour day to keep costs down. I think that our delegate ought to be instructed. . . ." "Fellow coöperators," a local politician has the floor, "we are interested in good quality at low prices. And we are for the workers too. And as for the long-suffering farmers, the backbone of the nation. . . . Let us not forget the fundamental principles laid down by the pioneers of Rochdale." "Yeah," it is Steve Bushwick speaking, "but the manager of our Cordon-Bleu low-priced automobile plant is hiring ex-prizefighters to beat up workers who are beginning to think about getting a union. I'm against this barbaric practice and I think that our delegate. . . ."

Under these conditions, upon what platform do the candidates for the delegacy stand? Do they kiss babies or, in the interests of hygiene, do they distribute to each mother in the association a package of best quality baby food? By all means, let there be consumers' organizations, advisory services and coöperatives to provide as extensive expression of consumers' interests as possible. But it cannot be expected that the organization of consumers can supplant the organization which arises around more intense producer interests.

The second largest economic group is those who work with their hands or minds for wages or salaries. Many of these also own producers' goods either as shares of corporate property or as small business enterprises. But there are from thirty to forty million people in the United States whose primary economic interest is in the wages or salaries they receive and the conditions under which they work. From these people arises the labor movement. To what extent are their interests identical with those of the whole community? Does the self-interest of these people direct them to apply the knowledge and techniques of the sciences which maximize the production and distribution of goods and services? Is the labor movement an institution suited to this end?

If the labor movement consisted of two or three million

relatively skilled workers strategically placed in the economic structure, there would be no special reason to believe that their self-interest would lead them toward the well-being of the community as a whole. As a minority group they could gain at the expense of the rest of the community by restricting their membership, limiting their output and establishing a scarcity value for their services. They might join with the owners or, more likely, the managers and financiers, in the establishment of two-sided monopoly practices. Monopoly finance and industry might even welcome such a labor movement as an instrument for consolidating their power. Minimizing, rather than maximizing, the production of goods and services would be the result. This would appear to the consumer in the form of higher prices, to the nonunion workers in the form of limited employment opportunities, and to the investor as reduced interest rates.

Suppose, however, that this organized labor movement should suddenly show signs of expanding to the point of including many more millions of industrial, agricultural, clerical and professional workers. Would not the self-interest of the members of such a labor movement lead them to destroy the monopolistic practices established by finance-management and the little labor monopolies in the strategic trades? Might not the proprietors of these monopolies be expected to show a somewhat frantic apprehension of the possibilities involved in the new movement? It is possible that this apprehension might be evidenced by such symbolic acts as refusing to sign trade agreements because they "inevitably lead to still further demands," [6] or by going through the somewhat dubious legal technicality of "suspending" the newer labor movement from the old? Might there not also be a good deal of personal

[6] This position was assumed by five of the independent steel companies in the spring of 1937, and was the cause of a strike in which eighteen persons were killed by midsummer and scores of others wounded and gassed.

pathos in this process if, for example, a newspaper reporter should inadvertantly address the leader of the older movement by the name of the new leader, with the result that the older leader takes his face in his hands and murmurs, "My God, man, my God." [7]

If the labor movement should come to include 25,-000,000 people with an average of two dependents each, what policies, resulting in maximizing the production and distribution of goods and services, would their self-interest lead them to adopt? It is primarily the business and pollitical policies of labor which are important in this connection. In previous chapters it has been indicated that the business policies of labor are directed toward the improvement of wages, hours and conditions. Are these policies consonant with social well-being? The establishment of minimum wages in competitive industries eliminates the relatively inefficient firms and concentrates production in the establishments which can afford to pay "living wages." It also eliminates the inefficient workers and forces society to recognize them as substandard or underprivileged groups which can be removed only by such remedial or preventative techniques as old-age pensions, more extensive liberal and technical education, hospitalization for the physically and mentally unfit, vocational rehabilitation and so on.

It has already been suggested that these are not new burdens upon society. They exist in a diffused or disguised form. Minimum wage policies force them into the open. The enforcement of minimum wages may actually reduce costs of production by increasing the physical efficiency of individual workers and reducing accidents, conscious or unconscious sabotage, labor turnover and industrial unrest. If the higher wages do result in higher labor costs which

[7] Reported in *Time* as having occurred in Mr. William Green's press conference on May 26, 1937, after he had announced that the A.F. of L. had issued a charter to the Progressive Mine Workers in opposition to the United Mine Workers. *Time*, June 7, 1937, p. 16, col. 2.

are passed on, under the competitive conditions assumed, in the form of higher prices, consumers may have to pay more for goods, but in the long run will gain from the reduced expenses of social pathology.

Under modified competition or monopoly conditions, the pushing up of wages squeezes out monopoly profits and effects a more equal distribution of income which in turn promotes the mass distribution of goods. If prices are raised each time wages are pushed up, the regulation of prices becomes a necessity. Workers organized as consumers or operating through the political machinery of the state are driven by their self-interest to recognize this problem.

If prices were held down while wage incomes were pushed up, the process might be carried so far as to eliminate all income from ownership. Owners might be compensated for their loss by governmental purchase of their holdings or, if ownership and management resistance were extreme, confiscation might result. This would leave the problem of providing capital for the maintenance and expansion of industry. The necessity for providing capital must be recognized if goods are to be produced at all. If private ownership were destroyed, capital could be provided by progressive income and inheritance taxation, the sale of government bonds recoverable at the death of the owner, or by keeping prices far enough above wages to provide an annual surplus to be diverted from the purchase of consumers' goods to the making of capital equipment.[8]

[8] It may be noted that a considerable proportion of American capital is already raised in these three ways. The sale of government bonds has been used to finance such projects as the T.V.A. These bonds or their equivalent are to some extent recoverable at the death of the holder through inheritance taxes. The government also raises some of its funds for capital investments through taxation. A large percentage of American capital is now saved by corporations rather than by individuals. Prices are maintained sufficiently high in relation to costs to provide a surplus which is "ploughed in" to plant and equipment instead of being distributed to shareholders. This maintenance of a high differential between

The self-interest of the labor movement with respect to hours leads in somewhat the same direction. The shortening of hours eliminates high cost producers, concentrates production in efficient plants, increases individual efficiency, and reduces many of the disguised costs of production up to a certain point which differs slightly in each occupation. Beyond this point, labor has a choice between the enjoyment of goods and the enjoyment of leisure. Leisure may be gained both by shortening the working day and by subtracting from the beginning and end of the working life. The amount of leisure enjoyed by the mass profoundly affects the types of goods produced. After the minimum requirements of life are satisfied, the enjoyment of the amenities and luxuries requires an increased amount of leisure. If labor elects to take advantage of improved methods of production by shortening the working life and the working day, changes result in the type of goods demanded by the mass. Without leisure, income in excess of bare living costs tends to go toward the purchase of quick stimulation. When the steel workers were on the twelve-hour day, seven days a week, quitting time found thousands of workers looking forward to "a quick shot of hot beer and gin, brother, I gotta have something to knock me out." The elimination of child labor, the provision of income for the people who have passed the best working years of their lives, and the thirty-five-hour week create a demand for education, books, roads, hobbies, group sports, parks, forest preserves and cultural or civic training.

The self-interest of labor leads it to demand "conditions." "Conditions" refer primarily to job control: the granting to labor of a share in the control of hiring and firing, promotions and layoffs and the orderly handling

---

costs and prices is also the chief method by which capital is raised in the U.S.S.R., although the Soviet Government also uses taxation and the sale of government bonds. Under any of these three methods, the process of capital formation tends to become collectivized instead of being left to the individual saver.

of grievances. There is a possibility here that the domocratic control of these matters might lead to the inefficient selection and rejection of the labor force said to be characteristic of "bureaucracy." Would not the pay roll of industry become padded with the favorites and the supporters of the labor leaders? Would this not reduce efficiency and minimize production? Perhaps it would. But there are contrary indications. Labor's interest in "conditions" lies chiefly in the establishment of regular rules of procedure which are understood by everyone; for example, that in the process of firing, the worker have the established right to appeal from what he considers the arbitrary action of a foreman. Appeal may be simply to higher management authorities, to outsiders or to a joint union-management board. Many industrial disputes arise from group sympathy with an individual's grievance. Industrial disputes do not produce goods. When the production of goods is semiautomatic, and little time is needed to learn the occupation, promotions and layoffs may just as well be based upon seniority as upon any other rule. The existence of the rule prevents rather than facilitates the padding of pay rolls with favorites by either the foreman or the union leader. The self-interest of labor leads it to magnify the small irritants and injustices of daily work. Organized labor compels managers to take the same attitude toward these sources of breakdown in the productive process that they take toward their inanimate machinery. The self-interest of labor compels personnel management to assume its real functions and prevents it from becoming a police force equipped with arbitrary powers and tear gas. The demand for "conditions" is fundamentally a demand for industrial democracy and for individual dignity expressed through the power of the group. There is some reason to think that industrial democracy need not inhibit the production of goods and services.

The self-interest of labor compels it to enter the political field to secure the adoption of social insurance, employment exchanges, educational facilities and other public services in addition to the regulation of wages, hours and prices. Clearly these institutions result in the distribution either directly or indirectly of goods and services. Can we produce these goods? Can society afford these services? Conservative statistical and engineering surveys report that American industry is technically capable of providing from three to four thousand dollars of income annually for every family in the country. An average of between one third and one half of that amount is actually distributed annually to American families. "We can produce but we can't consume." "Poverty amid plenty." These are commonplaces which are statistically verifiable. If we cannot immediately organize economic life in such a way as to eliminate unemployment, old-age dependence and so on, can we not afford to palliate their consequences through social insurance? The costs are there whether they are recognized or not. Should they be formally recognized and dealt with in the open, or left to fester unnoticed in obscurity?

Not merely the self-interest, but the very existence of the labor movement compels it to struggle for the maintenance of the civil liberties. Free speech, a free press, freedom of assembly, freedom for group action upon common interests—these are the prerequisites for the useful existence of the labor movement. Without these, the labor movement goes underground as does any other social group driven by powerful social compulsions. From the underworld emerge violence, terrorism, plots and counterplots, bridges are dynamited, the *Los Angeles Times* Building is destroyed, children are burned to an ash at Ludlow, bullet-riddled men crumple behind the flimsy wall of a shack at Centralia, the red ore of Mesabi is stained a deeper red and the ghost of Molly Maguire rides again. The labor movement can be destroyed. Legal interdict, militia, "embattled" citizens "called to arms" and provided with company tear gas and guns, concentration camps, compulsory "arbitration," strong-arm squads and private armies—these can do the trick. The question is whether this is the intelligent, scientific approach.

"The self-interest of the workers," yes. Their self-interest leads toward the fullest possible production and distribution of goods and services, the provision of leisure and the kind of satisfactions that leisure makes possible, and the preservation of the civil liberties. But what about the leaders? Can the followers control the leaders? Will the labor movement really be a democracy or will it evolve into one more form of despotism? [9] In social life there are no absolute blacks and whites. Perhaps democracy will not emerge lily-white from the new labor movement. But what are the alternatives? Territorial political life reduced to flag waving with group economic interests, imperfectly perceived, doing a kind of fan dance behind the flag? Financial oligarchy compelled by "natural law" to compensate for some of its major shortcomings? Against these alternatives, may not the labor movement be recognized as an effort to reassert the forms and practices of democracy in an industrialized society? Any democracy may fail, however, even though its forms and practices are adopted to the economic society from which it emerges. Ultimately, the intelligence and education of the mass determine the success or failure of a democracy. The economic objectives of the labor movement are those which provide the physical conditions in which education may flourish. The labor movement itself develops its own educational techniques. The physical and mental effort involved in establishing industrial democracy in an atmosphere of conflict is an experience in civic education which cannot be gained from the textbooks. Still, the effort may fail. If it does, even the effort may have been of value.

[9] In this connection compare John Strachey's *The Theory and Practice of Socialism* with Leon Trotsky's *The Revolution Betrayed.*

Taxicab drivers accused of throwing stench bombs and tipping over strike-breakers' taxicabs are rounded up by Chicago police.

Pickets during the 1937 Briggs Manufacturing Co. strike throw unexploded tear gas bombs back at the police during an attempt to break a mass picket line.

Appendix

Union Membership and Affiliation in the United States, 1936–1937

I. Unions Affiliated with The A.F. of L.

A. Extraction of Minerals

	Membership
Progressive Mine Workers of America	15,000
Quarry Workers' International Union of North America	20,000
Tri-State Mine and Smelter Workers' Union . .	6,000
Total	**41,000**

B. Manufacturing and Mechanical Industry

I. BUILDING TRADES:

Asbestos Workers, International Association of Heat and Frost Insulators and	2,500
Bricklayers, Masons, Plasterers' International Union of America	65,000
Bridge, Structural and Ornamental Iron Workers, International Association of	22,700
Carpenters and Joiners of America, United Brotherhood of	300,000
Electrical Workers, International Brotherhood of .	172,000
Elevator Constructors, Operators and Starters, International Union of	10,200
Engineers, International Union of Operating . .	42,000
Granite Cutters' International Association of America	5,000
Hod Carriers, Building and Common Laborers Union of America, International	99,600
Lathers' International Union, Wood, Wire, and Metal	8,100
Marble, Stone and Slate Polishers, Rubbers and Sawyers, Tile and Marble Setters' Helpers and Terrazo Workers' Helpers, International Association of	5,500

Membership

Painters, Decorators and Paperhangers of America,
Brotherhood of   80,100
Plasterers' and Cement Finishers' International
Association of United States and Canada, Opera-
tive   18,400
Plumbers and Steamfitters of the United States and
Canada, United Association of Journeymen . .   33,000
Roofers, Damp and Waterproof Workers' Asso-
ciation, United Slate, Tile and Composition . .   4,000
Sheet Metal Workers' International Association . 16,200

Total Building Trades   884,300

2. CHEMICAL AND ALLIED INDUSTRIES:

Powder and High Explosive Workers of America,
United   200

3. CIGARS AND TOBACCO:

Cigar Makers' International Union   7,000
Tobacco Workers' International Union   11,000

Total   18,000

4. CLAY, GLASS, STONE AND CEMENT:

Brick and Clay Workers of America, United . .   5,500
Glass Bottle Blowers' Association of the United
States and Canada   10,800
Glass Cutters' League of America, Window . .   1,300
Glass Workers' Union of North America, Ameri-
can Flint   5,300
Paving Cutters' Union of the U.S.A. and Canada,
International   2,000
Potters, National Brotherhood of Operative . . . 11,000
Stone Cutters' Association of North America, Jour-
neymen   5,000

Total   40,900

Membership

5. CLOTHING TRADES:

Boot and Shoe Workers' Union	29,300
Garment Workers of America, United	39,500
Glove Workers of America, International . . .	1,700
Hatters, Cap and Millinery Workers International Union, United	23,900
Total	94,400

6. FOOD AND LIQUOR:

Bakery and Confectionery Workers' International Union of America	32,500
Brewery Workmen, International Union of United	42,000
Meat Cutters and Butcher Workmen of North America, Amalgamated	30,000
Total	104,500

7. FURNITURE AND WOODWORKING:

Carvers' Association of North America, International Wood	400
Coopers' International Union of North America .	2,600
Upholsterers, Carpet and Linoleum Mechanics' International Union of North America	10,200
Total	13,200

8. JEWELRY TRADES:

Diamond Workers' Protective Union of America	300
Jewelry Workers' Union, International	6,000
Total	6,300

9. LEATHER MANUFACTURE:

Leather Workers' International Union, United . .	2,500
Pocketbook and Novelty Workers, International Ladies' Handbag	500
Total	3,000

10. METALS AND MACHINERY:

Blacksmiths, Drop Forgers and Helpers, International Brotherhood of	5,000
Boilermakers, Iron Shipbuilders and Helpers, International Brotherhood of	18,000
Carmen of America, Brotherhood of Railway . .	65,000
Engravers' Union, International Metal	200
Firemen and Oilers, International Brotherhood of .	23,600

Membership

Foundry Employees, International Brotherhood of   3,500

Horseshoers of United States and Canada, International Union of Journeymen   200

Machinists, International Association of   138,000

Metal Polishers' International Union   5,600

Molders' Union of North America, International .   22,200

Pattern Makers' League of America   4,200

Stove Mounters' International Union of North America   3,000

Wire Weavers' Protective Association, American   300

Total   288,800

11. PAPER AND PRINTING:

PAPER:

Paper Makers, International Brotherhood of . . .   11,600

Pulp, Sulphite and Paper Mill Workers, International Brotherhood of   15,700

Wall Paper Crafts of North America, United . .   900

Total   28,200

PRINTING:

Bookbinders, International Brotherhood of . . .   13,100

Lithographers of America, Amalgamated . . .   7,200

Photoengravers' Union of North America, International   9,100

Plate Printers', Die Stampers' and Engravers' Union of North America, International   1,000

Printing Pressmen and Assistants' Union of North America, International   33,700

Siderographers, International Association of . . .   100

Stereotypers' and Electrotypers' Union of North America   8,300

Typographical Union, International   75,500

Total   148,000

12. MISCELLANEOUS MANUFACTURES:

Broom and Whisk Makers' Union, International .   200

Membership

C. Transport and Communication

1. WATER TRANSPORT:

Longshoremen's Association, International	61,400
Masters', Mates' and Pilots' National Organization .	2,900
Seamen's Union of America, International . . .	14,200
Total	**78,500**

2. AIR TRANSPORT:

Air Line Pilots' Association	900

3. STREET AND ROAD TRANSPORT:

Street and Electric Railway and Motor Coach Employees of America, Amalgamated Association of	76,700
Teamsters, Chauffeurs, Stablemen and Helpers of America, International Brotherhood of	210,900
Total	**287,600**

4. RAILROAD TRANSPORT:

Clerks, Freight Handlers, Express and Station Employees, Brotherhood of Railway and Steamship	89,200
Conductors, Order of Sleeping Car	1,900
Maintenance of Way Employees, Brotherhood of	41,800
Porters, Brotherhood of Sleeping Car	5,500
Switchmen's Union of North America	8,900
Total	**147,300**

5. COMMUNICATION (other than United States Post Office):

Telegraphers, Order of Railroad	35,000
Telegraphers' Union of North America, Commercial	2,000
Total	**37,000**

D. Trade

1. ADVERTISING:

Bill Posters and Billers of America, International Alliance of	1,400

2. RETAIL SELLING:

Clerks' International Protective Association, Retail	18,500
Total	**19,900**

Membership

E. *Professional, Semiprofessional and Recreational*

Actors and Artistes of America, Associated . . .	5,500
Draftsmen's Unions, International Federation of Technical Engineers, Architects and	1,400
Musicians, American Federation of	100,000
Stage Employees and Moving Picture Machine Operators of the United States and Canada, International Alliance of Theatrical	24,200
Teachers, American Federation of	15,400
Total	**146,500**

F. *Government Service*

1. FEDERAL, STATE AND MUNICIPAL:

Fire Fighters, International Association of . . .	29,100
Government Employees, American Federation of	21,400
Master Mechanics and Foremen of Navy Yards and Naval Stations, National Association of . .	100
State, County, and Municipal Employees, American Federation of	11,400
Total	**62,000**

2. UNITED STATES POST OFFICE:

Letter Carriers, National Association of	52,500
Letter Carriers, National Federation of Rural . .	500
Mail Association, Railway	21,000
Post Office Clerks, National Federation of . . .	36,000
Total	**110,000**

G. *Personal Service*

Barbers' International Union of America, Journeymen	40,800
Building Service Employees' International Alliance	42,000
Cleaning and Dye House Workers, International Association of	4,800
Hotel and Restaurant Employees' International Alliance and Bartenders' International League of America	107,100
Laundry Workers' International Union	7,000
Total	**201,700**

Membership

H. Agriculture

Sheepshearers' Union of North America   800

I. Local Trade and Federal Labor Unions (1406) .   232,700

Total A.F. of L. Membership   2,995,900

II. Unions Affiliated with the C.I.O.

A. Extraction of Minerals

Mine, Mill and Smelter Workers, International
Union of   45,000
Mine Workers of America, United   600,000
Oil Workers' International Union   100,000

Total   745,000

B. Manufacturing and Mechanical Industry

1. GLASS, BRICK AND CLAY:

Brick and Clay directly affiliated local unions (29)
Glass Workers of America, Federation of Flat .   17,000

2. CLOTHING TRADES:

Clothing Workers of America, Amalgamated . .   225,000
Fur Workers' Union of the United States and
Canada, International   30,000
Ladies' Garment Workers' Union, International .   250,000
Shoe Workers of America, United   52,000

Total   557,000

3. TOBACCO:

Tobacco directly affiliated local unions (10)

4. CHEMICALS:

Chemicals, soap, etc., directly affiliated local unions
(19)

5. FOOD AND LIQUOR:

Bakery, Food, Dairy directly affiliated local unions
    (90)
Meat Packing directly affiliated local unions (49)

6. LEATHER:

National Leather Workers' Association   15,000

7. FURNITURE AND WOODWORKING:

Furniture directly affiliated local unions (33)
Lumber directly affiliated local unions (59)
Woodworkers of America, International   100,000

8. METALS AND MACHINERY:

Aluminum Workers of America   15,000
Automobile Workers of America, International
    Union United   400,000
Die Casting Workers' League, National . . . . *No report*
Marine and Shipbuilding Workers of America, In-
    dustrial Union of   20,000
Metal Products directly affiliated local unions (19)
Radio, Electrical and Machine Workers of America,
    United   140,000
Steel and Tin Workers, Amalgamated Association
    of Iron   490,000
                                            _____
                                Total   1,065,000

9. PAPER:

Paper and Paper Bag directly affiliated local unions
    (37)

10. RUBBER:

Rubber Workers of America, United   75,000

Membership

11. TEXTILES:

Textile Workers of America, United   450,000

C. Transport and Communication

1. TRANSPORT:

Longshoremen and Warehousemen's Union, International   20,000
Marine Engineers' Beneficial Association, National   6,500
Maritime Union, National   40,000
Transport Workers' Union   80,000
Inland Boatmen of the Pacific . . . . *No report*

Total   146,500

2. COMMUNICATION:

Communications Association, American   8,000

D. Trade

Retail Employees of America, United   40,000

E. Professional and Semiprofessional

Architects, Engineers and Chemists, Federation of .   6,000
Newspaper Guild of America   14,000
Office and Professional Workers, United   25,000

Total   45,000

F. Government

Federal Workers, United   5,000
State, County and Municipal Workers of America .   30,000

Total   35,000

G. Personal Service

Laundry directly affiliated local unions (36)
Hotel and Restaurant directly affiliated local unions (25)

H. Agriculture

Cannery, Agricultural, Packing and Allied Workers of America, United   100,000

Membership

I. Miscellaneous

225-250 other directly affiliated local unions

Total Membership of all directly affiliated local
unions, including those listed under industrial
groups   225,000

Total C.I.O. Membership   3,623,500

III. Unions Not Affiliated with the A.F. of L. or the C.I.O.

A. Manufacturing

Engravers and Sketchmakers, Friendly Society of .	800
Leather Workers' International Union of America, United	1,180
Shoe and Allied Craftsmen, Brotherhood of . . .	13,000
Textile Operatives, American Federation of . . .	6,000

Total   20,980

B. Transport and Communication

1. WATER TRANSPORT:

Licensed Officers of the United States of America, United	2,000
Sailors' Union of the Pacific	20,000

Total   22,000

2. RAILROADS:

Brakemen-Porters, National Association of . . .	125
Conductors, Brotherhood of Dining Car	1,000
Conductors of America, Order of Railway . . .	50,000
Dining Car Employees, Brotherhood of	2,700
Dining Car Employees, National Brotherhood of .	1,100
Engineers, Grand International Brotherhood of Locomotive	59,000
Firemen and Enginemen, Brotherhood of Locomotive	60,886
Porters, Brakemen and Switchmen, Association of Train	700
Railroad Workers, American Federation of . . .	20,000
Signalmen of America, Brotherhood of Railroad .	12,000
Station Employees, Brotherhood of Railroad . .	1,100
Train Dispatchers' Association, American	2,415

Membership

Trainmen and Locomotive Firemen, Association of
Colored Railway   3,000
Trainmen, Brotherhood of Railroad   116,274
Yardmasters of America, Railroad   1,440
Yardmasters of North America, Railroad . . . . *No report*

                                   Total   331,740

3. COMMUNICATION:

Telephone Workers, International Brotherhood of   5,400

C. *Government*

1. FEDERAL, STATE AND MUNICIPAL:

Federal Employees, National Federation of . . .   64,000

2. UNITED STATES POST OFFICE:

Letter Carriers' Association, National Rural . . .   35,579
Mail Service, National Council of Officials of the
Railway   330
Postal Employees, National Alliance of   4,800
Postal Supervisors, National Association of . . .   6,415
Postmasters of the United States, National Associa-
tion of   5,000
Postmasters of the United States, National League
of District   17,000
Post Office Clerks of the United States, United Na-
tional Association of   45,000
Post Office Employees, National Association of
Substitute   3,000
Post Office Laborers of the United States, National
Association of   2,500
Post Office Motor Vehicle Employees, National
Federation of . . . . *No report*

                                   Total   119,624

D. *General Organizations*

American Labor Alliance   8,000
Industrial Workers of the World   34,000
Master Workmen of America . . . . *No report*

                                   Total   42,000

SUMMARY

Industry	A.F. of L.	C.I.O.	Not Affiliated
Extraction	41,000	745,000	
Manufacturing	(1,630,000)	(2,279,000)	(20,980)
Building	884,300		
Clothing	94,400	557,000	13,000
Metals	288,800	1,065,000	800
Printing	148,000		
Rubber		75,000	
Textiles		450,000	6,000
Woodworking	13,200	100,000	
All Other	201,300	32,000	1,180
Transport and Communication	(551,300)	(154,500)	(359,140)
Water	78,500	66,500	22,000
Air	900		
Street	287,600	80,000	
Railroad	147,300		331,740
Communication	37,000	8,000	5,400
Trade	19,900	40,000	
Professional	146,500	45,000	
Government	(172,000)	(35,000)	(183,624)
Federal, State, Municipal	62,000	35,000	64,000
Post Office	110,000		119,624
Personal Service	201,700		
Agriculture	800	100,000	
All Others	232,700	225,000	42,000
Totals	2,995,900	3,623,500	605,744
Grand Total		7,225,144	

THE figures for the A.F. of L. are taken from the 1937 Executive Council Report to the A.F. of L. convention and are therefore based upon the average membership for the year 1936-37. Since the A.F. of L. increased its membership by about 800,000 during this period, the average for the year understates the membership at the end of the period. In its October, 1937, convention the A.F. of L. gave out an unitemized report of 3,271,726 members as of August 1, 1937.

The figures for the C.I.O. are taken from the report of Director John Brophy to the October, 1937, conference of C.I.O. unions in Atlantic City. The total C.I.O. membership given in the *Summary* above is about 100,000 smaller than the total figure announced at the C.I.O. conference because the *Summary* total does not include the membership of the Typographical and Hatters' unions which continue to pay per capita tax to the

A.F. of L. although their presidents are charter members of the committee.

The figures for the nonaffiliated unions are taken from the *Handbook of American Trade Unions* (full citation in Notes and Bibliography). These figures are based upon 1935 reports and probably understate considerably the present membership of many of these unions, especially those on the railroads.

The total present membership of the American labor movement is therefore somewhat more than seven and a half millions.[1]

[1] Between October, 1937, and August, 1938, the C.I.O. gained three new national unions: the United Furniture Workers of America, the Marine Cooks and Stewards of the Pacific, and the Quarry Workers' International Union. Organizing committees were also set up for department-store workers, optical workers, packing-house workers, toy and novelty workers and utility workers. The expectation is that these committees will eventually expand into national unions in their respective industries.

In spite of severe depression and unemployment, C.I.O. membership held up remarkably well. By maintaining wages and actively assisting unemployed workers in securing relief, the C.I.O. has been able to maintain the loyalty of its new recruits. In spite of decreases in dues payments from unemployed members and the continuance of an expensive organizing campaign, the C.I.O. was reported to be keeping its nose above water financially in March, 1938. This fact in addition to the C.I.O.'s remarkable record of victories in N.L.R.B. elections is evidence of a degree of stability which might not have been expected of mass production unions. In Board elections, C.I.O. unions appeared in 557 cases and of these they won 455.

Between October, 1937, and July 5, 1938, the membership of the A.F. of L. increased from 3,271,726 to 3,554,584. (The latter figure was reported to the author by Secretary Morrison on July 14, 1938.) Of this total July membership, 151,565 were contained in 1,521 local trade and federal labor unions. Comparison with 1937 figures shows that the number of these directly affiliated locals increased from 1,406 to 1,521 but that their membership declined from 232,700 to 151,565. Their average membership, therefore, was considerably smaller. This loss, however, was more than offset by unitemized gains in the membership of the 102 national and international unions. The A.F. of L. was also successful in its Board elections, but less so than the C.I.O. Its unions took part in 453 elections and of these won 254. The average number of workers participating in A.F. of L. elections was 297 as compared with 527 in the case of C.I.O. unions, but A.F. of L. unions secured larger majorities. Of the 208 elections in which C.I.O. unions opposed A.F. of L. unions, C.I.O. unions won 160. (The figures for Board elections are from N.L.R.B. Press Release R-1073, *Summary of All N.L.R.B. Elections from October, 1935.*)

Notes and Bibliography

CHAPTER I

GENERAL SOURCES

HARDMAN, J. B. S., ed., *American Labor Dynamics* (New York, Harcourt, Brace & Co., 1928), Part II.

International Ladies' Garment Workers' Union, *Handbook of Trade Union Methods* (New York, 1937).

New York Times, News stories and articles on strikes and organizing.

Union News Service, 1936–37, official news agency of the C.I.O., Washington.

PAGE 21, LINES 8–16

A.F. of L. Convention *Proceedings*, 1936, p. 46.

CHAPTER II

PAGE 44 (FOOTNOTE 2)

FELDMAN, HERMAN, *Problems in Labor Relations* (New York, Macmillan, 1937), pp. 255–262.

PAGES 45–49

WARE, NORMAN J., *The Labor Movement in the United States, 1860–95* (Appleton & Co., 1929).

PAGES 49–52

BRISSENDEN, P. F., *The I.W.W., A Study of American Syndicalism* (New York, Columbia University Press, 1920).

GAMBS, J. S., *The Decline of the I.W.W.* (New York, Columbia University Press, 1932).

PARKER, CARLTON, *The Casual Laborer and Other Essays* (New York, Harcourt, Brace & Howe, 1920).

PAGE 52

HARDMAN, J. B. S., *op. cit.*, Part I.

DAUGHERTY, CARROLL R., *Labor under the N.R.A.* (New York, Houghton Mifflin Co., 1934).

BROOKS, R. R. R., "Labor under Section 7a," *Workers' Education Quarterly*, Vol. 11, No. 4.

345

PAGES 55–60

A.F. of L., Convention *Proceedings*, 1934, 1935, 1936.
C.I.O., *The Case for Industrial Organization* (Washington, 1936).
GREEN, WILLIAM, *President Green Sounds Warning against Continued Existence of C.I.O.*, A.F. of L. (Washington, 1936).
New York Times, May 24, 25, 26, 27, June 3, 4, 7, 1937.

CHAPTER III

PAGE 64

New York Times, March 4, 1937.

PAGES 69–73

DUNN, ROBERT, *The Americanization of Labor* (New York, International), Chap. V.
HOWARD, SIDNEY, *The Labor Spy* (New York, International, 1924).
LaFollette Committee, *Hearings before a Subcommittee of the Committee on Education and Labor, United States Senate*, 74th Congress pursuant to S. Res. 266, Parts I, II, III.
LEVINSON, E., *I Break Strikes* (New York, McBride, 1935).

PAGE 72, LINES 18–21

New York Times, Jan. 28, 1937.

PAGE 76, LINES 12–19

New York Times, Jan. 5, Mar. 15, 1937.

PAGE 76, LINES 33–36

Life, Feb. 15, 1937.

PAGE 77, LINES 25–37

MR. GEORGE SOKOLSKY, in an article in *Commentator*, summarized in *Reader's Digest*, April, 1937, p. 30. Mr. Sokolsky, however, has now assumed an open and vocal antiunion position.

PAGE 79, LINES 16–29

SULLIVAN, E. D., *This Labor Union Racket* (New York, Hillman-Curl, 1936).

PAGE 82, LINES 17–34

New York Times, Feb. 11, 13, 18, Mar. 2, 6, 1937.

PAGES 83–85

WITTE, E. E., *The Government in Labor Disputes* (New York, McGraw-Hill, 1932).

COHEN, E. E., *The Yellow Dog Contract* (New York, International).

PAGES 85–89

EPSTEIN, A., *Insecurity, A Challenge to America* (New York, Random House, 3d [revised] ed., 1936), pp. 141–162.

PAGES 90–94

FAIRLEY, LINCOLN, *The Company Union in Plan and Practice* (New York, Affiliated Schools for Workers, 1936).

PAGES 95–98

American Civil Liberties Union, Annual Reports.

BARRON, ROSE, *They Gave Their Freedom* (New York, International Labor Defense, 1935).

Committee for the Defense of Civil Rights in Tampa, *Tampa, Tar and Terror* (New York).

GOLDBERT AND LEVENSON, *Lawless Judges* (New York, Rand School Press, 1935).

HOPKINS, E. J., *Our Lawless Police* (New York, Viking Press, 1931).

JAMESON, JACK, *Night Riders in Sunny Florida* (New York, Workers' Library, 1936).

Labor Research Association, *Labor Fact Book*, Vol. III, Chap. IX.

LaFollette Committee Reports (exact citation above), Parts I, II, III.

PICKARD, WALT, *Burlington Dynamite Plot* (New York, International Labor Defense).

SMALL, SASHA, *Ten Years of Labor Defense*.

SOLOW, HERBERT, *Union Smashing in Sacramento* (New York, National Sacramento Appeal Committee, 1935).

WHIPPLE, LEON, *The Story of Civil Liberties in the United States* (New York, Vanguard Press, 1927).

CHAPTER IV

GENERAL SOURCES

ADAMIC, LOUIS, *Dynamite* (New York, Viking, 1931).

BROOKS, R. R. R., *The United Textile Workers of America* (manuscript in Sterling Library, New Haven, Conn., 1935), pp. 371–391.

CANTWELL, ROBERT, *Land of Plenty* (New York, Farrar & Rinehart, 1934).

C.I.O., *How the Rubber Workers Won* (Washington, 1936), Publication No. 6.

DAUGHERTY, CARROLL, *Labor Problems in American Industry* (New York, Houghton Mifflin, 1933), Chap. XIII.

GOLDBLOOM, *et al.*, *Strikes under the New Deal* (New York, League for Industrial Democracy, 1936). Contains an excellent bibliography of magazine articles on strikes.

HARDMAN, J. B. S., ed., *op. cit.*, pp. 128–168.

LUMPKIN, GRACE, *To Make My Bread* (Macaulay, 1932).

New York Times, news stories and articles in Sunday magazine section on 1937 automobile and steel strikes.

ROLLINS, WILLIAM, *Shadow Before* (McBride, 1934).

SEIDMAN, JOEL, *Sit Down* (New York, League for Industrial Democracy, 1937).

STEINBECK, JOHN, *In Dubious Battle* (Covici Friede, 1936).

VORSE, MARY HEATON, *Strike* (Boni & Liveright, 1930).

YELLEN, SAMUEL, *American Labor Struggles* (Harcourt, Brace, 1936).

CHAPTER V

PAGES 133–149

National Labor Relations Board, 161-D-130, Case No. C-145. In the Matter of Remington Rand, Inc., and Remington Rand Joint Protective Board of the District Council of Office Workers. (As far as possible, the author has verified this material by personal investigation in Middletown, Conn.)

PAGES 152–153

BONNET, C. E., *Employers' Associations in the United States* (New York, Macmillan, 1922).

LaFollette Committee (exact citation above), especially Part III.

PAGE 156 (FOOTNOTE 14)

WILSON, WALTER, *American Legion and Civil Liberty* (New York, American League against War and Fascism, 1936).

PAGE 156 (FOOTNOTE 15)

MORRIS, GEORGE, *The Black Legion Rides* (New York, Workers' Library, 1936).

PAGES 155–156

See references to pp. 90–91.

PAGE 161

For a technical description of the mechanics of tear gas manipulation, see LaFollette Committee Reports, Part II.
In general, see references for Chaps. III and IV.

CHAPTER VI

GENERAL SOURCES

A.F. of L., Convention *Proceedings*, 1934, 1935, 1936, *Weekly News Service* (Washington, 1935–37).

BIMBA, ANTHONY, *The Molly Maguires* (New York, International, 1932).

BROOKS, R. R. R., The United Textile Workers of America (cited above).

C.I.O., *Union News Service* (Washington, 1936–37).

CUMMINS, E. E., *The Labor Problem in the United States* (New York, Van Nostrand, 1932).

DAVIS, HORACE, *Labor and Steel* (New York, International, 1933).

DAUGHERTY, CARROLL R., *Labor Problems in American Industry* (New York, Houghton Mifflin, 1933).

ELIEL, PAUL, *Labor Problems in Our Steamship Business, Yale Review*, Spring, 1937 (New Haven, Conn.).

FOSTER, WILLIAM Z., *Unionizing Steel* (New York, Workers Library, 1936).

GLUCK, ELSIE, *Introduction to American Trade Unionism* (New York, Affiliated Schools for Workers, 1935).

HARDMAN, J. B. S., ed., *op. cit.*, Part III, Secs. 1, 2, 3.

HARDY, JACK, *The Clothing Workers* (New York, International, 1935).

LABOR RESEARCH ASSOCIATION, *Labor Fact Book* (New York, International, Vols. I, II, II, 1936).

MUSTE, A. J., *The Automobile Industry and Organized Labor*, Christian Social Justice Fund (Baltimore, 1936).

New York Times

ROCHESTER, ANNA, *Labor and Coal* (New York, International, 1931).

STEWART, ESTELLE, *Handbook of American Trade Unions*, United States Department of Labor, Bureau of Labor Statistics, Bulletin No. 619, 1936.

WARE, NORMAN J., *Labor in Modern Industrial Society* (New York, Heath, 1935).

PAGE 180 (FOOTNOTE 4)

HORSLEY, ALBERT (alias Harry Orchard), *Confessions and Autobiography* (McClure, 1907).

ADAMIC, LOUIS, *Dynamite* (New York, Viking, 1931).

PAGE 185, LINES 14-21

Time, June 7, 1937, pp. 13-14.

CHAPTER VII

PAGE 221 (FOOTNOTE 3)

LAFOLLETTE COMMITTEE REPORTS (exact citation above), Part II, p. 611, Exhibit 235.

PAGES 224-225

STEWART, ESTELLE, *Handbook of American Trade Unions*, United States Department of Labor, Bureau of Labor Statistics, Bulletin No. 618, p. 37 *et seq.*

CHAPTER VIII

PAGE 233, LINE 29 ET SEQ.

HARDMAN, J. B. S., ed., *op. cit.*, Part IV.

PAGES 233–234

EPSTEIN, A., *Insecurity, A Challenge to America* (New York, Random House, 3d [revised] ed., pp. 141–162).

PAGES 233–234

STEWART, ESTELLE, *op. cit.*, pp. 24–29.

PAGE 234 (FOOTNOTE 1)

A.F. of L. Convention *Proceedings*, 1936, pp. 60–64.

PAGES 238–239

Brookwood College, *Brookwood, Labor's Own School* (Katonah, New York, 1936).

PAGES 240–241

Bryn Mawr Summer School, *Shop and School* (New York, Affiliated Schools, 1936 [with apologies to Helena Cooper and Ethel Gregory]).

PAGES 241–242

International Ladies' Garment Workers' Union, *I.L.G.W.U. Songbook* and victrola records. Educational Department, I.L.G.W.U., 3 W. 16th St., New York City.
Rand School, *Rebel Song Book* (New York, Rand School).
International Publishers, *Red Song Book* (New York, International).

CHAPTER IX

GENERAL SOURCES

FOSTER, WILLIAM Z., *Misleaders of Labor*.
FELDMAN, H., *Problems in Labor Relations* (New York, Macmillan, 1937), pp. 245–248.
HARDMAN, J. B. S., ed., *op. cit.*, Part IV.
New York Times.
Standard texts on Labor Problems.
Union Periodicals.
WARE, N. J., *Labor in Modern Industrial Society* (New York, Heath, 1935), pp. 23–51.

PAGE 265, LINES 2–6

A.F. of L. Convention *Proceedings*, 1936, p. 37.

PAGE 267, LINES 8–17

"It Happened in Steel," *Fortune*, May, 1937, p. 91.

PAGE 268, LINES 3–6

The Labor Standard (Fall River), Feb. 21, 1879.

PAGE 272, LINE 19

FLYNN, JOHN T., *Graft in Business* (New York, Vanguard Press, 1931).

PAGES 271–274

"History of Organized Felony and Folly," *Wall Street Journal* (New York, 1922).
SULLIVAN, E. D., *This Labor Union Racket* (New York, Hillman-Curl, 1936).
New York Times, News reports on Dewey racket trials.

PAGE 272, LINES 9–18

New York Times, April 18, 1937.

PAGE 274, LINES 25–36

WARE, N. J., *Labor in Modern Industrial Society* (New York, Heath, 1935), pp. 43–46.

CHAPTER X

PAGES 278–291

MACDONALD AND STEIN, *The Worker and Government* (New York, Affiliated Schools, 1935).

PAGES 283–284

BERLE AND MEANS, *The Modern Corporation and Private Property* (New York, Macmillan, 1934).

PAGES 291–293

A.F. of L., *Legislative Achievements* (Washington, 1935).
Non-Partisan Declarations (Washington, 1935).

PAGES 293–307

A.F. of L. Convention *Proceedings*, 1934, 1935, 1936.
HILLQUIT v. WOLL, *Should the Workers Form a Party of Their Own?* (New York, Rand School, 1932).
PORTER, PAUL, *Which Way for the Socialist Party* (Milwaukee, Socialist Party of Wisconsin, 1937).
SEIDMAN, JOEL, *A Labor Party for America?* (Katonah, New York, Brookwood College, 1936).
Social Economic Foundation, *A Labor Party for the United States* (New York, 1936).
THOMAS v. BROWDER, "Which Road for American Workers, Socialist or Communist?" *Socialist Call*, New York, 1936.

CHAPTER XI

SELECTED READINGS

Waste and Exploitation

BRANDEIS, LOUIS, *Other People's Money* (Frederick A. Stokes, 1932).
CHASE, STUART, *Rich Land, Poor Land* (McGraw-Hill, 1936).
FLYNN, JOHN T., *Security Speculation* (Harcourt, Brace, 1934).
HARDING, T., *The Popular Practice of Fraud* (Longmans, Green & Co., 1935).
LAMB, RUTH DE F., *The American Chamber of Horrors* (Farrar & Rinehart, 1936).
LOWENTHAL, M., *The Investor Pays* (Alfred A. Knopf, 1933).
RORTY, JAMES, *Our Master's Voice, Advertising* (John Day, 1934).
WINKLER, M., *Foreign Bonds, An Autopsy* (Roland Swain, 1933).

Concentration of Economic Power

BERLE AND MEANS, *The Modern Corporation and Private Property* (Macmillan, 1934).

COREY, LEWIS, *The House of Morgan* (C. H. Watt, 1930).
—— *Crisis of the Middle Class* (Covici Friede, 1935).
JOSEPHSON, MATTHEW, *Robber Barons* (Harcourt, Brace, 1934).
LAIDLER, HARRY W., *Concentration of Power in American Industry* (Crowell, 1931).
LUNDBERG, FERDINAND, *Imperial Hearst* (New York, Equinox Coöperative Press, 1936).
MEYERS, GUSTAVUS, *History of Great American Fortunes*, Modern Library (New York, 1936), 2 Vols.
O'CONNOR, HARVEY, *Mellon's Millions* (John Day, 1933).
ROCHESTER, ANNA, *The Rulers of America: A Study of Finance Capital* (New York, International, 1936).
THOMPSON, C. D., *Confessions of the Power Trust* (Dutton, 1932).
WINKLER, JOHN K., *Incredible Carnegie* (Vanguard, 1931).
—— *Morgan the Magnificent* (Vanguard, 1930).
—— *The DuPont Dynasty* (Reynal & Hitchcock, 1935).

Comparative Civilizations

CHASE, STUART, *Government in Business* (Macmillan, 1935).
CHILDS, MARQUIS, *Sweden, The Middle Way* (Yale University Press, 1936).
COREY, LEWIS, *The Decline of American Capitalism* (Covici Friede, 1934).
DUTTE, R. PALME, *Fascism and Social Revolution* (International, 1935).
FLORINSKY, M. I., *Facism and National Socialism* (Macmillan, 1936).
SCHUMAN, FREDERICK, *The Nazi Dictatorship* (Alfred A. Knopf, 1936).
SOULE, GEORGE, *The Coming American Revolution* (Macmillan, 1934).
STEFFENS, LINCOLN, *Autobiography* (Harcourt, Brace, 1931).
STRACHEY, JOHN, *The Coming Struggle for Power* (Covici Friede, 1933).
—— *Socialism in Theory and Practice* (Covici Friede, 1936).
TROTSKY, LEON, *The Revolution Betrayed* (Doubleday, Doran, 1937).
WOOTTON, BARBARA, *Plan or No Plan* (Farrar & Rinehart, 1935).

Index